THE INTERLOPER

THE INTERLOPER

Lee Harvey Oswald
Inside the Soviet Union

PETER SAVODNIK

BASIC BOOKS

A MEMBER OF THE PERSEUS BOOKS GROUP

New York

Copyright © 2013 by Peter Savodnik
Published by Basic Books,
A Member of the Perseus Books Group

Books published by Basic Books are available at special discounts for bulk pur-
chases in the United States by corporations, institutions, and other organizations.
For more information, please contact the Special Markets Department at the
Perseus Books Group, 2300 Chestnut Street, Suite 200, Philadelphia, PA 19103,
or call (800) 810-4145, ext. 5000, or e-mail special.markets@perseusbooks.com.

Designed by Timm Bryson

A CIP catalog record for this book is available from the Library of Congress.
ISBN: 978-0-465-02181-9
10 9 8 7 6 5 4 3 2 1

To my mother and father

CONTENTS

ACKNOWLEDGMENTS

Many people helped bring this book to fruition, and I have, no doubt, forgotten some of them. Those whom I have not forgotten are:

Friends and/or fellow journalists who offered criticism, humor, and generosity: Miriam Elder, Dan Shea and Yulia Golobokova, Stephen Bierman, Charles Case and Will Mauldin. Thank you also to Andrew Kramer, for raising some thoughtful questions, and Julia Ioffe, for putting me in touch with her lovely grandmother Emma Bruk, who gave me a tour of Botkinskaya Hospital, where she was once a doctor and Lee Harvey Oswald was once a patient.

In Moscow, Sima Horunzhaya and Tatyana Voronina helped unearth former KGB officers and Intourist guides, and Lena Kamenskaya and her husband, Sasha, told me the way things really were in the time of Nikita Khrushchev. In Minsk, I was helped by Olga Nenadovets, Katya Lysenko, Katya Yakukhina, Nikolai Ovsianko, and Tatyana Schastnaya. Eduard Sagindikov, the current resident of Apartment 24, Kommunistichiskaya Ulitsa, put up with innumerable visits and queries.

I am grateful for my editor at Basic Books, Lara Heimert. Roger Labrie also offered excellent editorial comments. My agent, Ted Weinstein, was a tireless advocate.

I am indebted to two of my former editors: Dick Reston, at *The Vineyard Gazette*, and Wayne Mogielnicki, at *The Daily Progress*, both of whom stoked my interest in Russia.

I am appreciative of the many engaging and provocative Oswald- and Kennedy-themed conversations I was afforded while teaching a winter term course in 2011 and 2012 at Middlebury College. I owe special thanks to my former teachers Murray Dry, Michael Kraus, and Allison Stanger for offering some of the best and most trenchant criticism I received; Stephen Donadio for his wonderful insights into the mid-twentieth-century American scene; and Tatyana Smorodinskaya and Michael Katz for expanding my knowledge of Russian literature and culture.

My sister and brother-in-law, Sabrina and Adam Schaeffer, offered great support, especially when I was in need of a place to sleep in Washington. So, too, did my in-laws, Dan and Diana Weber, who gave me plenty of encouraging words and somehow never took offense when I excused myself to write. My beautiful wife, Kate, has been at the very center of this endeavor from the start: she walked the streets of Minsk with me, read several drafts of the book, figured out before I did what needed to be rewritten or cut, and suffered through innumerable conversations about Oswald, who has been the third person in this relationship since we met. Her love and devotion make this book as much hers as it is mine.

Finally, I owe my greatest thanks to my mother and father. Their limitless enthusiasm and love and wisdom helped sustain this project through many long nights in the former Soviet Union.

INTRODUCTION

This book makes three arguments: First, that Lee Harvey Oswald acted alone in murdering John F. Kennedy. Second, that the more important question, the question that we should have spent the past half century debating but have not (satisfactorily), is why Oswald felt compelled to kill the president and what this tells us about him, the United States, and the Cold War. Third, that we can learn about why Oswald killed the president by examining the nearly three years he spent in the Soviet Union, from October 1959 to June 1962, during which time he traveled to Moscow, tried to kill himself, moved to the city of Minsk, worked at a radio and television factory, made friends, enjoyed the company of several young women, married, and became a father.

The Interloper is about Oswald's Soviet period: why he ventured to the USSR in the first place, what he did there, whom he met, how he was affected by his time there, and why he left. Most of the information comes from interviews I conducted with people who knew Oswald—coworkers, friends, relatives of friends, neighbors, and acquaintances, mostly in Minsk but elsewhere as well, including the Marine Corps and Dallas. My research benefited mightily from the US National Archives' more than five million pages of letters, testimonies, CIA and FBI reports, maps, photographs, and other documents related to the JFK assassination, and I was helped by several Russians and Belarusians who shared with me photographs, letters, passports, and housing and work papers from the late fifties and early sixties. Most of this later material is newly reported and sheds fresh light on the events leading up to the tragedy in Dallas.

There are three factors that make Oswald's Soviet period so important. He lived in the Soviet Union longer than anywhere else, except for one of his many childhood homes (about which he had little say). The Soviet chapter of his life represented the culmination of Oswald's uneasy development, and his experiences there offer a much more three-dimensional view of the man than those of any of his other addresses. And it is in the Soviet Union that Oswald tried, unsuccessfully, to put an end to a pattern of "interloping" from one address to another. This was among his most important failures in a life that was a series of failures.

By "interloping" I am referring to Oswald's repeated attempts to flee from his old life and to insert himself into a new one adorned with new people and a new landscape and a new language or accent—with the hope, however desperate, that *this* time he might find a permanent home. In each instance he failed, and with each failure his sense of not fitting in—his alienation—intensified greatly. Oswald's interloping was foreshadowed by his fragmented and frenetic childhood, but it did not really take shape until his late adolescence. That was when he began to jump, of his own volition, from one new home to the next. First, he enlisted in the Marines; then, he defected to the Soviet Union; then, he returned to the United States; then, he fled to Mexico (with the intention of heading on to Cuba or back to Russia); then, finally, he returned, once again, to the United States. In all of these cases, his jumping, or interloping, was meant to lead to a happy resolution, and in all of them, it did not. What distinguished his Soviet chapter from the others was that it was in the Soviet Union that Oswald came closest to ending this progression of people and places. It was in Moscow, and especially in Minsk, that the whole process of Oswald's nearly constant movement was laid bare and that Oswald, unable to fit in, was confronted with the awful realization that this movement, this hopeless wandering, would never stop. It was there that the desperation and fury coursing through his whole life were most fully and powerfully on display. And it was there that his eventual assassination of the president was most clearly foreshadowed.

The much-maligned Warren Commission—the President's Commission on the Assassination of President Kennedy, chaired by Chief Justice

Earl Warren—seems to have grasped the profundity of Oswald's Soviet period. "It should be remembered," the commission notes in its report, "that he was not yet 20 years old when he went to the Soviet Union with such high hopes and not quite 23 when he returned bitterly disappointed. . . . His return to the United States publicly testified to the utter failure of what had been the most important act of his life." His widow, Marina Oswald (née Prusakova), backed up this conclusion. In her testimony before the commission, she indicated that her marriage, which had never been very happy, worsened markedly after she and Lee returned to the United States.[1]

Alas, the public discourse has not made room for this kind of Oswald. He has rarely been viewed as a total person; his assassination of the president has never been understood in the context of his frequent moving and searching. That is because the discourse has never really assumed the *fact* of Oswald's sole responsibility for the planning and execution of the murder. Instead, it has revolved around the *question* of whether he was the lone gunman. It has always insisted on a degree of uncertainty, which is to say that Oswald has been intriguing or newsworthy only insofar as he has helped to clear up   or prolong—that uncertainty. His importance has been limited to his participation in the detective story: where he was, what he was doing, the people he knew. We have avoided delving deeply into Oswald the man, with all his contradictions and incongruities, because that seemed to be a secondary concern that had little to do with the mystery of the president's death. Oswald has always been one-dimensional, hard to know, aloof, amorphous—an instrument or expression of darker forces.

The irony of all this is that it is Oswald the man who helps us to disentangle the mystery. It is the facts of his life, and especially his life in the Soviet Union, that tell us what we need to know to conclude that he alone was responsible for killing President Kennedy.

The Interloper is an attempt, at long last, to make sense of this person we have never known. It is an attempt to understand Oswald so that we might better understand how this lonely figure could so alter history. He was fascinating, grotesque, pitiful, and self-involved, and he could be insightful and decent. He was a product of his moment, but he was also his own construction. He accomplished almost nothing until he accomplished this one, awful thing. There are reasons for this, and they are not buried in government vaults in Moscow, Havana, or Washington, DC. They are not part of a cover-up or a subterfuge or a military-industrial complex that believed John F. Kennedy stood in the way of its war profiteering or its secret ambitions to overthrow Fidel Castro. They are to be found in the story of Oswald's life inside the Soviet enigma, which can lead us to the heart of this man who has occupied an oversized place in the public consciousness for so long.

It was in the Soviet Union, and especially in Minsk, that Oswald gave voice to his greatest ambitions and desperations, and it was there—most importantly—that he sought to end his pattern of migrating from one life to another, his interloping. Prior to his defecting to the Soviet Union, almost all of Oswald's life had been a series of moves, and almost all of these moves were prompted by his mother, the perennially unstable Marguerite Oswald. Each lurch reinforced the notion that Oswald did not belong anywhere, that he was an outsider without any roots or sense of identity no matter where he went. (That his father died before he was born only exacerbated this feeling, as Oswald himself suggested.) To escape this permanent rootlessness, he dropped out of high school to enlist in the Marine Corps, but the Marines failed to provide him with the stability and sense of purpose he was after. So he turned to the Soviet Union. In Russia Oswald hoped, finally, to impose some order on his life, to take charge of it, and to achieve some sense of permanence. He fully expected that this would be the final move. This would mark the end of history, as it were.

Oswald's Soviet period embodies the whole spectrum of his emotions, strivings, successes, and failures. In this place, we can glimpse the real Oswald: The spurned adolescent, having failed to find a home or sense of purpose in America, sets out for Russia. Once in Russia, he is deeply wounded when he discovers that he is unwanted there, too. But then he trundles on, he persists—there is nothing else for him to do—and he achieves something he has never before achieved: a sense of place. But gradually he suspects that this place is not what he imagined it would be—not only is it cold and unloving, but it's also distrusting, hostile, bureaucratic, mean—and he starts to want to leave. With this new desire to flee, to move once again, comes an even more painful realization: the cycle he had sought to break, the seemingly endless cycle of lurching and fleeing that he had sought to squash, has in fact not been squashed. He is trapped inside himself. And so Oswald leaves the Soviet Union broken, enraged, and confused.

There is an important corollary to all this: with each failure to settle— in the Dallas–Fort Worth area, in New Orleans, and in New York, where he spent his childhood; in the Marines; and in the Soviet Union—Oswald was made more aware of his outsiderness, his status qua interloper. And with this awareness came anger building to fury. The fury mounted. The velocity of his emotions ratcheted up. The violent outbursts became more violent. It was as if Oswald were moving toward something—a resolution. This resolution might end in any number of ways, but it pointed to an inescapable bloodshed. Oswald's short life was riddled with violent flare-ups—mostly fights and self-inflicted wounds—but he did not seem to crave any of that. He was not a bully or a thug. He did not enjoy violence, but violence found him; it forced itself on him when he was no longer able to avoid it. So it was with his interloping. He had sought to escape the cycle of lurching and trespassing nonviolently by moving to a foreign country and finding a new life there that would be divorced from the old one, but the lesson he likely took away from Russia was that even that action was ineffective. Enveloping himself in a radical ideology and parachuting himself into this country that was so different from, and so at odds with, his own was insufficient. If he were to escape himself once and for all, it would almost certainly involve something destructive, not because he wanted that but because there was no other way out.

There was, in all this, a great deal of desperation. That was what infused the Soviet period with such intensity and consequence, and that was what made his decision to leave Minsk so traumatic.

By the time Oswald returned to the United States, thirty-two months after arriving in the Soviet Union, his desperation had morphed into something much darker and with a momentum and force it had previously lacked. During the seventeen months between his return to the United States and the assassination, that darkness intensified even more. With each lurch, whatever hopes he had left of transcending himself seem to have dimmed, and by November 1963 he seems to have intuited that he was close to putting an end to it all. There is no indication that he had any animosity toward Kennedy—in fact, Oswald had indicated he thought favorably of the president—but that was not the point. The point was Oswald, and everything that was wrong with him.

PART ONE

BEFORE MINSK

1

IN SEARCH OF A
NEW COUNTRY

L EE HARVEY OSWALD'S CHILDHOOD DID NOT TAKE PLACE IN
any one town or city. He was always provided for, but he was also, in
a way, homeless—without a stable backdrop of buildings or even people.
By the age of seventeen, he had moved twenty times. Almost all of these
moves happened because of his mother, Marguerite. Often he shuttled
between Dallas–Fort Worth and New Orleans, but he also lived in New
York. His briefest stay, in Manhattan, lasted six weeks; his longest, in Fort
Worth, four years. He averaged 10.2 months per address. (This did not
include stints with family or friends who filled in when Marguerite was
absent, or his three-week detainment at a home for troubled youths, in
the spring of 1953.) Not surprisingly, nearly all of these homes were rent-
als or places owned by other people who let them live there for free.[1]

Lee's father, Robert Edward Lee Oswald, had been an insurance pre-
mium collector, and he died of a heart attack in August 1939, two months
before his son was born. His death and absence from the boy's life might be
regarded as the defining trauma of Oswald's entire life, setting in motion
a youth of chaos and frenzy. Marguerite and Lee rarely changed addresses
because of a new opportunity, but rather because of a failure or crisis that
almost always crept up suddenly. (Nearly half of the moves that took place
between addresses numbers 7 and 21, when Lee was of school age, took
place during the school year.) Mostly their hopscotching was prompted

by Marguerite's run-ins—with men, landlords, family, or employers. Often an infidelity or job termination was involved. In some cases, Lee's older brother, Robert, or older half brother, John Pic, moved with him; in other cases, it was just Lee and Marguerite. Some moves were more traumatic than others: Lee spent 1943—the year he turned four—at the Bethlehem Children's Home in New Orleans. But from late 1945 to mid-1946 he lived in a comfortable brick house in Benbrook, a Fort Worth suburb, with his mother and Edwin Ekdahl, her new husband. Ekdahl was well off—this was probably why Marguerite married him—and he had an evident fondness for Lee. For a little less than a year, he was the closest anyone ever came to being a father figure to the little boy. Ultimately, this relationship, and the one between Marguerite and Ekdahl, was a failure, too.

Marguerite was hardly capable of playing the role of one parent, let alone two. She was unreliable, frantic, harried, hectoring, needy, and prone to irrational outbursts. Throughout Lee's childhood, she vacillated between two poles—that of the self-involved, self-imagined victim in search of love and support, and that of the doting, controlling mother. She either paid very little attention to Lee's wants and needs—yanking him out of school, moving him away from what friends he had—or fawned over him in an effort (obvious to all, including Lee) to compensate for her selfishness. That selfishness, and her inability to provide any semblance of stability and normalcy for her youngest son, is clearly reflected in Lee's constant moving. Her compensatory "love" comes through, as will be seen, in her letters to Lee.[2]

This homeless youth cannot be stressed enough if we are to understand the unstable man Lee Harvey Oswald was to become. Over the years, the pinball-like movement generated not so much relationships or attachments but a murky tableau of schools, teachers, neighbors, accents, faces, and skylines. There was no single, overarching configuration of people and spaces that governed Oswald's childhood universe. There was only a whir of disjointed impressions. When someone asked him where he came from, he couldn't say, so he said whatever he felt like. Nor could he recall or explain how, exactly, he and his mother had proceeded from address number 1 to 2 to 9 to 20. Most everything about his childhood felt arbitrary and fleeting.[3]

Address number 14, while especially short-lived, marked an important juncture and revealed the first glimpse of the emotionally volatile young man Lee Harvey Oswald was to become. In August 1952, Marguerite and Lee moved out of address number 13, in Fort Worth, to live with John Pic and his wife, Margy, in New York. The Pics didn't know why Marguerite and Lee had come or when they planned to leave. Still, they were happy to see them. Margy's mother, who lived with her daughter and son-in-law in the railroad apartment on the Upper East Side, was in Norfolk, Virginia, visiting her other daughter for the month, and the Pics said Marguerite and Lee could stay in her room. The last time John had seen his half brother had been in October 1950, when Lee was not yet eleven. At that time, Lee had been more attached to his mother. (Until he was ten, the two slept in the same bed.) Now, he was going on thirteen and appeared less bound to her. Pic, who had a strained relationship with Marguerite, sensed an opening.

When he recalled this brief period, during his testimony before the Warren Commission, Pic sounded remorseful. It was as if he had never really known Lee but had wanted to. His father, Edward John Pic Jr., had married Marguerite in 1929; John Pic had been born in 1932; sometime around then, Edward Pic and Marguerite had divorced; and soon after, Marguerite had married Robert Oswald Sr. John Pic told the commission that the week Marguerite and Lee arrived in New York, he took time off from work to show his half brother the city—the Museum of Natural History, the Staten Island Ferry, and Polk's Hobby Shop.[4] But from the start of the Oswalds' visit, the Pics were uneasy, and they had reason to be. Marguerite and Lee showed up at their place with several suitcases and a television set. John and Margy expected they would visit for a week or two—John told the Warren Commission that he thought it made sense that they should come in August so Lee wouldn't miss the beginning of the school year in Fort Worth. But after a few days it became clear that Marguerite planned that they would stay for good.

Margy was nineteen. She had recently given birth and, presumably, was still nursing. Marguerite didn't pay for any of their groceries even though John made only $150 per month in the coast guard—he was on the security detail at Ellis Island. When he mentioned the groceries to his mother, she became livid. There was also the not unimportant question of space. Mrs. Fuhrman, Margy's mother, would be home from Norfolk soon. It would have been one thing if it had been their apartment, but it was Mrs. Fuhrman's. John was angry. Why hadn't Marguerite said anything before she and Lee came all the way from Texas? John and Margy wouldn't have minded if it were only Lee, even with the baby and Mrs. Fuhrman. They later said they liked having Lee around, although he could be quiet, and it could be hard to know what he was thinking. The truth was, Pic said, this behavior was very much typical of his mother. It was deceptive and manipulative, and it made Margy upset and infuriated him.[5]

Then an incident took place that was, perhaps, an early indication of Lee's capacity for violence. All of the anger in the small apartment made for a combustible atmosphere at a time of year, late summer, when it was already hot and humid, and tempers were more prone to flare up. The apartment, which had probably been built in the 1880s, was on Ninety-Second Street, between Second and Third Avenues. It was north of the old money and south of East Harlem. The ventilation was anemic, and it was shadowy and cluttered, without private spaces.

For reasons that they could not agree on, Lee apparently hit his mother and pulled a knife on Margy. This took place during an argument between Marguerite and Margy, which Pic called "the big trouble," and it was the first in a stream of violent outbursts over the next eleven years. The argument started with a disagreement about the television set, but, naturally, it wasn't really about that. Pic indicated to the Warren Commission that the argument was about who mattered more to Pic: his wife or his mother. Marguerite enlisted Lee, and suddenly Lee pulled out a pocketknife. The order of events is unclear: either Lee threatened Margy, and then he hit his mother, or vice versa. It is also unknown how much time elapsed between these events, although it's believed that they took place within a few moments of each other. This would explain why John remembered them as a single incident.

Marguerite blamed the whole blow-up on her daughter-in-law. In her testimony before the Warren Commission, Marguerite told J. Lee Rankin, the commission's general counsel, that Margy "didn't like me, and she didn't like Lee. So she—what is the word to say—not picked on the child, but she showed her displeasure. And she is a very—not, I would say so much an emotional person—but this girl is a New Yorker who was brought up in this particular neighborhood, which I believe is a poor section of New York. . . . And this girl cursed like a trooper. She is—you cannot express it, Mr. Rankin—but not of a character of a high caliber." Marguerite said the argument had to do with John and Lee carving little ships out of blocks of wood. Margy, she said, was upset that there were wood chips on the floor. "So there was, I think now—it was not a kitchen knife it was a little pocket knife, a child's knife, that Lee had," Marguerite said. "So she hit Lee. So Lee had the knife—now, I remember this distinctly, because I remember how awful I thought Marjory was about this. Lee had the knife in his hand. He was whittling." After Margy slapped Lee, he apparently threatened Margy. "He did not use the knife," Marguerite recalled. "He had an opportunity to use the knife." She did not mention the television set, nor did she say anything about Lee hitting her. John Pic said, in his testimony before the Warren Commission, that he was not, in fact, home when the "big trouble" occurred. And he stressed that, before everything happened, his wife had liked Lee very much.[6]

After the fireworks had subsided, it seemed—to John Pic and Margy, at least—that something had changed permanently. It was as if the aloofness they had sometimes perceived in Lee had coalesced into a jumble of furies. Now, more than before, he seemed to be in a state of continuous conflict. John and Margy couldn't have him or Marguerite living with them any longer. After that, Lee never really talked to his brother again, even though he would sometimes ask about him. A schism had been opened: Lee was no longer just angry but dangerous, and it was impossible to go back to the way things had been.

The Warren Commission Report indicates that it was at about this time, toward the end of 1952, that Lee was confronted by an intense and bitter loneliness. He and Marguerite were now living on East 179th Street, in Manhattan, and he was enrolled at Public School 117. He hated it. Of the sixty-four days he was enrolled there, he showed up for just fifteen and received mostly failing grades. Marguerite then enrolled him at Public School 44, but he refused to go. In February 1953, the Pics visited Marguerite and Lee, and Marguerite asked her older son how she might persuade her youngest son to accept psychiatric care, but nothing was done. Soon after, Lee was declared a truant, and a judge sent him to Youth House. He was evaluated by a psychiatrist, a social worker, and a probation officer.

The social worker, Evelyn D. Siegel, observed "a rather pleasant, appealing quality about this emotionally starved, affectionless youngster which grows as one speaks to him." According to the Warren Commission Report, Siegel

> thought that [Oswald] had detached himself from the world around him because "no one in it ever met any of his needs for love." She observed that since Lee's mother worked all day, he made his own meals and spent all his time alone because he didn't make friends with the boys in the neighborhood. She thought that he "withdrew into a completely solitary and detached existence where he did as he wanted and he didn't have to live by any rules or come into contact with people." Mrs. Siegel concluded that Lee "just felt that his mother never gave a damn for him. He always felt like a burden that she simply just had to tolerate." Lee confirmed some of those observations by saying that he felt almost as if there were a veil between him and other people through which they could not reach him, but that he preferred the veil to remain intact. Disturbingly, he admitted to fantasies about being powerful and sometimes hurting and killing people, but refused to elaborate on them. He took the position that such matters were his own business.[7]

All of this appears to have left him exposed and vulnerable to a world of ideas he could not have been expected to understand.

There was little, if anything, in Lee's childhood that suggested he might one day embrace radical politics. But by the time he reached early adolescence, there was an obvious emptiness in his life, a desire for something real and deeply felt to compensate for the home that was sorely missing. Of course, this desire was never fulfilled, and a conflict seems to have emerged pitting Lee against the world—not just New York but the world in a more general and ill-defined sense. He was angry and alone, he was becoming more violent, and he was in dire need of a community or surrogate father who could teach him self-respect and self-discipline.[8]

We can, perhaps, better understand Lee's early embrace of Marxism, however superficial, if we view it through the lens of his childhood and early adolescence. Marxism, and especially Marxist revolution, offered discipline and purpose, and it was shot through with a vocabulary and mood that comported with Lee's mounting rage. Marxism would do for him, or so he seems to have intuited, what his parents should have done: it offered a home. Because this particular "home" was a place that no one else in his life—family, neighbors, and classmates, to say nothing of tens of millions of other Americans—wanted to live in, it was probably even more appealing. It was something that he alone could possess. Up until Lee left for the Soviet Union, almost everyone who met him (social workers, teachers, fellow marines) called him "withdrawn" or "quiet." They thought he didn't want to spend time with them. A likelier explanation is that he simply wanted to be with his "family," which amounted to people with whom he thought he shared something. These were the revolutionaries he imagined living far away, in Russia or Cuba—the same people he would one day move halfway around the world to be with.

Lee's interest in Marxism started to develop within a year of returning to New Orleans from New York, in January 1954. By then, the gulf separating Oswald from his mother was probably unbridgeable, he had very little extended family to speak of, and he had no friends or place that he thought of as home. According to the Warren Commission Report, Lee started to teach himself about Marxist theory when he was fifteen. In Moscow Oswald told a reporter from United Press International, Aline Mosby, without much in the way of context, that he ran into or encountered an "old lady" who "handed me a pamphlet about saving the Rosenbergs," suggesting that this was a catalyzing moment. Oswald did not say where or when this encounter took place. He only said that it stuck with him, implying that it was this momentary interaction with a stranger, presumably in a public place, that sparked his interest in radical politics and ultimately led him to travel to the Soviet Union. He repeated this claim, about studying Marx, in a letter to his brother written at about the same time that he met with Mosby.[9]

It should be noted that the chronology of events, as related by Oswald, is a tad confusing. Demonstrations on behalf of Julius and Ethel Rosenberg, who were members of the Communist Party and convicted of spying for the Soviet Union, started in earnest in early April 1951, after they were sentenced to die, and continued through mid-June 1953, when they were executed. Oswald's comment suggests that, at some point between the ages of eleven and thirteen, he happened on a pro-Rosenberg demonstrator or volunteer—presumably, in New York, where the couple enjoyed more support than in Fort Worth—and that it was this brochure that prompted him to start thinking about Marxism. He then, apparently, pondered its meaning or forgot about it for two years and, at fifteen, started reading Marx's *Capital*.

There was nothing in Lee's record to suggest that he could have made sense of Marx. His student records from Beauregard Junior High School, in New Orleans, where he spent the 1954–1955 school year, show that he was a mediocre student, and his only friend at the time, Edward Voebel, never said anything to the Warren Commission about Oswald being a particularly voracious reader. His highest grades at Beauregard were in Civics (he received an 85 and a 90) and Art (85 and 90). In English, he received a 68 and 72; General Math, 70 and 70; and General Science, 73 and 85. He missed nine days of school, and when he was there, he was often in trouble. John Neumeyer, who was a year behind Oswald at Beauregard, recalled getting into a fight with Lee. By then, the violent impulse that had led Lee to hit his mother and pull a knife on his sister-in-law in New York had begun to manifest itself more often, and Lee had become more withdrawn. Neumeyer, in an interview with the FBI after the assassination, noted that Lee "went by the nickname 'Yankee' and did not seem to get along with other students." Neumeyer said that he "had heard Oswald often became involved in fights."[10]

A few months after leaving Beauregard, Oswald started the tenth grade at Warren Easton High School. A few weeks later, just before his sixteenth birthday, he dropped out. It was at this time, at Beauregard and Warren Easton, that Oswald apparently was struggling to make sense of the labor theory of value, the rise of the proletariat, and other complex Marxist concepts. He was on a journey that would lead him away from his country, his past, and his mother.[11]

On October 26, 1956, Lee Harvey Oswald reported for duty at the Marine Corps Recruit Depot in San Diego. He was assigned to the Second Recruit Training Battalion. He had turned seventeen eight days earlier. He had wanted to join when he was sixteen, but the Marines wouldn't let him, so he had to wait a year. (His half brother, John Pic, had joined at sixteen by submitting a false affidavit from his mother stating that he was seventeen. Oswald had tried the same tactic but had failed.) His brother, Robert Oswald, had been a marine, too, and he had given Lee a Marine Corps manual. Lee spent the next year memorizing it.[12]

It might seem odd that someone who had found solace in Karl Marx would join the Marine Corps, but there was a logic to this. Lee had been drawn to Marxism for psychological reasons. He had not arrived at it intellectually. He had not migrated toward his radicalism gradually or reflectively, even if he believed he had. He had leapt at it, acting on reflex, because it filled a void. The Marine Corps had a similar appeal, and, unlike any political theory, it offered something concrete and immediate: he could go far away from home *now*. Certainly, these two competing forces gave rise to a contradiction, and during his time in the Corps Oswald became increasingly aware of it, as conversations with fellow marines would make clear. But that contradiction was not a problem in the fall of 1956. In fact, on October 3 of that year, Lee sent a handwritten letter to the Socialist Party of America requesting information about the party's youth league. This did not stop him, three weeks later, from reporting for duty in California. The allure of starting a new life, whether that meant enlisting with the Marines or embracing an ideology that was alien to his upbringing, was what mattered most.[13]

The Marines of the 1950s inhabited a world that was mostly cordoned off from the rest of America. There was a certain code of conduct and a regimen that distinguished Marine Corps life from life outside the Corps. But that regimen was not so different from that of other branches of the military. Most important was the mentality that had given rise to the Corps daily rhythms. It was this almost defiant insularity, this unwilling-ness to be cowed by external forces—politics, the popular culture—that set the Marines apart. This was made clear by the Ribbon Creek incident, which took place six months before Oswald arrived at boot camp. The incident, during which six marines drowned, exposed the toughness and even brutality of Marine Corps life, and it underscored the secretive na-ture of an organization that was very reluctant to explain itself to the outside world. It is hardly surprising that the Marines would have ap-pealed—at least at first—to Oswald, who was himself insular, defiant, and disinclined to listen to other people.[14]

Oswald, however, was unlike most of his fellow marines. He came from a world that had been dominated by a woman and included a raft of men who flitted in and out of his life. There was very little about him that was conventionally, or stereotypically, male. He didn't like sports. He preferred playing chess or Monopoly to hanging out with other boys. He liked to listen to the radio and read, and he had a stamp collection. He had few close friends. He'd never had any girlfriends. By contrast, most of the seventeen- and eighteen-year-olds who enlisted in this cloistered frater-nity in the mid and late 1950s came from homes that were intensely male. They had grown up in the shadow of veterans everywhere, surrounded by

fathers, uncles, older brothers, teachers, and coaches who had fought at
Normandy, Iwo Jima, and Inchon, and they intuited or had been told that
the only way they would ever gain the respect of these men would be to
serve and, more than that, to fight.[15]

Without knowing much about what he was about to embark on, Oswald was shipped to boot camp at San Diego. Recruits lived in Quonset
huts. They went to bed at ten p.m. and woke at five thirty a.m. In the early
morning, said Ray Elliott, who went to boot camp at San Diego one year
after Oswald did, recruits were expected to "rake the grass." ("They called
it grass," Elliott said, "but I didn't see any grass. It was dirt. You took one
of those leaf rakes that's made of steel, and you made precise lines and cut
it off at the sidewalk. There would be an inspection. It seemed senseless
to me, but we had to do it every day.")[16] They were trained in boxing and
judo and spent three weeks on the rifle range, and they were forced to live
inside very narrow parameters: they spoke, got out of bed, and ate when
someone else said they could. And always—always—there was the sense
of a lingering brutality, the possibility of a fight, bloodshed, the brandish-
ing of a blunt masculinity.

After boot camp, Oswald was shuttled from one base to another—first
Jacksonville, Florida; then Biloxi, Mississippi, and El Toro, California;
then back to San Diego. On August 22, 1957, he boarded the USS *Bexar*
in San Diego.[17] The *Bexar* (pronounced "bear") was a transport ship that
specialized in amphibious assault. The marines lived in quarters that were
more compact than those of the sailors assigned full-time to the *Bexar*:
The sailors had bunks stacked four high; the marines—the ship's cargo—
had bunks stacked six and eight high. The sailors had toilets; the marines
had two wooden slats that formed a crude, toilet-like contraption. Everyone, sailors and marines, suffered through the late-summer heat together.
There was no air-conditioning except in the electronics stations.

On board the *Bexar*, Oswald spent his time brooding and reading—his
reading list included Whitman's *Leaves of Grass*—or teaching Specialist
Daniel Powers, his commanding officer, how to play chess. Powers, who
was three and a half years older than Oswald, was married and had two

children, and later, on the base in Japan, he played football and baseball. Oswald was not an athlete. He was teaching himself Russian, and he
had sharp opinions and a sardonic quality. "He was a guy who was never
sought out," Powers said. "Was he intelligent? Yes. He was quick on the
uptake. But he felt inferior, like he was being persecuted—an introvert.
We called him Ozzie Rabbit because he was shy."[18]

Everyday Oswald and Powers would sit on the deck of the USS *Bexar*—
Ozzie Rabbit from everywhere and nowhere versus the linebacker from
Owatonna, Minnesota; the splintered subject versus the All-American,
floating across a vast and shapeless ocean, sunburned and staring at their
chessboard. They paid almost no attention to each other, Powers because
he seemed to be loosely tethered to the moment, Oswald because he
seemed to be tethered too tightly.

But most of the time, Oswald enjoyed being alone. It was as if he were
always engaged in a conversation with himself. Sometimes, when he felt
like it or when he was interrupted, Oswald would stop talking to Oswald
and pay attention to someone else, briefly and from a distance. But he
was not allergic to people. He had joined the Marines because he wanted
to escape his mother, and this was the best way he knew how. He was
not an obvious fit. He weighed 135 pounds and stood five foot eight. He
didn't talk much about women; he didn't know how. He rarely drank. He
was quiet, with a funny, surly smile that sometimes lapsed into a stare or
grimace that seemed to point to an untapped well of thoughts and anger.
Sometimes, it was as if he didn't hear things other people said—or didn't
care. What he cared about, more often these days than before he enlisted
in the Marines, was telling people what he thought and why he was right.
With plenty of free time and his mother far away, Oswald was able, for
the first time, to think seriously about the man he might become and the
path he would take to get there.[19]

On September 12, the *Bexar* docked at Yokosuka, Japan. Oswald had
been assigned to Marine Air Control Squadron 1, or MACS-1, at Atsugi
Air Base, an hour and a half (by train) south of Tokyo. He was a radar operator, and he lived with his squadron in the barracks near the northwest

corner of the base. Atsugi had been built by the Japanese before World War II and then occupied by the Americans. It encompassed more than 1,200 acres and was peppered with three- and four-story barracks, two-lane roads, football fields, baseball fields, mess halls, rolling lawns, hangars, radio towers, and a runway for the jet fighters and cargo and radar planes that supported the aircraft carriers, battleships, destroyers, cruisers, and other ships that patrolled the Western Pacific. There were also bowling lanes and a nine-hole golf course. To a budding Marxist, it was the embodiment of American imperialism.[20]

After North Korea invaded South Korea, in June 1950, the United States had transformed Atsugi into its major base of operations in the Far East. By November of that year, the navy had begun work on a six-thousand-foot runway where the old, Japanese-built airstrip had been, and, within months, it had repaired or razed many of the 220 buildings left by the Japanese at the end of the war in the Pacific. After the Korean War, in the mid-fifties, Atsugi's mission shifted. Instead of fighting a narrowly defined proxy war, it was now enlisted in the prolonged, global struggle against the Soviet Union. That was when the navy started sealing the walls of the Japanese army–built caves—moisture was their top concern—and installing gravel pathways in the underground tunnels. The Americans believed the base below the base could withstand a direct nuclear strike.

It was also at about this time that the CIA introduced to Atsugi the U-2 spy plane. Later, in Moscow, Oswald would tell the KGB that he knew all about the invisible planes flying above the Soviet Union. This looked to be a great coup for the Soviets—Oswald arrived in Moscow in October 1959, when the U-2s were still in operation—but the American defector had nothing to offer. He had been part of a radar outfit that provided support to the U-2s, and his barracks, which were white and consisted of two stories, with small windows and a large tree outside, were near the hangar where they kept the planes, but that was all. "The Soviets knew about the U-2 long before Oswald showed up," said Gene Poteat, an electrical engineer and a former CIA intelligence officer who worked on the U-2 program toward the end of its operational life span, in 1959 and

1960. "They had been tracking it with their radar. They knew every flight it took. They just couldn't do anything about it. Their fighter planes could not fly that high, and their missiles couldn't either."[21]

As had been his pattern throughout his life, Oswald was not good at settling into new places. Six weeks after arriving at Atsugi, he was opening his locker when a Derringer .22-caliber pistol fell to the ground and discharged. The bullet hit him in the left elbow. Another marine, Paul Edward Murphy, rushed in to find him staring at his arm. Oswald glanced at Murphy and said, "I believe I shot myself." He spent two and a half weeks at a naval hospital, and then he and his squadron left Atsugi for the next four months, on maneuvers.[22]

While he was at sea, Oswald traveled to Subic Bay, in the Philippines; Ping Tung, in northern Taiwan; and Corregidor, which is situated in the mouth of Manila Bay and was the site of one of the most important early World War II battles between the Americans and Japanese. Oswald's travels across the South Pacific seem to have had a limited impact on him, but it's noteworthy that he later referred to them in the autobiographical note at the start of his essay "The Collective," his longest and most important piece of writing. Written after he left the Soviet Union, it draws on his notes and recollections from his experiences in Minsk. Oswald apparently aspired to write a full-fledged book about his Soviet period, and "The Collective" was meant to be the first chapter or two. That project never came to fruition.[23]

Oswald's South Pacific maneuvers also came up in a November 1959 letter to his brother, Robert. The letter, which reads like Communist Party pap, asserts, predictably, that the United States is an imperial power that subjugates foreign peoples in the service of its empire. There is a marked absence of any nuance or balance, any consideration of other viewpoints, any discussion of the Cold War or the bellicosity of the Soviet Union. Oswald does not indicate what happened while he was on maneuvers in the South Pacific that led him to view the US presence there with such hostility. Daniel Powers, his commanding officer, recalled that most of the marines seemed to enjoy themselves. He added that Corregidor, more than the other places they visited, left the most vivid impression on many of the marines who traveled there in the winter of late 1957 and early 1958. It was luscious and beautiful, and it had seen some of the bloodiest fighting of the war. Oswald's fellow marines spent considerable time swimming there, despite the coruscated tanks, jeeps, and ambulances at the bottom of the water. The scene did not seem to leave much of an impression on Oswald, who does not refer to it in his writings.[24]

A few weeks after Oswald returned to Atsugi, on March 18, 1958, he was convicted of possession of an unregistered, private weapon—the .22-caliber. His sentence was handed down on April 29: twenty days of hard labor and a $50 fine. He was also reduced to the rank of private from private, first class. His confinement was suspended for six months, but two months later he was found guilty again, this time for pouring a drink on a noncommissioned officer and using "provoking words" with him at the Bluebird Café in Yamato. Oswald was sentenced to hard labor for twenty-eight days. He also had to pay a $55 fine, and the suspension of his previous sentence was withdrawn. On August 13, he was released from confinement. In his semiannual review, he received poor marks from his superior officers. 1.9 out of 5 for conduct, and 3.4 for proficiency It would seem that Oswald, always the outsider, always the loner, was ill-suited to the discipline and close quarters of military life.[25]

In late 1958, Oswald's tour in Japan ended, and he was shipped back to the United States. By chance, he nearly crossed paths with his half brother, whom he hadn't seen in years. John Pic had left the coast guard in 1956 and immediately joined the air force, and on November 10, 1958, he arrived in Japan. Eight days before, Lee had left Yokosuka for San Francisco on the USNS *Barbet*. Pic said he had received a letter telling him that Lee was in Japan, but he couldn't remember whether the letter had come from his half brother Robert or his mother, with whom he was no longer speaking. Whoever it was thought he might want to see Lee.[26]

Oswald was sent to the Marine Corps Air Station at El Toro, in California, and from the moment he arrived, in December, he seemed determined to leave the Marines as soon as possible and to defect to the Soviet Union. It's unclear when his interest in Marxism hardened into a desire to go to the Soviet Union, and when this desire sharpened into a plan. He never says anything about this evolution in his diary, which doesn't begin until after he arrived in Moscow, or in his other writings, which include almost no autobiographical detail. What characterizes this period—from his arrival at El Toro to his discharge from the Marines nearly ten months later—are all the lies he told. He had lied before, and he would lie promiscuously in the Soviet Union—about his family, work, nationality, sexual prowess, and reason for venturing to Russia. But those later lies and half-truths were more scattered, and they were playful or arbitrary. They were not part of a plan. During the six months or so prior to his departure for the Soviet Union, he hewed to a plan that had been building in his head since late 1958, shortly before he was sent to El Toro. He lied to his superiors in the Marines, to the admissions officers at Albert Schweitzer College in Switzerland, and to the passport clerk at the Santa Ana Superior Court. And he lied to his mother. These were not complicated lies. He didn't have to remember what he had told whom. Mostly, he lied by omission.[27]

As Oswald's conversations with fellow marines make clear, he was not good at deception. In fact, as he inched closer to leaving the Marine Corps, he found it harder not to talk about, or hint strongly at, his impending departure, which would seem to undermine the whole point of lying. "He is said to have had his name written in Russian on one of his jackets," the Warren Commission Report observes, "to have played records of Russian songs 'so loud that one could hear them outside the barracks'; frequently to have made remarks in Russian or used expressions like 'da' or 'nyet,' or addressed others (and been addressed) as 'Comrade'; to have come over and said jokingly, 'You called?' when one of the marines played a particular record of Russian music." Nelson Delgado, a fellow marine, told the Warren Commission that he had shared with Oswald an admiration for Fidel Castro. According to the Commission's report, "Oswald told Delgado that he was in touch with Cuban diplomatic officials in this country; which Delgado at first, took to be 'one of his . . . lies' but later believed."[28]

Some of the men in Oswald's Marine squadron—Kerry Wendell Thornley, John Donovan, Nelson Delgado, Henry Roussel—were familiar with his political ideas. Some of them called him Oswaldskovich.[29] Thornley told Albert E. Jenner Jr., the Warren Commission assistant counsel who questioned him, that his first memory of Oswald was of him sitting on an upside-down bucket discussing religion with some marines at El Toro. "It was known already in the outfit that I was an atheist," Thornley said. "Immediately somebody pointed out to me that Oswald was also an atheist."

MR. JENNER. Did they point that out to you in his presence?

MR. THORNLEY. Yes.

MR. JENNER. What reaction did he have to that?

MR. THORNLEY. He said, "What do you think of communism?" and I said . . .

MR. JENNER. He didn't say anything about having been pointed out as being an atheist?

MR. THORNLEY. No: he wasn't offended at this at all. He was—it was done in a friendly manner, anyway, and he just said to me—the first thing he said to me was with his little grin; he looked at me and he said, "What do you think of communism?" And I replied I didn't think too much of communism, in a favorable sense, and he said, "Well, I think the best religion is communism." And I got the impression at the time that he said this in order to shock. He was playing to the galleries, I felt. . . . He was smirking as he said this and he said it very gently. He didn't seem to be a glass-eyed fanatic by any means.

A few moments later, Thornley told Jenner, "I still certainly wouldn't—wouldn't have predicted, for example, his defection to the Soviet Union, because once again he seemed idle in his admiration for communism. . . . [I]t seemed to be theoretical. It seemed strictly a dispassionate appraisal—I did know at the time that he was learning the Russian language. I knew he was subscribing to *Pravda* or a Russian newspaper of some kind from Moscow. All of this I took as a sign of his interest in the subject, and not as a sign of any active commitment to the Communist ends."[30]

Oswald's last six or seven months at El Toro, before his departure for the Soviet Union, are particularly revealing. On March 19, 1959, he applied to Albert Schweitzer College, in Churwalden, Switzerland, hoping to begin study in the spring term of 1960. On his application, Oswald stated that he wished to study philosophy and "to live in a healthy climate and Good moral atmosphere." He also indicated that he had a long-standing interest in psychology, football, tennis, stamp collecting, and "ideology," and, oddly, that he had taken part in a "student body movement" in school meant to combat juvenile delinquency. His application was accepted, and on June 19, he sent a registration fee of $25 to the college. About two months later, on August 17, he asked the Marines for a "dependency discharge" on the grounds that his mother, who had recently turned fifty-two, needed help. (He was required to serve until December 7 of that year to make up for the time he had spent in military prison.) On August 28, the Dependency Discharge Board recommended that Oswald's request be approved, and soon after, it was.

On September 4, he applied for a passport at the Superior Court in Santa Ana, California. On his passport application, he stated that he planned to leave the United States on September 21 to attend the Albert Schweitzer College and the University of Turku in Finland; he also said that he wanted to visit Cuba, the Dominican Republic, England, France, Germany, and Russia. Six days later, he received his passport. The next day, September 11, he was released from active duty and transferred to the Marine Corps Reserve. On September 14, he arrived home, in Fort Worth, and three days after that, he left for New Orleans. In New Orleans, Oswald went to Travel Consultants, Inc., and filled out a Passenger Immigration Questionnaire. He said that he was a "shipping export agent" and that he would be overseas, on vacation, for two months. Then he paid $220.75 for room and board on the freighter SS *Marion Lykes*, which would depart three days later for Le Havre, France.[31]

The Marine Corps had failed to deliver Oswald from his past, and now he was doing what he had always done—moving. He had watched his mother do this from his earliest childhood, and then he had done the same thing by enlisting; when the Marines turned out not to be what he had expected, he copied his mother yet again and moved. The roots of this move could be traced back at least two or three years, to his time at Beauregard and Warren Easton. But there was a critical difference between his decision to enlist in the Marines and his decision to defect to the Soviet Union: the military had been handed down to him by his brothers. He had taken an interest in the Marines because he wanted to get away from his mother, and the Marines had offered him the easiest way out. But he had found Russia all by himself. No one had given him that, and there was a feverishness, a territoriality, about this move that was absent from his first encounter with the Marines. The Soviet Union would be his entirely, and nobody would ever be able to take it away from him.

2

THE GREAT ESCAPE

O SWALD'S MANY LIES, ABOUT WHO HE WAS AND WHERE HE was going, would persist for the next several weeks. Mostly he would lie by omission. He would tell no one about his plan to defect to the Soviet Union and generally sidestep conversations that might reveal too much information about his past or his future. It was as if he were afraid that he might be caught or forced to turn around. He seemed filled with anticipation, guarded, and a little fearful.

In the early morning of September 20, 1959, the *Marion Lykes* left New Orleans. There were only four passengers on board the freighter: Oswald; Billy Joe Lord, a twenty-two-year-old airman (third class) from Midland, Texas; George B. Church, a junior high school teacher from Tampa who had been a lieutenant colonel in the army; and Church's wife, who is referred to by the Warren Commission as Mrs. George B. Church. Oswald roomed with Lord, who was planning to attend college in France. Lord, like the Churches, told the Warren Commission that Oswald had told them he was thinking about studying in Switzerland. Lord said that he and Oswald had talked about religion and that Oswald had told him that science proved that God did not exist. (Lord thought Oswald said this because he noticed Lord had a Bible.) Lord called Oswald "extremely cynical."[1]

George Church said all the passengers ate at one table but that Oswald "missed quite a few meals because he was seasick much of the time." The one conversation Church had with Oswald had to do with the

Depression. "Oswald appeared quite bitter as to the hard time his mother had suffered during this period," Church testified. "I tried to point out to Oswald that I had lived through and survived the Depression and that millions of people in the United States also had suffered during those years. This, however, made no impression on Oswald." Mrs. Church was also put off by Oswald. "Upon completion of the voyage aboard the S.S. *Marion Lykes*, I obtained the address of Bill Lord for the purpose of perhaps later writing him or sending him Christmas cards," Mrs. Church said. "I also requested Oswald's address and he questioned the purpose of my request." Eventually, Mrs. Church said, Oswald "reluctantly" gave her the Fort Worth address of his mother, who did not know where he was at that moment. Marguerite knew he was overseas—he had told her, in a letter that he mailed before boarding the *Marion Lykes*, that he had booked passage on a ship to Europe—but very little else. He had stressed that "my values are very different from Robert's or your's. It is difficult to tell you how I feel, Just remember this is what I must do. I did not tell you about my plans because you could harly be expected to understand."[2]

From Le Havre Oswald traveled to London, and from London he flew to Helsinki. In contrast with what he had told the passport office, studying in Switzerland was not on his agenda. In Helsinki, he checked into the Torni Hotel, and the next day, he moved to the Klaus Kurki Hotel, about ten minutes away, by foot. The weather was typical for October—chilly, with temperatures in the high thirties and low forties, and intermittent rain. Outside the hotel was a narrow street made of cobblestones. There was a café. It was gray and quiet.[3]

On Monday, October 12, Oswald applied for a visa at the Soviet embassy in Helsinki. The embassy was about a twenty-minute walk from Oswald's hotel, and it was situated in the middle of what looked like a park: lovely, rolling, and blanketed with trees and surrounded by walls and wrought-iron fences. It was near the water, facing south. Two days later, on October 14, the embassy issued him visa #403339. It was valid until October 20; according to Oswald's passport, it would later be extended by forty-eight hours, until October 22.[4]

At 12:25 p.m., October 15, Oswald's train pulled out of Helsinki and headed toward the Soviet border. At about 6 p.m., the train was scheduled to arrive at Vainikkala, just west of the border. In Vainikkala, the train changed engines, from a Finnish steam engine to an older, slower, Russian diesel. Then the train shuffled on a few miles to the border, where there was a cluster of two- and three-story buildings with fences wrapped snuggly around them. It had been cloudy and raining intermittently since Oswald had left Helsinki. The train stopped, and the people on board, in neighboring cars and hallways and in-between spaces, waited for something to happen. Outside, the guards spoke Finnish. After a while, the train began to move again, and the buildings and the guards' voices receded as the train was enveloped by a thick band of trees—spruces, ferns, birch trees, pine trees—and patchy clumps of grasses, fences, peasant homes, and radio towers. Then the forest opened up, and Oswald would have been able to see lights on the other side of a clearing, which was actually a river. A transformation had taken place. Suddenly, the fences were rusted, the peasant homes looked like they might collapse on themselves, and the power lines sagged and listed. That was how the passengers on the train knew they were in Russia.[5]

The train arrived at its first stop inside the Soviet Union, the town of Vyborg, at 8:35 p.m. The station at Vyborg, which still stands, had been built out of big, yellow-green bricks; columns had been fitted into the external walls and molding. Just beyond the station was a red-brick smokestack, and then another. The smokestacks bordered a factory or mill. The train stopped, the doors opened, and guards marched inside. The guards carried handguns. On the platform were soldiers with rifles. Oswald had a "hard seat"—the Soviets used "soft" and "hard" to designate first and second class because there were no classes in the officially classless Soviet Union—but there is no sign that he was fazed by the guards or the discomfort of riding in a train at night without anywhere comfortable to stretch out or sleep. Only "soft seats" were good for sleeping, but, naturally, they cost more.[6]

At 9:40 p.m., the train left Vyborg. It arrived in Leningrad about three hours later, and forty-seven minutes after that, it left Leningrad for Moscow. By the next morning, the train was just north of the capital.

There is no indication—from his diary entries, letters, or subsequent writings or from his conversations prior to his departure for the Soviet Union—that Oswald knew much about his fellow passengers. He didn't know what they did for a living, where they had been born, what they ate for dinner, or what kind of cigarettes they smoked. As it turned out, they tended to smoke unfiltered cigarettes that came in thin, squarish boxes with pictures or drawings of things you never saw on cigarette boxes in the United States: workers mopping the sweat off their brow, hammers and sickles, and Laika the space dog.

When Oswald arrived in Russia in 1959, Nikita Khrushchev was at the apex of his power. Two years earlier, he had secured control of the party and the tentacle-like apparatus of the sprawling Soviet state. His most serious rival, Lavrenty Beria, the head of the NKVD (the predecessor of the KGB) under Stalin, had been dead for years. The so-called Anti-Party Group, including Georgy Malenkov and Vyacheslav Molotov, had been marginalized back in 1957. For now, there was no one who could threaten Khrushchev's hold on power. This gave the Soviet premier the chance to move beyond the sharp, fiercely ideological antagonism of the early Cold War period and to look toward a new era of "peaceful coexistence" with the West. He had signaled his intent in 1955, when he went to Yugoslavia and declared that, Stalin notwithstanding, there were, in fact, different "roads to communism," and he had reaffirmed it the next year at the Twentieth Party Congress. It was at the Twentieth Party Congress that Khrushchev made his famous, or infamous, "secret speech," in which he denounced Stalinism and turned the communist world upside down.[7]

With that in mind, in September 1959 Khrushchev had embarked on his first, and highly successful, trip to the United States. During his thirteen-day visit, the Soviet premier met a farmer in Iowa, visited a supermarket in San Francisco, was detained in an elevator in the Waldorf-Astoria, lunched with movie stars in Hollywood, and discussed the future of Berlin with President Eisenhower at Camp David. He left the United States with a sense of possibility.[8]

We can't be sure how much of this new spirit had filtered down to the long-suffering Soviet people or, for that matter, to Oswald. As far as he was concerned, he was moving—defecting—to the great American nemesis, the USSR. Apparently, it did not matter to Oswald, or he was not entirely aware, that the Soviet Union was ruled by a totalitarian state with a dark and blood-soaked past, that that state retained mind-numbing powers of thought control, that the masses had been cowed and manipulated, that paranoia and ignorance of all things Western coursed through Soviet culture. It cannot be stressed enough that, at the height of the Cold War, Lee Harvey Oswald was not simply seeking out a new life in a new country; he was going to the country that was the arch enemy of his own. His move cannot be seen, in this light, as just a move. It must be seen as a refutation of the place he came from. Oswald was not only eager to start over. He was filled with anger and even rage.

Oswald's timing was impeccable. Nineteen days after Khrushchev returned to the Soviet Union from the United States, Oswald arrived in Moscow. From the moment Khrushchev left the United States until, seven months later, a Soviet missile shot down a U-2 spy plane flying seventy thousand feet above the Ural Mountains, there was a period of warming between the two countries, a window. Priscilla McMillan, an American journalist who reported from the Soviet Union in the 1950s, said, "Oswald was very much the beneficiary of a favorable turn in U.S.-Soviet relations that took place in 1959. . . . The Russians were careful not to tamper with that up to the announcement by Khrushchev on May 6 [1960] of the downing of the U-2." During the same period, jamming of Western radio signals stopped.[9]

Had Oswald turned up at the Soviet embassy in Helsinki one month earlier, or eight months later, he might very well have been denied a visa. At the time of his arrival, there was reason to think that the superpowers were on the verge of a permanently altered relationship, though surely that had not figured into Oswald's calculations. But that hope for better relations was quixotic and ill-informed. The United States and the Soviet Union were fundamentally incompatible with each other. This was not simply a matter of geopolitics or conflicting ideas about how their respective spheres of influence should be demarcated. It was a question, almost, of physical properties—thermodynamics. Both sides seemed to acknowledge as much. The communists, starting with Khrushchev, appeared to believe that world revolution was inevitable. The United States, meanwhile, had built its foreign policy around a policy of containment—with the understanding, prescient in hindsight, that, in time, the Soviet Union would collapse on itself. Both sides intuited that, efforts at peaceful coexistence notwithstanding, the two systems could not coexist indefinitely without coming into conflict. Eventually, there would have to be a resolution of historical and even "scientific" forces.[10] The window through which Oswald happened to slip, in other words, was not a sign of things to come but an aberration born of unique circumstances in Moscow and Washington. Conveniently, Oswald seems to have been entirely ignorant of this window and its fleeting nature. It was very important to him that Russia was America's bête noire. That was the point.

At five minutes to nine on the morning of October 16, Oswald stepped off the train at Moscow's Leningradskiy Train Station. Waiting for him was Rima Shirokova, a guide from Intourist, the Soviet travel agency. Her job was to escort Oswald to the Hotel Berlin, give him a tour of the city, and, of course, report on him to the KGB.[11]

The Berlin was in the center of Moscow. It was housed in a small building on the corner of Pushechnaya Ulitsa and Ulitsa Rozhdestvenka. Across the street was the largest toy store in the Soviet Union, Dyetskiy Mir, or Children's World, which had opened two years earlier. Immediately diagonal from Children's World was the Lubyanka, the headquarters of the KGB. According to Irina Gavrilova, an Intourist guide in the 1970s and, today, the concierge at the hotel, there were eighty-six rooms at the Berlin, and only ten of those came with "modern conveniences," meaning a sink and toilet. The hotel had a compact dining room and a dance floor. On the second floor, next to the reception, was a stuffed bear that stood about three and a half feet tall.[12] Oswald registered with the hotel, saying he was a student.[13]

The KGB was aware that Oswald had arrived in Moscow but was mostly uninterested in him, according to Yuri Nosenko, who was then the deputy chief of the Tourist Department in the Second Chief Directorate of the Committee for State Security, or KGB. According to an FBI report, Nosenko, who defected to the West a few months after the Kennedy assassination, told the FBI that when he turned up in Moscow, "Oswald was not regarded by the KGB as being completely normal mentally nor was he considered to be very intelligent." Nosenko added that "it was the desire of the KGB that Oswald depart from Russia as early as convenient but no effort was made to curtail his visit or to inconvenience him during his stay in Russia."[14]

From the start, Oswald made it clear that he wanted to become a Soviet citizen. He told Shirokova, soon after arriving at the train station, that he had no intention of staying just six days, as his visa indicated. "She is flabbergassted," Oswald wrote in his diary of his time in the USSR, "but aggrees to help." Shirokova informed her superiors that Oswald wanted to become a Soviet citizen, and they are believed to have notified the Visa and Registration Department, which was a division of the Interior Ministry, or MVD. Shirokova was told to tell Oswald that he had to write a letter to the Presidium of the Supreme Soviet requesting citizenship, and that she would help him. He mailed the letter that same day. (It's unclear, from Oswald's diary and the Warren Commission Report, whether all this took place on October 16, the day Oswald arrived in Moscow, or on October 17.) October 18 was his twentieth birthday. Shirokova gave him a copy of Fyodor Dostoevsky's *The Idiot*, which may have left Oswald wondering what the Russians thought of him. Inside the book, Shirokova had inscribed, "Dear Lee, Great congratulations! Let all your dreams come true!"

The next day, October 19, a man named Lev Setyayev, who said he was a reporter with Radio Moscow, interviewed Oswald in his hotel room, Room 320, about American tourists' impressions of Moscow. The story was never broadcast—probably because there was no story. According to the Warren Commission's report, Setyayev was thought to have been working for the KGB. His job (like that of Shirokova, Oswald's Intourist guide; of the woman who was stationed on Oswald's floor at the Hotel Berlin, known as a *dzhurnaya*; and of any number of people watching him) was to feed the security organs information about the American who claimed to hate America and to want nothing more than to live in the Soviet Union. Evidently, that claim seemed far-fetched to party operatives. It was, as we shall see, the beginning of intense spying on Oswald by the KGB during his entire time in Russia.[15]

On October 21, the day after Oswald's visa was originally set to expire, he visited the Visa and Registration Department. The department wanted to know why he wanted to live in the Soviet Union. This conversation, according to former KGB officers, would have involved a three-step process: First, they would determine whether he was working for the Americans (meaning the CIA, military intelligence or some other intelligence-gathering agency). Then, after they had determined that he was not working for the Americans, they would consider whether he might be useful to them. Then, if they decided he would not be useful, they would order him to leave.[16]

When he arrived at the Visa and Registration Department, Oswald was not given much hope. Oswald wrote in his diary: "Oct. 21. (mor) Meeting with single offial. Balding stout, black suit fairly. good English, askes what do I want?, I say Sovite citizenship, he ask why I give vauge answers about 'Great Soviet Union' He tells me 'USSR only great Literature wants me to go back home' I am stunned I reiterate, he says he shall check and let me know weather my visa will be (extended it exipiers today)."[17]

Oswald went back to the Berlin to wait for the Russians' decision. In fact, it had probably already been made. According to an undated letter from the Presidium of the Supreme Soviet to the Communist Party's Central Committee, the real seat of power in the Soviet Union, "State Security" (meaning the KGB) had strong feelings about the American. The letter, which was released by Russian authorities in 1999, states:

> U.S. national Lee Harvey Oswald, who came to the USSR as a tourist on October 15 of this year, has applied to the Presidium of the Supreme Soviet of the USSR for Soviet citizenship.
>
> According to his application, Lee Harvey Oswald (b. 1939), a native of the United States, served with the occupation forces in Japan after

graduating from a three-year U.S. Navy school [*sic*]. Oswald writes in the application: "I request that I be granted citizenship in the Soviet Union because I am a communist and a worker. I have live in a decadent capitalist society where the workers are slaves. I have no desire to go to any other country." . . .

The Committee for State Security of the Council of Ministers of the USSR deems it inadvisable to grant Oswald Soviet citizenship.

In our opinion, there are no grounds for approving Oswald's request for Soviet citizenship and for permitting him to remain as a permanent resident in the Soviet Union.

Comrade K. Ye. Voroshilov agrees with this opinion.[18]

By early evening, according to Oswald's diary, it was official. "Eve. 6.00 Recive word from police official," he wrote. "I must leave country tonight at 8.00 P.M. as visa expires. I am shocked!! My dreams! I retire to my room. I have $100 left. I have waited for 2 year to be accepted. My fondes dreams are shattered because of a petty offial; because of bad planning I planned to much!" Oswald was so despondent, he turned his violent energies on himself. "I decide to end it. Soak rist in cold water to numb the pain. Then slash my left wrist. . . . I think 'when Rimma comes at 8. to find me dead it will be a great shock." Then he adds (apparently unironically), "somewhere, a violin plays, as I wacth my life whirl away. I think to myself. 'how easy to die' and 'a sweet death, (to violins) about 8.00 Rimma finds my unconscious (bathtub water a rich red color) she screams (I remember that) and runs for help."[19]

When Rima Shirokova came to Oswald's room and he didn't answer, the KGB broke in, and they found him on the bathroom floor. They carted him out of the Berlin, and an ambulance sped him off to Botkinskaya Hospital, a little north of the center of Moscow. The hospital was in what Russians would call a prestigious neighborhood, and it was in the capital, and this meant it was almost certainly one of the best hospitals in the country. It had a quiet, stately feel to it. It looked more like a college campus than a hospital.[20]

The wound, on his left wrist, was not serious. Still, he was treated with great care. No one is believed to have bothered him with questions about his visa or when he planned to leave the Soviet Union. He was fed hot meals. His wound was bandaged and rebandaged. He was visited by Rima Shirokova and Rosa Agafonova, the translator from the Hotel Berlin. And he met with numerous doctors, including more than one psychiatrist.

The psychiatric evaluations in Oswald's medical file indicate that none of the doctors who saw him thought he was especially depressed or unstable. While the psychiatrists did not go so far as to contend that Oswald did not intend to kill himself, at least one of them suggested that suicide was not his overriding concern. "A few days ago [the patient] arrived in the Soviet Union in order to apply for our citizenship," Maria Ivanovna Mikhailina stated in her report. "Today he was to have left the Soviet Union. In order to postpone his departure he inflicted the injury upon himself." Mikhailina added, "According to the interpreter, there were no mentally sick people in his family. He had no skull trauma, never before had he made attempts to commit suicide. . . . He claims he regrets his action." Another evaluation, signed by I. G. Gelershtein, reported: "His mind is clear. Perception is correct. No hallucinations or delirium. He answers the questions [illegible] and logically. He has a firm desire to remain in the Soviet Union. No psychotic symptoms were noted. The patient is not dangerous for other people."[21]

When released from Botkinskaya, on October 28, Oswald was moved from the Berlin to the Hotel Metropol, next to Karl Marx Ploshchad, or square. The Metropol was bigger and grander than the Berlin, and it was closer to Red Square. Irina Gavrilova, the former Intourist guide, said the reason they moved Oswald probably had to do with vacancies. The Berlin, she said, was always filling up because it had a cozier feel to it, especially in the fall and winter.[22]

If Oswald had hoped that his attempted suicide would persuade the KGB to rethink its position on his request for citizenship, he was wrong. Nosenko, the KGB officer who oversaw the Oswald case while Oswald was in Moscow, told the FBI that "upon Oswald's release from the hospital Oswald was again informed he could not remain in the Soviet Union, whereupon Oswald declared if this were true he would commit suicide. Nosenko said that at this point the Second Directorate of the KGB 'washed its hands of Oswald.'"[23]

Over the years, there has been speculation that Oswald returned to the United States in 1962 as a kind of Manchurian candidate who had been programmed to spy (or kill) for the KGB or even the CIA. There are many political and practical reasons why this theory does not make sense. But perhaps the most compelling argument against the claim that Oswald was recruited by an intelligence agency so that he might wreak havoc in the United States is Oswald himself and, more to the point, his psychology. As Oswald's suicide attempt illustrates, he was difficult and irascible and, at times, histrionic, self-pitying, and reckless. He could hardly have been counted on to do or finish anything. That a professional, clandestine organization would rely on Oswald to pull off what would have been one of the most dangerous operations ever—the assassination of an American president—is absurd.[24]

PART TWO

MINSK

3

THE FAUX REVOLUTIONARY

O THER AMERICANS HAD DEFECTED TO THE SOVIET UNION. They had started coming to Moscow during the 1917 revolution and the civil war, from 1917 to 1922—this was before moving to the Soviet Union was called "defecting"—and thousands of other fellow travelers, intellectuals, writers, journalists, and curious observers had arrived after the Bolsheviks had secured power, in the twenties and thirties. With the end of World War II and the start of the Cold War, the number of Americans traveling to Russia plummeted, but in 1959 there was something of an uptick. In September of that year, Robert E. Webster, a plastics technician from the Cleveland-based Rand Development Corporation (not to be confused with the RAND Corporation, the US Air Force–sponsored, quasi-governmental research institution in Santa Monica, California), had defected and been granted a Soviet passport. (Webster had traveled to Moscow to help prepare for the American National Exhibition, at which Vice President Richard Nixon would debate the merits of capitalism and socialism with Khrushchev in an American-style kitchen.) About the same time, Nicholas Petrulli of Long Island, who, like Oswald, had entered the Soviet Union at Vyborg by train, showed up at the US embassy in Moscow to declare that he was surrendering his American citizenship. Richard Snyder, the consular officer who would advise Oswald to take a few days to think before doing the same thing, administered the oath of renunciation to Petrulli.[1]

But there was only a superficial resemblance binding Oswald to other, recent defectors. All of them had had trouble building a life for themselves in the United States; most of them had professed communist sympathies. But these similarities masked more important and less visible nuances. Oswald's migration to the Soviet Union was not born of whim or circumstance—work, legal trouble, a sexual entanglement—but rather emerged as a slowly developing idea, the outlines of which first appeared two or three years earlier. There was a much greater emotional and psychological momentum to it, and there was a decisiveness and a feeling—as his suicide attempt shows—that he had to be in the Soviet Union, that this was his only option. John McVickar, one of the consular officers at the US embassy in Moscow who handled the Oswald case, called people like Webster and Petrulli "tentative defectors." Not Oswald. "Oswald, I think it's safe to say, he seemed to be somewhat more determined about what he wanted to do, and maybe it looked like he had thought about it more in advance," McVickar said in an interview. "That was partly because he had made his decision when he was in the States."[2]

Oswald had much bigger ambitions than his fellow defectors. He imagined that he would move to the Soviet Union and join the cause. This sentiment comes through in a letter from Oswald to his brother, Robert, that was dated November 26, less than six weeks after Oswald arrived in Moscow. "These people," he reported, "are a good, warm, alive people These people would never think of war, they wish to see all peoples live in peace but at the same time they wish to see the eonomicly enslaved people of the west free, they believe in their Ideal and they support their government and country to the full limit." He did not expect that he would actually do any fighting, but he did make it clear that he was willing to. In his letter to his brother, Oswald stipulated the terms of their future relationship, or "arrangement." He wanted Robert to understand, first and foremost, that "in the event of war I would kill *any* American who put a uniform on in defense of the American government—any American."[3]

Oswald conceived of his defection as metabolic, and he expected that it would transform not only his own life but his relations with everyone he had ever known. "I want to, and I shall, live a normal happy and peaceful life here in the Soviet Union *for the rest of my life*," he informed Robert. "My mother and you are . . . *not* objects of affection, but only examples of workers in the U.S. You should not try to remember me in any way I used to be, since I am only now showing you how I am. I am not all bitterness or hate, I came here only to find freedom, In truth, I feel I am at last with my own people." He imagined himself taking part in a global revolution: he started his letter by explaining why he and his "fellow workers and communist's would like to see the present capitalist government of the U.S. overthrown." Like the Bolsheviks who overthrew the Romanov dynasty four decades earlier, he was filled with an almost incomprehensible fury and sanctimoniousness, disdain, and, of course, a naïveté and lack of historical or political perspective.[4]

Oswald was not a revolutionary. Among other things, he lacked the consciousness, the historical awareness, of the firebrand. But he was oblivious to that, and it would take many months before the realities of Soviet life forced him to reconsider his defection. Most other defectors figured out quickly that they had made a mistake—maybe because they had been "tentative" about their defection to start with—and, after a month or two, after the end of a short-lived relationship and the onset of depression or loneliness, they were clamoring to leave. In Oswald's case it would take him more than a year to reach that point.[5]

What was most important about his new home, the Metropol, was that Oswald did not know how long he would be there. It was a sort of purgatory. The KGB, as if to heighten this sense of in-betweenness, made a point of not giving any hints about what might come next. Oswald knew nothing about the status of his case or what was being said or done about it.

The Metropol was lavishly appointed, even regal, but it had lost some of its sheen. It was a five-minute walk from the Berlin, and it was closer

to the Kremlin and catty-corner from the Bolshoi Theater. It was more
tsarist and Russian than Soviet in style. The hotel had opened in 1901,
sixteen years before the Bolsheviks seized power. It had long enjoyed a
famous clientele: heads of state, railroad titans, famous poets and musicians, revolutionaries, government ministers, and members of the
nomenklatura. Everything about the Metropol was oversized: the hallways, the ceilings, the staircases, the rugs, the marble columns, and the
doors, which were tall and thick. Like so many buildings in the center
of Moscow, it seemed to lumber. In the lobby, a five- or six-piece band,
mostly brass, played Russian folk songs. The most popular song, the one
it seemed to play most nights, when the foreigners had a drink or black
tea, was "Moskva Vechera," or "Moscow Nights."[6]

Oswald's room was on the second floor, facing Teatralniy Proezd. He
had a view of the Bolshoi. "Hotel Room 214 Metropole Hotel," he wrote
in a diary entry dated October 29, one day after his discharge from Botkinskaya. "I wait. I worry I eat once, stay next to phone worry I keep fully
dressed."[7]

He spent most of his time in Room 214 in a state of great anxiety. Soon,
he hoped, the people at Intourist or Rima or someone would tell him
where he was going next.[8]

On October 31, a Saturday, he became overwhelmed with fear. He
thought that if he renounced his American citizenship, the Soviets would
be more inclined to let him stay and eventually become a Soviet citizen. "I
make my dision," he wrote in the diary entry dated October 31. "Getting
passport a 12:00 I meet and talk with Rimma for a few minutes she says;
stay in your room and eat well, I don't tell her about what I intend to do
since I know she would not approve. After she leaves I wait a few minutes
and than I catch a taxi. 'American Embassy' I say."[9]

At the embassy, a white-and-mustard-colored building that faced the
fifteen-lane Garden Ring, he met with Richard Snyder, the consular officer. Snyder shared an office with another consular officer, John McVickar.
"There were six of us," McVickar wrote in an unpublished essay on his
encounter with Oswald. "Two officers, myself and Consul Dick Snyder, an

American secretary, and three Russian ladies, all very agreeable and competent, the one in charge especially so." Oswald, surrendering his American passport, said he wished to renounce his citizenship and live in the Soviet Union. Snyder wasn't about to grant Oswald his request so fast.[10]

Oswald wrote that Snyder "warnes me not to take any steps before the soviets except me, says I am a 'fool', and says the dissolution papers are along time in preparing (In other words refuses to allow me at that time to dissolve U. S. Citiz. I state 'my mind is make up' From this day forward I consider myself no citizen of the U. S. A. I spend 40 minutes at the Embassy before Snyder says 'Now unless you wish to expound on your Maxist belifes you can go.'" Then Snyder advised Oswald to spend the weekend mulling over his future. He said that Oswald could renounce his citizenship on Monday. He stressed that doing this kind of thing was very serious, and he told Oswald that if he felt just as strongly on Monday about severing his ties with the United States, he should come back then. Whatever sympathy Snyder or McVickar may have had for Oswald was "extinguished," as McVickar put it in a memo written after the assassination, when Oswald told the Americans that he planned to share with the Soviets information about US military radar systems that he had learned while in the Marines. The meeting lasted less than an hour. Oswald left the embassy enraged and "elated": "Returning to my hotel I feel now my enorgies are not spent in vain. I'm sure Russians will except me after this sign of my faith in them."[11]

It should be noted that there is evidence that the recent spike in defections to the Soviet Union had caused some alarm at the US embassy. A cable from the embassy to the State Department reports: "LEE HARVEY OSWALD, UNMARRIED AGE 20 PP 1733242 ISSUED SEPT 10, 1959 APPEARED AT EMB TODAY TO RENOUNCE AMERICAN CITIZENSHIP . . . SAYS ACTION CONTEMPLATED LAST TWO YEARS. MAIN REASON 'I AM A MARXIST'. ATTITUDE ARROGANT AGGRESSIVE. . . . IN VIEW PETRULLI CASE WE PROPOSE DELAY EXECUTING RENUNCIATING UNTIL SOVIET ACTION KNOWN OR DEPT ADVISES."[12]

After Oswald left the embassy, Snyder and McVickar immediately began talking to American reporters in Moscow about his case, hoping to generate a few newspaper articles back home that might prompt Oswald's family to take action—and, one imagines, save them the trouble of filling out the paperwork involved in this sort of international brouhaha. No more than a half hour or so after Oswald left the embassy, the first reporter, A. I. Goldberg, from the Associated Press, knocked on his hotel-room door. "2:00," Oswald wrote, "a knock a reporter by the name of Goldstene wants an interview I'm flabbergassed 'How did you find out? The Embassy called U.S.' He said. I send him away I sit and relize this is one way to bring pressure on me." A half hour later, another reporter, Aline Mosby, from UPI, turned up. "I answer a few quick questions after refusing an intervine," Oswald wrote. "I am surprised at the interest." He apparently answered a few questions from another correspondent, R. J. Korengold, and then tucked in for the night.[13]

The consular officers had accomplished their goal. The next day, Oswald's mother, Marguerite, and brother, Robert, read about him—no doubt to their astonishment—in the newspapers. On November 1, Oswald wrote, "more reporters, 3 phone calls from brother, mother, now I feel slighty axzillarated, not so lonely." When his mother telephoned, Oswald either refused to take the call or hung up on her.[14] On November 1, at 1:31 a.m., a telegram from Robert arrived at the US embassy for his brother:

FORT WORTH TEX

LEE HARVEY OSWALD US EMBASSY MOSCOW

LEE THROUGH ANY MEANS POSSIBLE CONTACT ME MIS-

TAKE KEEP YOUR NOSE CLEAN LOVE YOUR BROTHER

ROBERT L OSWALD

7313 DAVENPORT FORT WORTH TEXAS[15]

The next morning, a secretary at the embassy's consular section typed the following memo:

TO: Mr. Snyder
FROM: Marie Cheatham
SUBJECT: Lee Harvey OSWALD
DATE: November 2, 1959

According to your instructions, I telephoned Mr. Oswald at 0930 at his hotel this morning informing him that the Embassy had received a telegram from his brother and asked if he could stop by the office today to pick up the message. He replied in the negative.

I again called Mr. Oswald immediately thereafter, as instructed by you, to ask him if I could read the message to him over the telephone. His room did not answer.

At 1105 I contacted Mr. Oswald at his hotel and asked him if I could read the messages from his brother, that I now had two telegrams for him. Mr. Oswald replied, "No, not at the present time," and hung up.[16]

Oswald didn't acknowledge the telegram for six days. Only then did he write his letter to Robert declaring that he was committed to the communist cause and planned to settle in the Soviet Union.

The next day, November 9, another telegram arrived for Oswald at the US embassy, this time from his half brother, John Pic.

LEE OSWALD
C/O AMERICAN EMBASSY
MOSCOW
PLEASE RECONSIDER YOUR INTENTIONS.
CONTACT ME IF POSSIBLE.
LOVE
JOHN
SGT. JOHN E. PIC,
TACHIKAWA AIRBASE, JAPAN.[17]

That same day, John McVickar, having tried unsuccessfully to hand-deliver Pic's telegram to Oswald, filed a confidential note in the embassy's Oswald file:

> I took a typed copy of the message from Pic down to the Metropole Hotel today to deliver to Oswald. I went directly to the room (233) and knocked several times, but no one answered. The cleaning lady told me that he was in the room and only came out to go to the toilet. She suggested that I ask the dejorney[18] in charge of the floor. The latter told me that he was not in his room. I decided not to leave the message, but to have it sent by registered mail. On the way out I phoned from downstairs, but no answer.
>
>   McV[19]

All the excitement surrounding Oswald failed to prop his spirits up. Just one day after reporting, in his diary, that he felt "axzillarated" from all the attention, he descended into self-pity. In his diary he wrote: "Nov. 2–15 days of utter loneliness I refuse all reports phone calls I remaine in my room, I am racked with dsyentary." With the hope, perhaps, that some more attention from a journalist or his family would make him feel better, Oswald called Aline Mosby, the UPI reporter. Mosby rushed over to the Metropol to interview him. "I give my story," he noted, "allow pictures, later story is distorted, sent without my permission, that is: before I ever saw and o.k'ed her story, again I feel slightly better because of the attention." Never mind that reporters do not customarily provide copies of their stories to the stories' subjects for their approval; Oswald did not know the rules but assumed he had been exploited.[20]

Nonetheless, it was, perhaps, because the Mosby story had given him a lift that Oswald decided, the next day, to grant an interview to Priscilla McMillan of the North American Newspaper Alliance. McMillan, who had been reporting from the Soviet Union off and on since the early fifties, had spent the second half of September following the Khrushchev entourage around the United States. She had had trouble obtaining a visa to return to the Soviet Union and had just turned up in Moscow, six weeks after Khrushchev's final stop, at Camp David, where the Soviet premier had met with President Eisenhower. After checking in to her hotel—McMillan was also staying at the Metropol—she stopped by the embassy to pick up her mail and ran into McVickar. "John McVickar was a personal friend," she told me. "He had known my older brother and sister growing up on Long Island, and I think he tried to look out for me a little. It was he who told me, my first day back at the embassy to pick up my mail after the Camp David visit, 'Oh, by the way, there's a defector in your hotel. He won't talk to any of us, but maybe he'll speak to you because you're a woman.'" A few days later, on November 16, McMillan knocked on Oswald's hotel-room door and asked to interview him. He agreed to come by her room later that evening.[21]

McMillan's first impression of Oswald was that he was naïve and seemed a little lost. "By 1959, not many people wanted to live in the Soviet Union," she said. "So here was somebody who was trying to come to the Soviet Union for the old-fashioned reasons. He wanted to talk about economics." McMillan recalled having stayed in Room 319, one floor above Oswald, who was then apparently staying in Room 233. She made tea. He arrived at nine p.m. and didn't leave until after one a.m.[22]

After McMillan interviewed Oswald, she had a conversation with McVickar. Referring to McMillan, McVickar wrote: "Her general impression of Oswald was the same as ours has been. His naïveté about what he can expect here is balanced by a rather carefully worked out set of answers and a careful reserve about saying things he feels he shouldn't. He made one interesting comment to her to the effect that he had never in all his life talked to anyone so long about himself." McVickar adds: "I also pointed out to Miss Johnson[23] that there was a thin line somewhere between her duty as a correspondent and as an American. I mentioned Mr. Korengold [a reporter Oswald had apparently spoken to earlier] as a man who seemed to have known this difference pretty well."[24]

At about the same time, in mid-November, the authorities paid Oswald a visit. According to Oswald's diary, an unidentified Soviet official came to his room at the Metropol. The official asked Oswald how he was feeling—it had been just two weeks since the American had been discharged from Botkinskaya—and then he notified Oswald that he could "remain in USSR till some solution in found with what to do with me." This, Oswald reported, "is comforting news for me."[25]

There is little, if anything, that suggests the Soviets had any nefarious or surreptitious reason for letting Oswald stay in Moscow. The simplest explanation, which is also the likeliest, is that they were afraid of a public relations fiasco. They had already determined that Oswald was not terribly valuable to Soviet intelligence, and they had tried to make him leave. But he had forced their hand by trying to kill himself, and now the US embassy was involved, and there had been articles about him in the American press. If something happened to Oswald—if they tried to deport him and he managed to end his life, once and for all—it might look bad. Or at least it would generate some ill will toward the USSR. It would complicate things, and that was not what Khrushchev wanted right now. Ever since his American tour, there had been an opening, an opportunity for what looked to be a lasting and meaningful rapprochement between the superpowers, and now there were plans for a US-Soviet summit in May in Paris.

The Soviet premier wanted to settle the Berlin question—East Germany was hemorrhaging émigrés in search of a better future in the West—and he wanted to inaugurate an era of improved relations between the superpowers. He wanted to break from the Stalinist past. But Oswald was a problem. A dead ex-marine in Moscow would muddy the politics, and it would be impossible to make progress on an agreement between the two countries if the politics were not just right. This was a hopeful period, but it was a fragile hope, and everything could collapse at any time. The best way to handle Oswald, in order to avoid any diplomatic blow-ups, was to give him what he wanted. The Soviets knew better than Oswald did that what he wanted—a new life—was a distant hope, that it would require making great sacrifices and rethinking his expectations and understanding of almost everything he had ever known. But that was unimportant for now. What the Soviets wanted was to give themselves time—a month, maybe two—and then, after everyone had forgotten about him, to move Oswald somewhere where he couldn't speak with as many journalists or create problems.

So for the next six weeks, the authorities went silent. Oswald was scared and alone. He appears to have done very little—he recorded almost nothing in his diary after having made several entries in November. The Americans lost track of him. "On December 1, 1959, the Embassy informed the Department of State that Oswald had departed from Moscow within the last few days," William T. Coleman, an assistant counsel to the Warren Commission, wrote in a memo to the commission's general counsel, J. Lee Rankin. But the embassy was wrong. Oswald was just hunkered down, waiting, cut off, confused. The idea that he might one day escape his mother had been gestating since he had been an angry young man in New York; it had deepened while he was in the Marines in San Diego, Jacksonville, and Atsugi; and it had turned into a plan while he was at El Toro. For at least a year, he had worked on the plan. He had tried to anticipate all the pitfalls he would run into and the things he would need: money, tickets, travel schedules, visas, hotels. Finally, he had embarked on his journey, and he had expected, with a childlike faith in the Soviet authorities, that his old life would soon be replaced by a new one. There was a myopic and magical quality to his thinking. Now he wasn't sure what would come next.[26]

As much as he tried to convey stoicism and sure-footedness, Oswald's lack of education and his immaturity and even meekness were obvious. "Right from the beginning, I saw that he was very, very young," McMillan later said. "I had seen people who had gotten trapped in the Soviet Union, and I had figured that would happen to him since he didn't know much about the country, and I figured he didn't know much about the language, and he seemed kind of hopeless. . . . As he was leaving [the hotel room], I said, 'I'm going to write my story tonight or tomorrow, and I'd be glad to show it to you.' I wasn't very professional. And he said, 'No, I trust you.' He also said he'd look me up before he left the hotel, but he never did."

McMillan's assessment of and even tenderness for Oswald was shared by many people who met him. Ruth Paine, with whom Lee and Marina Oswald stayed in Dallas in 1963, said of Lee *after* he had spent two and a half years in the Soviet Union, married, and become a father: "He did not seem very mature and, I would say, not very comfortable or confident about who he was. I guess you could say there was something adolescent about him, especially in what seemed to be his efforts to figure out what he should do in life and how to achieve a life that satisfied him, where he felt valued." Many of the people he would later encounter in the Soviet Union, particularly the older, married men at the plant where he worked, viewed him as a wayward nephew in need of a warm meal, a little guidance, and maybe a bit of discipline. Oswald, to them, was a young man who needed some male supervision and, better yet, a wife. He seemed pitiable, lost, and a little sad.[27]

The weeks stretched out across December, uneventful but fraught with uncertainty. Usually Oswald sat on his bed or at a small table, where he studied Russian grammar. He had nowhere to go, and even if there had been somewhere he wanted to see, he was unsure whether he should leave his room. He saw few people except for Rima Shirokova, a handful of other Intourist representatives, and, on New Year's Eve, Rosa Agafonova, the translator from the Hotel Berlin. It's unclear even now what, exactly, the KGB was doing. Oleg Kalugin, formerly one of the most senior officers in the KGB, and Tennent Bagley, who ran CIA counterintelligence operations in the Soviet Union in the 1960s, both agreed in separate interviews that the KGB probably spent this period answering several questions: Where, exactly, would Oswald live? What would he do? Who would watch him? Whom would he be allowed to come into contact with? What, if any, problems or dangers would all this create? Also, Bagley said, the KGB may have wanted to see how Oswald, with very little money and few contacts in the Soviet Union, would react to these circumstances. There was a surreality to Oswald's life at the Metropol, where the everyday tempos and behaviors of the guests and hotel staff did not comport with those of the Russians on the other side of the looking glass. The organs, as the Soviet security services were sometimes referred to, may have wanted to see if the American would tire of Russia and ask to go home. Oswald thought his commitment to the communist cause would be well received by the Soviet authorities, but Bagley disagreed. He thought they would have viewed his determination and rigidity with alarm. This was not how most people responded to this sort of pressure.[28]

The organs' logic was clear, Kalugin and Bagley said. It was the same logic to which they had always adhered: no one told the truth, ever. Just as the state concocted elaborate myths—about the revolution, the purges, the war, the numerous national security threats it faced—so, too, did people. The American, Oswald, was not—could not—be the person he said he was. Possibly, he was useful. More likely, he was dangerous. Most likely, he was both.[29]

Oswald's familiarity with current events, and the clarity and emotional force with which he could discuss these events, camouflaged his ignorance of deeper historical and philosophical matters. Conversations with McMillan, Aline Mosby, and the US consular officer Richard Snyder, as well as his letters and other writings, indicate that he could discuss the latest newspaper headlines—a demonstration, a speech—and he could attach pat, ideological explanations to these events, but he couldn't go much further than that. This often had the effect of generating an initial interest in Oswald by Russians who encountered him that would peter out after a few weeks or months—for example, Rima Shirokova and Rosa Agafonova, who were, at first, curious about or even intrigued by the American but eventually found themselves caring for him in the way an older sister might. Nor was this only a matter of youth or immaturity. This was not a phase that Oswald eventually grew out of. It was characteristic of the way he comprehended the world.[30]

The faux sophistication that Oswald displayed when talking or writing about geopolitics or the Soviet premier, for example, may explain why a handful of authors have argued that Oswald possessed a keen, if underdeveloped, intellect and, in fact, great insight into world politics. According to this line of thinking, we shouldn't assume that Oswald's humble beginnings and paltry education barred him from making sense of the Soviet idea or the Cold War. On the contrary, Oswald's "ignorance" was simply a lack of conditioning or cultural programming that, far from hobbling him, enabled him to peer deeply into the hypocrisies of his age. Like Rousseau's Emile, removed from the corrosive and blinding forces of civilization, Oswald, unshaped by any university or corporation, freed of any bourgeois need for acceptance, was actually deeper and wiser than so many Americans who had been co-opted by a postwar culture that valued conformity at the expense of thought.

Possibly the best-known writer in this camp is Norman Mailer, whose *Oswald's Tale: An American Mystery* portrays Oswald as intelligent, alienated, at sea—the existential wanderer who refuses to be subjugated by an uncomprehending society. According to Mailer, Oswald's move to the Soviet Union and his assassination of the president point to the marginalization he had suffered at the hands of an uncomprehending establishment.

Of course, this has a discomfiting corollary: however much we are horrified by President Kennedy's death, that death is but a rejoinder to the grotesque soullessness of contemporary America. It is not entirely to be condemned, and it may even be praised, Mailer implies, in that it reflects the wisdom and courage of those who reject convention and material comfort in the service of authenticity. "Who among us can say that [Oswald] is in no way related to our own dream?" Mailer asks. "If it had not been for Theodore Dreiser and his last great work, one would like to have used 'An American Tragedy' as the title for this journey through Oswald's beleaguered life." There's something jarring about Mailer's tone. We sense in his description of Oswald a veiled respect for the assassin as rebel and seeker.[31]

Alas, the claim that Oswald was wiser than he appeared is just plain wrong. Lacking much insight into himself or Soviet political identity, he had little understanding of the profound differences between his state of mind and that of the people he encountered—Intourist guides, translators, bellhops, waiters, doctors, nurses, taxi drivers, party officials, and the hordes of anonymous faces that enveloped him at the hotel restaurant or the museums he may have visited, or on the street.[32]

More to the point, Oswald's writings and many of the conversations he had in the months before and immediately after his arrival in the Soviet Union make it clear that he did not really grasp that the revolution he had traveled thousands of miles to join had been consumed by a massive and terrifying violence a quarter of a century earlier and that the last reverberations of that violence had only subsided six years earlier, with Stalin's death.

This ignorance is most clearly reflected in his November 26 letter to his brother Robert. "Happiness is not based on oneself," Oswald wrote. "It does not consist of a small home, of taking and getting, Happiness is taking part in the struggle, where there is no borderline between one's own personal world, and the world in general I never belived I would find more material advantage at *this* stage of development in the Soviet Union than I might of had in the U.S. . . . I have been a pro-communist for years and yet I have never met a communist, instead I kept silent and observed, and what I observed plus my Marx'ist learning brought me here to the Soviet Union. I have always considered this country to be my own."[33]

Then he lectured his brother about his new home (which, at the time, had not said what it planned to do with him). "You probably know little about this country so I will tell you about it," he wrote. "I did find, as I suspected I would, that most of what is written about the Soviet Union in America is for the better part fabrication. The people here have a seven hour work day now and only work till three o'clock on Saturdays with Sunday's off. They have socializism which means they do not pay for their apartments or for medical care the money for these come's from the profit they help to create in their labor, which in the U.S. goes to capitailist."[34]

Toward the end of his letter, Oswald wrote: "Do not let me give you the impression I am on another world, these people are so much like Americans and people the world over. They simply have an economic system and the Ideal of communism which the U. S. does not have. I could never have been personly happy in the U.S. . . . I have no money problems *at all*. My situation was not nearly as stable then, as it is now, I have no troubles at all now along that line."[35]

He ended with a brief description of the center of Moscow, which must have sounded very much like another world to his brother, in faraway Texas. "It is snowing here in Moscow now, which makes everything look very nice, from my hotel window, I can see the Kremlin and Red Square and I have just finished a dinner of [Cyrillic writing] meat and potatos. So you se the Russians are not so different from you and I."[36]

If there is anything about Oswald that is far-seeing it is that the language he used to describe the United States anticipated the language that American radicals, six or seven years later, embraced. But this was born not of a shared insight or intelligence but a shared ignorance. Oswald's simplicity, like that of later campus revolutionaries, was not, as it turns out, deep or exceptional; it ignored or was ignorant of huge swaths of American history and political and cultural life. "I remember well the days we stood off-shore at Indonesia waiting to surpress yet another population," he wrote to his brother. "I can still see Japan and the Phillipines and their puppet governments. . . . I will ask you a question Robert, What do you surport the American government for? What is the Ideal you put forward? Do not say 'freedom' because freedom is a word used by all peoples through all of time. Ask me and I will tell you I fight for Communism."[37]

One wonders how Oswald conceived of "freedom" and "communism," or, for that matter, "happiness." "Happiness," he stated, is not the pursuit of selfish ends—it is "not based on oneself." "Happiness is taking part in the struggle," which is to say, fighting, killing, starving, and dying. It is to join the group, the collective. It is to surrender oneself, utterly, to something infinitely bigger and nobler than oneself—without knowing, of course, what the cost of that surrender might be or where this experiment might lead. He sounded like a Bolshevik, an angry, unreformed Marxist who had not yet been tempered by the nightmare of Stalinism.

Outside the Metropol, hitherto unimaginable things were taking place.

For decades, under Stalin, Russians had lived in a separate, walled-off universe. It was during this period that the most basic categories of Soviet consciousness—the ways in which people constructed the world and imagined themselves in it—had been revolutionized and then hollowed out by the state, with its all-consuming paranoia and cynicism. It had become so dangerous to think certain thoughts—one could never be sure what might slip out accidentally, consciously or unconsciously, in one's sleep, in the middle of a heated conversation—that people had been conditioned to think differently. They had expunged from their minds certain words or thoughts, and they had imbibed an ever-shifting vernacular that reflected the whims and political sensibilities of the supreme leader. Russia, as it had existed prior to the terror and the war, had been eviscerated, and what was left was not a radicalized mass of peasants and workers, as the Bolsheviks had imagined them, but a shadow of a people.

Oswald had learned some of the old vocabulary—he was familiar with terms like "capitalism," "imperialism," and "proletarian dictatorship"—but he seems not to have grasped that this vocabulary was outdated, that these words sounded stilted or ironic to Russians in the late 1950s, by which point very few of them believed any longer in the revolution they symbolized. When he tried to display his solidarity with the cause, he sounded ignorant of people and events that were very real to all Russians: the purges, the show trials, the famines, collectivization, the five-year plans, the war, the occupation of Central and Eastern Europe, and the creation, over three or four decades, of a vast network of informants and spies who had made it impossible to speak or act or even think the way people once did before the revolution.

Now the Soviet Union was becoming a country that no one had ever imagined it would become. Six and a half years after Stalin died, in early 1953, a new series of words and developments had entered the national lexicon: the *ottyepel*, or thaw; the "secret speech"; the rehabilitation of hundreds of thousands of Gulag prisoners; the Hungarian uprising and the Warsaw Pact's violent suppression of it; the uprisings in East Germany and Poland; and the reawakening of Russian culture. Oswald sounded unaware not only of the calamity of Stalinism but of the reassessment of communism that the calamity and its end had prompted. His whole disposition—the revolt against America, the inexplicable fondness for "the worker"—seemed out of step with a country that had recently hosted the American National Exhibition and was seeking peaceful coexistence with the West, albeit tentatively.

In retrospect, there appears to have been something unavoidable about the whole metamorphosis—the loosening of central authority, the proliferation of new freedoms and fissures, the birth of a conspicuous

consumer culture. Before Stalin's death, there had been nothing inevitable
about these developments. Then, it seemed as if the country had been
submerged in an endless cold. But the moment Stalin died, on March
5, 1953, the uncoiling had begun. Stalin's death, more than anyone else's
in the whole life span of the Soviet Union, prompted a furious questioning and fragmentation. The questions most people asked were not
explicitly political; they had less to do with the nature or organization
of the state and more to do with the way they were now expected to
lead their lives. Which decisions could they make for themselves? Who, if
anyone, would tell them what to say, or which opinions to hold, or which
people to avoid? Under Stalin, any right-thinking Soviet citizen would
have avoided Oswald, an American, for fear of being branded a traitor or
counterrevolutionary. Now, a few years later, they weren't sure whether
they should stay away or give in to their curiosity and talk to him.

Mostly, Russians wanted to know if they would ever live in a normal
country. Stalin's image had always seemed to represent two contradictory
statements: nothing is permanent; I am forever. Now he was gone, and
they were reconstructing their country around his absence. This meant
they had to reimagine themselves, and few people knew how to do that.
They had very little experience in that area. If someone were to ask them,
"What kind of country do you live in?" they probably would have answered, "A very good one" because now they had things—apartments,
household products—they had never had before, and there was no war,
and they could launch dogs into outer space. But if someone had said,
"But what kind of country is this? What is its essence?" they probably
would not have known how to reply. They were no longer certain about
where they were. The Soviet Union was changing rapidly, and no one
knew exactly what it would become.

Oswald, with his one-dimensional understanding of Soviet life, could
not possibly have grasped the powerful, churning, contradictory forces
that had seized this new Russia. His embrace of a caricatured workers'
paradise was obsolete. (In fact, it had never existed.) He was unknowingly
wading into a country that was not the place he expected it to be. He was
an outsider still, but he did not know it.

4

A BOLSHEVIK AMONG
THE BOURGEOISIE

To BE SURE, SOVIET RUSSIA WAS HARDLY A CAPITALIST SO-
ciety, and it had not abandoned all of its socialist ideals. There were
chronic shortages of basic goods, few civil liberties, and an expectation
that the needs of the state took priority over those of the individual. But
there was a yawning gap between the place Oswald was in and the place
he thought he was in. He had journeyed to Moscow in search of a cause,
but instead of revolutionaries, he met tour guides, translators, police informants, bureaucrats, doctors, nurses, waiters, and taxi drivers. He was
full of rage toward his native land and ready to do battle against it. But
the Russians he met were mostly courteous and temperate. They listened
to whatever he had to say. They were pleasant, if at times a little brusque.
In Moscow in late 1959 there was a conspicuous dearth of revolutionary
fervor.

For several months, Oswald either did not know enough to realize he
was not where he thought he was, or he managed to delude himself. In
his letters and diary entries at this time, everything, all of his energies and
maneuverings, had to do with himself and his cause: becoming a citizen
of the Soviet Union. The apparent seriousness and even ferocity of his
cause are striking. On December 17, more than two weeks *before* he was
informed of what was to become of him, Oswald wrote to Robert: "I will
be moving from this hotel, and so you need not write me here. I have

chosen to remove all ties with my past, so I will not write again, nor do I wish you to try and contact me, I'm sure you understand that I would not like to recive correspondence from people in the country which I fled. I am starting a new life and I do not wish to have anything to do with the old life."[1]

Just as important as Oswald's rigidity, or obsession, was his apparent unawareness of the circumstances of this particular moment. He seems not to have appreciated that Moscow was the center of the Khrushchev thaw and that, in 1959, it was an exciting place but also deeply ambivalent about itself.

More than anywhere else in the Soviet Union, Moscow had opened up, but it was unsure what would happen if it went too far. It was exhilarated by the new freedom, however limited that may have been, but it feared that the old forces would return with a great violence. It was the capital and cultural-spiritual epicenter of a country run by men who grasped that Stalinism, as a governing system and state of being, could not persist indefinitely, yet they were themselves descendants and even instruments of terror. In the wake of Stalin, these conflicts and contradictions defined not only the Soviet state and Soviet society but the character of individual men and women. These contradictions were embodied in the personalities at the apex of Russian political and cultural life—Khrushchev, the KGB chiefs Alexander Shelepin and Vladimir Semichastny, the writers Boris Pasternak and Ilya Ehrenburg, the editor Alexander Tvardovsky, and, later, the poet Yevgeny Yevtushenko—and they were reflected in the cadence and timbre of everyday life. They were inescapable.

Moscow did not feel like a city as much as a *bolshaya deryevna*—a big village. This was how many Muscovites imagined the capital, and it was how they contrasted it with Leningrad, which had always been thought of as a city of poets and canals—the Venice of the North. Moscow was no Venice. It was sprawling and inelegant, and its center was riddled with narrow streets that weren't so much quaint as tangled. Everywhere there were trams, government ministries, institutes, factories, dormitories, parks, and riverfronts. There was also a smattering of state-run cafés and *gastronomes*, and starting in 1958, there was the circular Moscow Pool, which had a diameter of nearly 425 feet and, for a time, was the largest swimming pool in the world. The pool had been built atop the ruins of the never-completed Palace of Soviets, which had been built atop the ruins of the Cathedral of Christ the Savior. Except for the beige, Stalin-era wedding-cake towers, often called the Seven Sisters, of which the tallest was nearly eight hundred feet, Moscow was horizontal. It lumbered.[2]

Four concentric ring roads imposed some semblance of order on the big village. The ring roads started in the center, wrapping around the medieval fortress that was the Kremlin. The second ring road, the Bulvar, was divided by a narrow strip of park. The third was the Garden Ring. The outermost ring, the MKAD, or Moskovskaya Koltsevaya Avtomobilniya Doroga, was a few months from completion when Oswald lived in Moscow; eventually it would form the approximate borders of the city. Taken together, the ring roads looked something like a bull's-eye, although the innermost three rings encompassed just 10 percent of Moscow, while the space between the third and fourth rings amounted to nearly 90 percent of the city's territory. Importantly, none of the ring roads, nor any of the city's other major arteries, such as Prospekt Mira, Leningradsky Prospekt, Leningradsky Shosse (pronounced "Shaw say"), or Kutuzovsky Prospekt, were meant to move large numbers of individual motorists. The Moscow road network, before and after the revolution, was more suited for military parades and other state-orchestrated demonstrations. It neatly illustrated the imposition of top-down power, what Russians sometimes called "the vertical," on an unruly mass. Oswald spent most of his time inside the third ring road, or Garden Ring. The Metropol was tucked just inside the innermost ring. The Berlin was one block outside it. The US embassy was situated on the Garden Ring. The only place where he spent much time outside the third ring was Botkinskaya Hospital, and he never would have gone there had he not tried to kill himself. What's more, he never spent any time outside the hospital grounds.

The cold, which arrived in early November and stretched until at least April or May, surely accentuated the feeling of oppressiveness that was already a part of Soviet life. It made it harder to leave one's home or visit with other people; it coated the streets and sidewalks with a ubiquitous, seemingly impenetrable ice; and it underscored the peasant-like nature of so much of Russian life, which was closer to the earth, muddier, messier, and more contingent than life in the West. Most of all, the cold was colored gray. It did not come with invigorating blue skies, but with an overpowering lifelessness that made people feel isolated and small. Nor was it just a matter of climate or temperature. It had a dark, almost magical quality that had been shaped and even celebrated by Russia's rich literary tradition. This idea of the Russian cold—the Russian condition—had contributed, however obliquely, to an autocratic tendency. It reduced the individual by making him wary of the outside world and subject to the whims and furies of external forces. It cannot be coincidental that both periods of meaningful liberalization in recent Russian history, after Tsar Nicholas I's death in the 1850s and after Stalin's in the 1950s, are described as a thaw.[3]

What Oswald failed to grasp was that the thaw of the late 1950s had given rise to something that would have been unimaginable just a few years before: a culture and even a way of thinking that existed outside the rigid confines of the state and its official ideology. Stalin's death had not simply made people wonder who would replace Stalin but what would replace Stalinism. Nowhere was this searching more deeply felt than in Moscow. For a half century, the city had been the locus of a great and often violent change in the name of abstract movements or causes (revolution, Bolshevism, Marxist-Leninism, the worker, justice, communist utopia) that rarely, if ever, had much to do with the pedestrian, private lives of ordinary people. Now, the revolutionary city, which had felt for so long as if it were at the mercy of other people (the Whites, the Reds, the Nazis, the Stalinists), was less violent and more open. It was possible for people to imagine carving out their own space.

True, Moscow was becoming an imperial metropolis from which a new cadre of leaders ruled half the planet; it had emerged from its defensive crouch into a world capital that was more boastful and prone to crass rivalries. But it was also more human and life-sized—the old, monumental architecture was being steadily subsumed by five-story apartment blocks—and it lacked the cynicism and surreality of the Stalinist period. It was more normal, at least by Western standards.[4]

The nationwide symbol of Soviet bourgeois culture in the late fifties and early sixties was the single-family apartment. The aptly dubbed *khrushchyovka*—a cheaply made apartment building usually constructed with cement panels and consisting of five floors—was the regime's answer to decades of inadequate housing. Khrushchev, who had been head of the party in Moscow before becoming premier, had been pushing for more low-cost, no-frills housing for years, but it was only after he was running the whole country that construction boomed, first in Moscow and later across the Soviet Union. In his first three full years in the Kremlin, construction doubled in Moscow: in 1954, 910,000 square meters of housing space were built; in 1957, 1.8 million. The first, newly configured *khrushchyovka* did not appear until the end of the decade, but it was quickly replicated. In 1959, a little more than 2.9 million square meters of housing space went up in the city; the next year, that figure jumped to a little more than 3 million.[5]

The new apartment was compact, with low ceilings, narrow corridors, and a small kitchen and bathroom. It was filled with a shadowy light, and it had central heating, plumbing, and electricity. It could not compete with its American counterpart, if there were any. Oswald would call the new apartments "many storied barracks." Still, there was some modicum of privacy, which meant families could grow and evolve the way they did in Western countries. Previously, tens of millions of mothers, fathers, grandparents, children, aunts, uncles, cousins, and hangers-on lived in even tinier, darker places that overlapped with those of other extended families, in wooden barracks or prerevolutionary apartments that had been converted to communal abodes, or *kommunalki*. This arrangement had given rise to a strange anthropology, an urban-village life that hovered between a Western-style, family-based order and a non-Western, tribal society. The *khrushchyovka* established a new order that was less communal and more private. It changed permanently the way Soviet citizens imagined personal space.[6]

The centerpiece of this new Soviet apartment, like that of many American homes, was the television set. Until the late 1960s, television was a mostly unheard-of luxury for Soviet citizens, but in Moscow, by the late 1950s, television was more widespread. In 1960 4.8 million Soviet households had television sets. A disproportionate number were in Moscow and Leningrad.[7]

Television programming veered in two opposite directions. On one hand, viewers wanted to be entertained. They wanted to watch soccer games, movies, ballet, and the opera. The old propaganda, with its triumphalism, had been replaced by the quintessentially Western desire to be sated and happy. This was reflected in high and low culture, with productions of *Yevgeny Onegin*, *The Cherry Orchard*, and *Swan Lake*, and children's programs that freed up housewives who now had a *khrushchyovka* to tend to. On the other hand, television programming revealed, if only briefly, the growing anxieties and yearnings of a society in the middle of profound, even metabolic changes. These tensions were most vividly captured in the live broadcast.[8]

One example of a late-fifties live broadcast run amok was shown on First Channel and involved hundreds of drunken Muscovites locking a television producer in a closet. More telling was a panel discussion on the United States broadcast on First Channel a few years later. The panel featured two journalists who had recently returned from America and who offered a few breezy, entertaining anecdotes. They were later censored by the producers, who felt their description of American life was too positive. The producers were particularly distressed by the journalists' description of the "motel," which they characterized as clean, accessible, and adjacent to a restaurant where one could order a tasty and filling meal for a reasonable price. Often, this sort of meal came with a "soft drink"—for example, a Coca-Cola—and something the Americans called a "bottomless cup of coffee."[9]

One of the most colorful and revealing moments of the Cold War took place in Moscow a few months before Oswald arrived there, and it displayed the gulf separating the radical Oswald from the new Moscow. The

American National Exhibition was part of a cultural exchange between the superpowers. In June and July 1959, there had been a Soviet exhibition in New York. Then, in late July, the Americans came to Sokolniki Park in Moscow. The exhibition was a sensation, drawing 2.7 million Soviet citizens from the capital and beyond.[10]

Most of those who came were ordinary Russians. They were fascinated by the things the Americans exhibited, the cars and canned goods and television sets, but, just as important, it was the idea of America—the way its people thought and the hopes and ideals that animated their lives—that excited the Russians. They were not uncritical of the United States—the modern art the Americans brought to Sokolniki did not sit right with most laypeople—but they resented the KGB agitators who had been planted in the crowd to ask questions about unemployment and lynchings in the South.[11]

Naturally, both the Soviets and the Americans viewed their exhibitions as opportunities to further their ideological and political interests. In New York the Soviets had displayed images or prototypes of big industrial and technological ventures: power plants, airplanes, tractors, and sprawling farms. The Americans appear to have had a two-pronged approach to debunking the myth of the communist state. First, they showcased those things that ordinary Russians craved most: consumer goods. The exhibition included pots and pans, nylons, cheeseburgers, Pepsi-Cola, Monopoly boards, a Polaroid camera, a drugstore, and a fashion show. Second, they addressed, with the artworks they displayed, the more abstract question of freedom. There were paintings by Edward Hopper, Mark Rothko, Joseph Stella, and Jackson Pollock; also on display were Alexander Calder's *Seven-Footed Beastie* and Bernard Reder's *Adam and Eve.* "It was a propaganda mission," said Lucia DeRespinis, an industrial designer who helped create the American exhibition and spent six weeks in Moscow before and during the exhibition. Referring to the geodesic dome that housed many of the exhibits, DeRespinis said, "It was supposed to [feature] what America had to offer. . . . It was supposed to be like a huge Macy's."[12]

At the center of the Americans' propaganda campaign was a 1,144-square-foot house. Splitnik, as it came to be known, had six rooms,

including one and a half bathrooms. It was compact but roomy, taste-
fully appointed, and ideally suited to a young family in the suburbs. It
had been built by All State Properties of New York, and it typified the
kind of houses that were then being showcased at Levittown and other
planned communities on Long Island. These houses came with a price tag
of $11,000 to $12,000, and most skilled workers with a Veterans Administration mortgage, which required no down payment, could probably
afford one. Ultimately, the house that was sent to the National Exhibition
in Moscow included a few modifications. Not only was it important to the
Americans that Soviet citizens think that this was how they actually lived,
but just as important was that Splitnik be accessible. To make room for as
many visitors as possible, the builders added a central corridor that was
ten feet wide. This made the interior look a little strange, but it also made
it possible to saw the house in half and show off its amenities. The revised
floor plan featured three bedrooms—the master suite encompassed 180
square feet and had a sink and toilet—and a dining room, living room,
and brick patio. The kitchen was "all-electric," with appliances from GE.
Many of the furnishings came from Macy's.[13]

The famous kitchen debate between Khrushchev and Vice President
Richard Nixon took place on July 24, 1959, less than three months before
Oswald arrived in Moscow. It revolved around the merits of capitalism
and communism. The "debate" was not a formal debate but a handful
of exchanges between Khrushchev and Nixon, who was inaugurating
the National Exhibition. Khrushchev dominated the first exchange, at
the RCA color-television studio, and Nixon, worried that he had looked
weak in front of the American television audience, was intent on putting
on a good performance in round two. William Safire, then a press agent
for All State Properties and a future speechwriter for Nixon, was at the
National Exhibition to promote Splitnik, and he helped choreograph the
second exchange in Splitnik's kitchen. Khrushchev, in his light-colored
suit, looked bumptious, irritated, jesting, and proud. Nixon, in a dark suit,
looked confident and more at home—which, in a way, he was. During the
confrontation at the RCA studio, the vice president had been ill at ease;

now he smiled and shook everyone's hand. The two men leaned against a white fence that was meant to cordon off the exhibit from the hordes of visitors. To their left was a washer-dryer made by GE and, on top of that, a box of SOS detergent. Behind Nixon was Leonid Brezhnev, the Politburo member who would one day help topple and then replace Khrushchev.[14]

"I want to show you this kitchen," Nixon told Khrushchev. "It is like those of our houses in California."

Khrushchev: "We have such things."

Nixon: "This is our newest model. This is the kind which is built in thousands of units for direct installations in the houses. In America, we like to make life easier for women . . . "

Khrushchev: "Your capitalistic attitude toward women does not occur under communism."

Nixon: "I think that this attitude towards women is universal. What we want to do is make life more easy for our housewives. . . . This house can be bought for $14,000, and most American [World War II veterans] can buy a home in the bracket of $10,000 to $15,000. . . . "

Khrushchev: "We have steel workers and peasants who can afford to spend $14,000 for a house. Your American houses are built to last only 20 years so builders could sell new houses at the end. We build firmly. We build for our children and grandchildren."[15]

The whole debate amounted to a weird asymmetry. It pitted a Soviet against an American on American terms and in an American kitchen. The asymmetry illustrated how far the center of gravity had shifted—toward the American and capitalism and away from the Soviet, Marxism, and the old revolutionary spirit that Oswald clung to so tenaciously. The desirability and even the morality of a comfortable middle-class lifestyle were no longer up for discussion. What mattered now was how best to achieve it.[16]

It's striking that the argument that Khrushchev made in the kitchen debate was well to the right of the argument made by Oswald in his November 26, 1959, letter to his brother Robert. In that letter, Oswald argued against the materialism of the capitalist West. "In this system," he wrote, "art, culture, and the spirit of man are subjected to commercial enterpraising, religion and education are used as a tool to surpress what would otherwise be a population questioning their government's unfair economic system and planns for war." He suggested that, in the future, Soviets could expect to live more comfortably—"I never belived I would find more material advantages at *this* stage of development in the Soviet Union than I might of had in the U.S."—but that is clearly not his overriding concern. Instead, it is "the struggle." Khrushchev, however, does not dispute that things—material advantages—are good. He takes that for granted. What he attempts to argue, rather feebly, is that socialism can produce more and better goods than capitalism can. There is no mention of anything theoretical or idealistic.[17]

Much more controversial than Splitnik were the artworks that were brought to Sokolniki and the Americans' not-so-subtle attack on Soviet repression of freedom of expression. While Khrushchev was willing to give some philosophical ground on the matter of material goods, his position on creative expression was closer to that of Stalin's.

The artworks were displayed on the second floor of a four-thousand-foot-long glass pavilion. The pavilion wrapped around the geodesic dome, which had been designed by Buckminster Fuller and was the crowning achievement of the National Exhibition. (From the air, the dome looked like an eye, and the pavilion resembled an eyebrow.) Soviet organizers had dispatched six movers from the Pushkin Museum, in Moscow, to help Edith Halpert, one of the exhibit's curators, hang the paintings.[18]

Among the most controversial paintings was Jackson Pollock's *Cathedral*, painted in 1947. *Cathedral* was typical of "high Pollock," the artist at his most frenzied and splattering. The painting fills a rectangular canvas that is nearly six feet high and three feet wide, and it is shot through with pale yellows and greens, as well as streaks of black that suggest blood flowing through veins. Despite the chaos, there is a uniformity of size and structure to all the streaks and capillaries—a geometry. The left side of the canvas is dominated by five black semicircles; the upper right-hand corner has more green. A jagged but perpetual motion courses through the angry channels and is reminiscent of a Möbius strip.

The point of exhibiting *Cathedral* and other abstract expressionist art-works such as Willem de Kooning's *Asheville II*, Rothko's *Old Gold Over White*, and many others, was to flaunt Americans' freedom of expression, their individuality, their independence from any overarching thought control. These artworks, and *Cathedral* most of all, conflicted sharply with the old Soviet-Marxist ethos, which called for order, uniformity, and clarity of purpose in its pursuit of revolution—the very same struggle that Oswald had traveled to Moscow to take part in. What was most important about them, at least in the context of the National Exhibition, was that they were primarily political, not esthetic or cultural, statements. In fact, it's possible, even probable, that many of the Americans behind the exhibition found Pollock's work disturbing, crude, or boring. But that was hardly the point.[19]

To Khrushchev, Pollock did not represent freedom of expression but a provocation. His artwork did not look like any artwork he had seen. He preferred socialist realism, with its cartoonish depictions of soldiers, factory workers, and combine operators. The people in those paintings were doing things that made sense to old-time Soviets like Khrushchev. They looked serious and hard-working. They were noble and patriotic. *Cathedral*, as far as the Soviet premier could tell, did not resemble any cathedral anywhere. It was confusing and even threatening. It looked to him, at least, like a Trojan horse: a piece of propaganda that only pretended to be an artwork. It was dangerous.[20]

Unlike Splitnik and the many consumer products the Americans exhibited at Sokolniki, artworks like *Cathedral* met mixed reactions from the Russians. The official party line had it that abstract expressionism reflected the mental illness that was eating away at American society. But many Russian artists who attended the exhibition were left, for the most part, inspired and a little saddened, convinced that the United States was at the forefront of groundbreaking, creative expression. In contrast, many of the ordinary people who visited the art exhibit were left confused or even repulsed. According to the United States Information Agency, the artworks drew the second highest number of negative comments, with the dearth of "science and technology" exhibits receiving the most criticism.[21]

That did not bother the Americans, who regarded the art exhibit as a great success. As Khrushchev appears to have intuited, the exhibit cast a spotlight on one of the reigning contradictions of Soviet life: the workers, having been liberated from their shackles by the revolution, were not, in fact, free to express themselves. At the same time, the exhibit ran the risk of reminding Russian artists and writers and other members of the intelligentsia that not only was the future in the United States but it had once been in Russia. It was bound to remind them that they had at one time been freer than they were now, and it seemed designed to encourage Soviet artists—and, by extension, all Soviets—to reclaim that freedom, to exercise a kind of expression and liberty that they had not known in nearly two generations. All this may explain Khrushchev's angry outburst, three and a half years later, at the famous, or infamous, Manezh exhibit, which featured avant-garde Soviet artists whom the premier found distasteful, hard to understand, and, worst of all, unpatriotic. The Americans had helped to inculcate a new Soviet art that could only be regarded as subversive.[22]

How did all this Cold War posturing impinge on Oswald's foray into the Soviet Union? The irony is unavoidable: a little more than two months after this exhibition—which had underscored Russians' hankering for a more comfortable, middle-class lifestyle and, especially among artists, for a more untrammeled, more individual freedom—Oswald arrived in Moscow ready to join the revolution. Just as Russians were giving voice to their inner bourgeois tendencies, the American Bolshevik, who had told his brother that happiness comes neither from things nor from oneself, arrived in the Russian capital. That the former hotbed of Bolshevism was not a hotbed of Bolshevism any longer seems to have eluded him.

The Soviets, like the Americans, were engaged in a struggle for world domination, but it was a struggle that no longer had obvious definition or meaning. Before the war, and especially before the purges and famines in the 1930s, the party had had great ambitions. The chief ambition had been not simply to industrialize, collectivize, and out-produce the West, but to create a new kind of human being—*Homo Sovieticus*. Oswald had come to Moscow wanting to become that person, but Moscow in the age

of Khrushchev did not offer the right climate for that kind of metaphysical reengineering.

On New Year's Eve 1959, Oswald went to his old home, the Hotel Berlin,
with the translator Rosa Agafonova, whom he had met there. "She has
the duty," he wrote in his diary. "I sit with her untill past midnight, she
gives me a small 'Boratin' clown, for a New Years present she is very nice
I fonud out only recently she is married, has small son who was born
crippled, that is why she is so strangely tender and compeling."[23]

A few days later, Oswald was plucked from his doldrums and told that
he would finally be leaving the Metropol. His great relief was tinged with
disappointment. "Jan 4. I am called to passport office and finilly given a
Soviet document not the Soviet citizenship as I so wanted, only a residence document, not even for foringuers but a paper called 'for those
without citizenship.' still I am happy. The offiar says they are sending me
to the city of 'Minsk' I ask 'is that in Siberia? He only laughes; he also tells
me that they have arranged for me to recive some money though the Red
Cross to pay my hotel bills and expensis I thank the gentlemen and leave
later in the afternoon I see Rimma She asks are you happy' 'Yes.'" He was
no longer an American, but he was not a Soviet. He was stateless.[24]

The next day he wrote: "I go to Red Cross in Moscow for money with
interrupter (a new one) I recive 5000. rubles a huge sum!!" Later, Oswald
would realize that the Red Cross in the Soviet Union was not the same
Red Cross as everywhere else. Like so many aspects of Soviet, or Russian,
life, it was a simulacrum of something from the outside world that was
meant to convey the impression of normalcy. As Oswald would indicate
in his third "untitled composition," the Red Cross in the Soviet Union
was simply an agency for distributing money at the behest of the security
organs. It was an extension of state power pretending to be an emergency
relief organization.[25]

Two days later, on January 7, he wrote: "I leave Moscow by train for
Minsk, Belorussia. My hotel bill was 2200. rubles and the train ticket to
Minsk 150. rubles so I have a lot of money I hope. I wrote my brother &

mother letters in which I said 'I do not wish to every contact you again. I am begining a new life and I don't want any part of the old.'"[26]

He was about to disappear into a Soviet void. For many months, the US embassy and the State Department would have no idea where he was or what he was doing. It would be more than a year before he made contact again with anyone in his family. The Americans would not even be sure whether he was still one of their own. In early 1960, someone in the State Department responsible for keeping tabs on him inserted a card in the Oswald file with the word "REFUSAL" at the top. "The reason for the refusal written on the card was that Oswald 'may have been naturalized in the Soviet Union or otherwise . . . expatriated himself,'" William T. Coleman would write in his memo to J. Lee Rankin, the Warren Commission's general counsel. Soon after the "REFUSAL" card was inserted in Oswald's file, the State Department sent an operations memorandum to the embassy in Moscow "stating that the Embassy should take no further action in the case unless the Embassy comes into possession of information or evidence upon which to base the preparation of a certificate of loss of nationality." There was no point in doing anything else until it became known which country Oswald belonged to. At the same time, State Department officials issued a so-called look-out card with his name on it. The United States was now officially ignorant of Lee Harvey Oswald's whereabouts.

5

MINSK TO THE
END OF THE LINE

O FFICIALLY, THERE HAD BEEN A CITY CALLED MINSK SINCE
the eleventh century, but the place they sent Oswald to was really
only fifteen years old. That was because the old Minsk had been flat-
tened by the Germans after they invaded the Soviet Union in June 1941.
Storming across the Belorussian countryside in their tanks, armored con-
vertibles, motorcycles, and long columns of goose-stepping soldiers, the
Germans had blown up, burned down, or otherwise eviscerated thousands of villages, farms, towns, and manufacturing hubs, including Minsk,
the capital of the Soviet Socialist Republic of Belorussia. There had been a
huge Jewish community in Minsk for centuries; before the war, it had included writers, artists, musicians, university professors, and party officials.
In the center of the city, the Germans walled off a ghetto for the Jews,
built a concentration camp called Masyukovshina, and killed, plundered,
and destroyed wantonly. On the eve of the war, there were roughly three
hundred thousand people in the city. By the end of the war, a little more
than 10 percent of the prewar population remained, and only five or six
buildings still stood in the whole of Minsk.[1]

In the years immediately after the war, villagers from across the smol-
dering Belorussian plain streamed into what was left of the old Minsk.
The Stalinist regime bestowed on Minsk the title "hero city"—there is a
monument outside the Kremlin that signifies as much—and they rebuilt

what had been an old, crammed, medieval tsarist trading center as a model communist city. It was broad, orderly, and boring, with placid hues and well-swept streets and sidewalks, and bisected by a narrow, slow-moving river that was good to look at but for not much else. The new Minsk was an unequivocal statement of the totalitarian impulse, stripped down and neatly fitted together, and without any history, energy, cultural edifices, or anything else that might feel busy, loud, urbane, or unexpected. The normal layering of the polis—the sediment-like building up of peoples, architectures, styles, and eras that stretched across decades and centuries in most cities—did not obtain. It felt inorganic. This feeling was intensified by its surroundings, which consisted of mostly gray-green countryside. Approaching Minsk from any direction, one did not pass from farmland to town to suburb to city; rather, one moved from farmland directly to the city. Even the people, most of whom had never left their villages until the war destroyed them, were like props in a Soviet diorama.

It was evening when Oswald stepped off the train in Minsk on January 7, 1960.[2] He did not know where he was, except that it was called Minsk. He seems not to have known in which direction he had been traveling (west), or how far he was from Moscow (408 miles), the Polish border (220 miles), or New York City (4,427 miles). He was probably unaware that he was in the Soviet Socialist Republic of Belorussia[3] and that he was due south of Lithuania and north of the Ukraine. He did not know anything about the geography or sociology of this particular subset of *Homo Sovieticus*, or about the regional economy, which revolved around a network of *kollektivnoye khozayistvo*, or collective farms. He did not know that he had been sent there because it was far from Moscow—the better to keep him away from anyone important, including not only Soviet officials but Western reporters—and small and self-contained, like a fishbowl. He also didn't know that he was now in the westernmost flank of the Soviet Union and that there were army bases tucked away in the green-black forests and air force jets constantly flying overhead. For many years, Belorussia had been a place that was between more important places. Now, it was an armed fortress, and it played a critical role in defending the whole country.[4]

Oswald was met at the station by two representatives of the Red Cross. They escorted him to the Hotel Minsk, on Prospekt Stalina. The boulevard was wide, with a handful of recently built low-lying buildings with neoclassical facades. They looked stately. Minsk, like Moscow, was a horizontal city. In recent years it had been infused with a new life, but it was still hemmed in by a quiet order that was absent in most cities, which overflowed with people, signs, colors, and movements. In his diary Oswald sounds less excited or curious than overwhelmed. He had never been anywhere like it before. It is a measure of how closely watched Oswald was that the day after he arrived, the mayor of Minsk, one Comrade Shrapov, made his introduction. Shrapov, Oswald wrote, "promisis a rent-free apartment 'soon' and warns me about 'uncultured persons' who somethines insuit foriengers." This red-carpet treatment was not unheard of. "Immigrants in the USSR," Oswald wrote, "are treated with more respect than the Russians treat each other. . . . This is part of the nation wide drive to impress all foriengrers as to the high level of life in the USSR."[5]

In his essay "The Collective," Oswald provided a lengthy description of the foreigner's first encounter with the city. This section is noteworthy because it includes some illuminating details about Oswald's new home and because it is the only section, in any of Oswald's writings, that concerns itself largely with the concrete and the mundane—as opposed to the more abstract, ideological questions he preferred to write about. "The arkatecual planning may be any thing but modern but it is the manner of almost all Russian citys with the airport serving as its . . . eastern boundry we find a large spead out township in apperance, city. Only the skyline [illegible] with factory looms and chimmlies betrays its industrial background." As one entered the center of the city, Oswald noted, one encountered the Hotel Minsk and the post office, which was built in 1955 "in the Greek style." "Next down the prospect are a clothing store, childrens store, the central movie house, the best one in mink seating 400 people in an small unventilated hall. Next to it stands a shoe store across from it the central barber shop. the main Drug Store and a [illegible]." A little farther down the *prospekt*, or boulevard, past the Ministry of Internal Affairs and the local KGB headquarters, was an unnamed restaurant—one of just five in the whole city. For two rubles one could have chicken, potatoes, and fried cabbage. Other dishes included beefsteak, potatoes and cabbage with macaroni, sweet rolls with coffee, and, in the summer, various fruits and salads with tomatoes.[6]

When Oswald woke up at the Hotel Minsk on the morning of January 8, it would have been helpful had the Red Cross, Comrade Shrapov, or Oswald's new interpreter, Roman Detkov,[7] given him a glossary of all the character types whom he was likely to encounter in a provincial Soviet city: workers, pensioners, students, musicians, apparatchiks, senior officials (or *nomenklatura*), and a small number of intelligentsia. Most of these people were quintessential Menchani, or "residents of Minsk." Menchani, like most people in the Belorussian Soviet Socialist Republic, were, above all, Soviet. They may also have been Belorussian, Polish, or Russian, but their primary identity was their ideology (unlike, say, the Baltic peoples to the north or the Ukrainians to the southwest, who had retained a national heritage and were in a permanent state of semiwar with the Soviet regime).

There were two overarching reasons for this. First, there had never really been a strong Belorussian national identity with which Sovietism had to compete. And second, the violent upheaval of the past quarter century, which included not only the German invasion but the collectivization, mass deportations, and purges of the 1930s, had destroyed most everyone who might have helped cultivate a national identity separate from the Soviet superstate. "There were no real citizens of Minsk left after the war," said Igor Kuznetsov, a historian at Belarus State University who has studied the impact of the Gulag and the war on Belorussian identity. There were only the peasants, who had just arrived, had no serious connection to any liberal tradition, and were inclined to be led by a strongman or "strong hand"—the *silniy ruyka*. In the 1950s and 1960s, more than half the people living in Minsk had been born in a village.[8]

The peasant-workers, many of whom spoke one or another rural dialect, were like their environment—flat. They wanted small things: a slab of meat, a few hundred grams of vodka, a pig, a goat, a few chickens, a body to lie next to at night—*stabilnost*. They embraced the Soviet Union and all of its symbols and mythologies because there was little else to embrace and because it had delivered them from the fascist invaders. "Most workers in Minsk," Oswald wrote, "come from peasent stock while repopulated the city at the end of the 2nd War.; like most Russinas they are warm hearted and simple but often stubborn and untrustworthy."[9]

Minsk was not the only flat place in the Soviet Union. Everywhere in the country there was a peasant-worker culture—a tasteless food filled with grease and mayonnaise; a colorless, overbearing architecture; a truncated alphabet and vocabulary made simple for the toiling masses—but in almost every place there was also a subculture, something genuine and rich that predated the communist ironing out of ancient civilizations. This underlying culture lent depth and a sense of humor and irony to peoples across the Soviet Union; it created a space between that which was real and organic and that which had been imposed.[10]

But in Belorussia, and especially in Minsk, there was no subculture. There was no deep tradition with its own artistic and intellectual inheritance, its own commercial practices, its own mores and rituals. There was nothing that connected present-day Menchani with previous generations. It was as if they had been severed from the past. It was as if the color, the blood, the *idea* of the city had been drained out of it. It was what might be called a fake city filled with fake city dwellers. People existed incongruously—far away from the villages and towns they had known and unable to return to them. They were a people, for the most part, who lived in a city without knowing *how* to live there. Here, if you dug beneath the surface of the peasant-worker culture, you found very little else.

Perhaps because there was no self-contained, underlying tradition, because there was nothing else to feel close to, Menchani, paradoxically enough, felt very close to Minsk. Indeed, their territoriality amounted to a substitute subculture, and, for this reason, it was not only a matter of geography. It had to do with a strange dichotomy at the heart of their identity. It was true that they had not been born or raised in the city and that there was an incongruity about their lives, a sense of displacement. But it was also true that *this* city was theirs more than anyone else's. They felt this connection very strongly. They were the ones who had lifted, hauled, swept, dug, and erected a new place out of the old. That was why they talked with great pride about Minsk. They were protective of their turf.

All this was of significance when it came to Oswald because it greatly impeded his efforts at fitting in. Soviets prided themselves on their cosmopolitanism, and in fact many cities in the Soviet Union had a rich blend of peoples, cultures, and histories—not only Moscow and Leningrad, but Kiev, Odessa, Tbilisi, Baku, and even to the east, beyond the Urals, in Siberia and the Russian Far East. In all these places, Oswald would have likely encountered a more colorful array of attitudes and opinions, a greater openness to outsiders, a greater disdain for Soviet authority. There would have been more opportunities to forge more enduring friendships, and he would have been permitted to indulge in his quasi-intellectual ambitions to a greater degree than in Minsk. The KGB would not have had trouble recruiting people to inform on Oswald, as was done in Minsk, and they would have monitored him constantly, but there would have been a greater ironic detachment between the people in his life—the friends, acquaintances, lovers, coworkers, and others who would have been recruited to report on him—and the security organs. There would have been plenty of smirking and dark humor, winks and nods, and these would have made Oswald's eventual realization that he was being watched very closely less traumatic than would be the case in Minsk. It would have made possible a secret solidarity with his new comrades, a feeling of shared repression. Oswald's experience in Minsk, by contrast, was one of gradually coming to the conclusion that he was all alone, that the Soviet Union was not the home he had hoped it would be.

Oswald, perhaps in an effort to mitigate his initial disappointment with a city that could never have compared with Moscow, described Minsk as a work in progress. "The reconstruction of Minsk is on interesting story reflecting the courage of its Builders. In a tolatitarian system great forces can be brought into place under rigid controls and support." He seemed to want to reconcile his ideology with his personal feelings about the city, to try to make sense of all the things that were naturally discomfiting—the "rigid controls"—in light of something that was much nobler and idealistic—"the reconstruction" and "the courage of its Builders."[11]

When I interviewed Tamara Pavlovna Soroko, who was born in 1944 and worked at the same factory where Oswald would work, she said she doubted that the American ever understood the real Minsk or appreciated the connection between Minsk and the Menchani. Their Minsk was not drab or quiet, which was how foreigners often saw it, but glorious. It was a triumph of great and innumerable sacrifices.[12]

Not surprisingly, none of the people who would become close to Oswald in Minsk were true Menchani. His three closest friends—Pavel Golovachev, Ernst Titovets, and Yuri Merezhinsky—were too educated or ambitious, or they came from members of the Soviet elite. Marina Prusakova, his future wife, was not sophisticated, and she was certainly not elite (her uncle from the Interior Ministry notwithstanding), but she wasn't a villager either, and her disposition and sensibility were more urban, more inclined to the hustle; there was a grittiness and garrulousness about her that did not jibe with her adoptive home. The woman he fell in love with before he met Marina, Ella German, was closer to the Menchani, but she was Jewish and therefore not of the old, Slavic peasant stock. Other people he spent a lot of time with included engineers at the factory where he would be employed, but they were not workers, and they were technically educated. Some had spent time in Moscow or were Jewish, and they had traveled; at least one, Alexander Ziger, had emigrated to the Soviet Union from Argentina.[13]

But most of Oswald's future coworkers were very much Menchani. What's more, as was often the case in the Soviet Union, workers from the same factory were assigned to the same apartment building or complex, which is to say that almost all of Oswald's neighbors on Kalinina Ulitsa (which would be renamed Kommunistichiskaya Ulitsa in late 1961 or 1962) worked at the factory and were Menchani. This meant that his everyday experiences in Minsk—coming in and out of his apartment, going to work, being at the factory, having lunch, making dinner, taking out the trash—were circumscribed by people who believed in the rightness of the Soviet system and were naturally suspicious of any outsiders and especially of any Americans, no matter how much those foreigners professed to be Marxists (or, better yet, *especially* if they professed to be Marxists).

Of all of Oswald's future coworkers, none was filled with a greater pride and none had a deeper feeling for the sensibility of Minsk than Leonid Stepanovich Tsagoiko. Tsagoiko worked in the same department as Oswald, and he recalled having seen the American most days. "We were on friendly terms," he told me.[14]

What was most important about Tsagoiko, like nearly everyone Oswald met at the factory, was something Oswald knew very little about—his experience of the war. Of course, Oswald would hear plenty of war stories, but he never learned the whole history, and he certainly didn't have any psychological understanding of what it had been like to be in Minsk during the invasion and then the occupation. This was not a problem in any day-to-day sense, but it meant that Oswald could never really grasp the shape and scope of the lives of everyone he spent most of his time with—and it meant that they had a very difficult time making sense of Oswald, who had not been through the things they had been through and didn't know very much about those experiences. The war was the organizing principle around which the Menchani had built, or been forced to build, their whole lives. It was the great demarcation. Events and people came either before or after it, and anything that came after was fundamentally different from whatever came before.

As Tamara Soroko, the woman who worked at the same factory as Oswald, said, the war had "created new people" out of those who were left behind. In the same way that Minsk had been hollowed out, she said, the people who had survived the shock and violence of the German occupation had been emptied of the places and people who had once filled their lives. Just as Minsk had rebuilt itself, so had the Menchani. They were tough.

In light of this history, there was bound to be a tension, or disconnect, between Oswald and the Menchani. The American had come to Minsk believing himself independent, strong—as tough as any Russian. Recall the letter Oswald wrote to his brother before departing for Minsk: "I have chosen to remove all ties with my past, so I will not write again, nor do I wish you to try and contact me, I'm sure you understand that I would not like to recive correspondence from people in the country which I fled. I am starting a new life and I do not wish to have anything to do with the old life." It turned out that starting a new life would be harder than he expected. It would require an extraordinary fortitude and perseverance, and it would require adapting to a world filled with people who possessed great strength and were not entirely sympathetic to someone who found it hard to be one of them.[15]

It was not simply that the Menchani had been affected by the war; it was that they had been brought to Minsk and granted a new future by it. The war had destroyed everything they had known, and then it had given them a life they could never have anticipated before it. In the case of Leonid Tsagoiko and his mother and brother, they had been uprooted from their home in the town of Ivenetz, west of Minsk, and, in fact, their address no longer existed. Even if it had existed, there were no longer any records indicating that they had ever lived there. This meant they could claim they were from Minsk, and this meant they could receive internal passports, which would enable them to travel most anywhere in the Soviet Union—which was among the most important benefits that came with being a resident of an officially recognized city. (Before the war, in Ivenetz, they had not had internal passports because only people in cities could get those. If they had wanted to go somewhere outside Ivenetz, they would have had to receive written permission.) As Tamara Soroko put it, saying you came from Minsk meant you were no longer a serf.

Naturally, Leonid Tsagoiko and his mother and brother were not the only ones who wanted greater mobility. Many, if not most, of the peasants who ventured to Minsk in the mid to late forties had the same goal. Indeed, Oswald must have heard as much from his coworkers: "The Collective" includes a detailed discussion of passports, identification papers, and places from which most Soviet citizens were generally barred.[16]

The process involved in obtaining residence papers underscored the extent to which the Menchani were untethered to any previous identity— and the extent to which they would come to embrace their new identity as proud Soviet citizens of the city of Minsk. The first and most important step in this process entailed getting a new birth certificate. "I went to the doctor," Tsagoiko said, "and, judging by my appearance, he said I was born sometime in the first half of 1930. Then he said I could choose a birthday, so I chose April 23 because it came exactly six months after my real birthday." According to Soroko, "People, and especially women, liked to pick dates that made them younger. One woman . . . they told her [mistakenly] she was five years younger than she was, so she picked a birthday that indicated this. Then, later, after she had been working for some time, she restored her old birthday. I don't know how she did this. This meant that one day she celebrated her fiftieth birthday, and the next week she became a pensioner." People generally stopped working at fifty-five.

This murkiness about who one was and where one came from was further exacerbated by the less-violent but nonetheless disruptive social dislocations wrought by the war. It has been noted by many Menchani that, like Soviet citizens elsewhere, they had acquired a second, or even a third, surname during the war. This pointed to the kaleidoscope of fathers and families many children had cycled through. Soroko, for example, said she had two last names. That was because her mother and father were not married when she was born, so Soroko got her last name from her mother. This was the name on her food card, which was issued to everyone after the war so they could contend with the food shortages. But then her father returned—he had been away, either fighting or working; it was never entirely clear—and her parents gave her his last name. Her father's name was the name she preferred; it was only proper, she said. But it was not the name that could get her food. For that, she needed to be someone else.

Soroko and Tsagoiko said this was common. Many Russian men had spent the war traveling around the country—fighting, running away, or living with another family. They had been serving on the front, or they had been imprisoned in a penal colony east of the Urals, in the far north or in central Asia. Then they were wounded, or they couldn't or didn't want to go home, and they married or just started sleeping with a woman from a nearby village. They had children, and then they had a second (or third) family. For a few years after the war, many of these men trickled back to Minsk. Sometimes they came with their new families. Some of Oswald's coworkers said that one of the reasons why the American attracted so much female attention in Minsk was that women thought he was stable and sober—the opposite of the postwar Soviet man, who seemed to many unmoored, aimless, and undependable.[17]

The immediate postwar period instilled in the Menchani a sense of belonging. Tsagoiko explained that there was no time for rest. He worked six days a week, and on Sundays everyone had to clear debris and plant trees. They would form assembly lines on the *prospekt* and the riverbank that were one-thousand-people, two-thousand-people, or even ten-thousand-people long, and they would move large piles of rocks and dirt. He remembered the sounds of the assembly line. They had shovels and small pickaxes. Everyone swore and heaved together; everyone perspired and bled. Most important, Soroko said, everyone had the same memories. When they talked about the new Minsk, they felt a combination of pride and solidarity. "This was a wonderful time," she said. Yes, there were food cards. And they had to live in the old barracks, which were like stables—damp, mildewy, dark, and hot. If they were lucky, they found a room in an apartment with other families and strangers. But this did not bother most Menchani. They thought of each other as members of the same family. Tsagoiko, like his coworkers at the factory, agreed that they were stronger then. Everyone knew what everyone else had suffered through, so they were kind to each other. "This was the time when there were no strangers in Minsk," Tsagoiko said.

By the time the American turned up, fifteen years after the war ended, the Menchani had made great progress. Oswald knew this in a way. He knew the city had been rebuilt after the war. In "The Collective," he wrote that "the design and structure of the city allready gives no idea of the condition of the capital of the Belerussian State in 1945." But his knowledge was mostly studied; it did not come from any firsthand exposure. Oswald lacked any of the shared memories, and, in fact, he could not imagine what it would have been like to have had these experiences, to have hunkered down and burrowed and pushed through and been enveloped by the destruction—to have survived. No one who had not been through a similar experience could have known about these things, and especially not an American who had grown up in a country that was at peace and was always looking forward, upward, that was, on some level, intensely ahistorical. As his friend Ernst Titovets said in an interview, Oswald lacked a "psychological understanding" of Minsk, and this made it much harder—at first—for him to grasp where he stood with the Menchani.

Instead, over time, Oswald would come to the realization that he was not a Menchan and never would be. He would discover this with a combination of unhappiness, dejection, and fear. But he did not know this in the beginning. In the first few months after his arrival in Minsk, he remained under the illusion that this place could be his home—the last place, the place that would end all of his interloping. At last, he would escape his mother, himself, the past, and he would not only embrace Marxism and the revolution but also be embraced. He would feel as if he had finally arrived in the place where he had always belonged, and the sense of a nauseous, frenetic motion would be over.[18]

But on a fundamental level that Oswald could not have been expected to apprehend, there was a vast psychological-cultural chasm separating him from the Menchani. It was as if they were immiscible liquids—the American and his Russian hosts. The American could insert himself into their lives, and he could learn some of their language, and he could spend long nights dining or going to concerts or forging close, even intimate relationships with them, and it would not be enough to close the gap. It came down to a feeling, Soroko said. It was a matter of *druygi* (friends) versus *znakomi* (acquaintants). This was a distinction, Soroko said, that Oswald, an American, could not understand because Americans called everyone their friend. Also, she said, Americans smiled constantly, and they moved their lips a great deal when they spoke, as if they were happy to see you, even if you knew they were not.

The Russian's personal universe was much smaller, Tsagoiko said—and, in this respect, he was backed up by most everyone I met in Minsk, Moscow, and elsewhere in Russia. It included, at most, two or three friendships. A friend, he said, was someone who was like a brother or a parent. This was the kind of person, Soroko said, who would do anything for you, if you asked, and would never ask why. A Russian friend of mine (a real friend, not an acquaintance) once explained it to me: "If I am in Vladivostok, and you are in Moscow, and I call you and say, 'Come here now'—it is a very long way, several time zones—you will come, and you will not ask why. Then you are a friend. Then you should come to my funeral, and I should come to yours."

The sharpness of this distinction between friends and acquaintances was a little blurry during the first years after the war. At that time, there was a strong feeling of solidarity among Menchani. This was when there was "friendship with everyone," as another one of Oswald's coworkers put it. In 1953, when Stalin died, this feeling started to subside, but it never went away entirely, and it was very much alive when Oswald arrived in January 1960. Even though people no longer talked about the war the way they used to, and even though there were no more assembly lines on the *prospekt*, and the bodies and rubble had been cleared, and the new, monumental buildings had risen out of the craters and smoke, they still thought about it and remembered. It was inescapable; it was a part of their collective memories.[19]

It was difficult, Soroko told me, for anyone who arrived in Minsk in 1960, in the age of Khrushchev, to become anyone's *druyg*. They did not mean to be thoughtless, she said. The experience of the war had been so intense, so acrid, bitter, and all-consuming, that it had changed everyone permanently. It was hard to understand people who had not been changed in the same way. She said it was as if people who had been through the war and people who had not had come from different countries. This meant, she said, that Oswald came from a country, the United States, that was "two countries away" from her own. It made it hard for such people to understand each other.

6

THE EXPERIMENTAL DEPARTMENT

T HE KGB APPEARS TO HAVE BEEN TROUBLED BY ONE THING: they still did not know—or they did not believe they knew—why he had come all the way to the Soviet Union. They thought that if he felt at home, he would be more open. So they gave him a job and, by Soviet standards, a spacious apartment, with a balcony and a view of the river, the Svisloch. They created a whole world for him. According to the FBI's report on Yuri Nosenko, the KGB officer who handled the Oswald case in Moscow, Nosenko said that after Oswald left Moscow, his file was "transferred to the regional office of the KGB at Minsk and that office was instructed to maintain a discreet check" on him. The security organs had not ruled out the possibility that he was a "sleeper agent" for American intelligence.[1]

On January 13, 1960, six days after he arrived in Minsk, Oswald showed up for his first day of work at the Experimental Department in the Minsk Radio Factory Named in Honor of the Fiftieth Anniversary of the October Revolution. Soon he would move into his new apartment, a seven- or eight-minute walk from the factory.[2]

The Minsk Radio Factory designed and manufactured radios and television sets for the entire communist world—from East Berlin to Warsaw to Moscow to Khabarovsk and Vladivostok. Oswald, in "The Collective," called the factory "a fine example of average, and even slightly better than average, working conditions." He said that it employed five thousand workers full-time and another three hundred part-time and that 58 percent of the employees were female. It's unclear just how many radios and television sets the factory manufactured each year. Oswald wrote that the factory churned out eighty-seven thousand radios and sixty thousand televisions, but he didn't indicate whether he was referring to a specific year or a rate of production. Oswald noted that the full employment rate that the Soviets were so proud of could be explained by a lack of automation in factories and a "democratic corps" of workers whose job was to shuffle reams of paperwork from one office to the next. The factory's crowning achievement, as of early 1960, when Oswald arrived, was the "combination radio-phonograph-television set," which, Oswald noted, was shown at the Soviet Exhibition in New York in 1959.[3]

The factory's Experimental Department occupied two stories; it had large windows and high ceilings, and the walls were painted pink, gray, and green. "Green," said Filip Lavshuk, then the department's junior foreman, "was good for your eyes. Every year, they would repaint the walls to make sure everything looked professional." It was important that the mood was uplifting, Lavshuk said. That was part of the socialist ethos. Lavshuk embodied this can-do spirit. "Loveook," Oswald wrote, mangling his name, "is much younger . . . enigetic, handson, quick, he climbed to his post through a night school degree and a sort of rough charm which he instintively uses in the presence of superiors."[4]

The Experimental Department's job was to come up with ideas for new televisions, which could then be turned into prototypes and shipped to the authorities in Moscow, where they would decide which ones would be mass-produced. The department was divided, roughly speaking, into two sections: a small group of engineers, who designed the new models, and two hundred or so metal-lathe operators and metal workers, whose job it was to turn the engineers' blueprints into reality. When Oswald first reported for duty, the department was working on the Belarus I and II models, said Sergei Skop, a coworker. Oswald mostly worked on the

Belarus III and IV, which had a screen just shy of sixteen inches. Lavshuk was especially enthusiastic about the Belarus V, which featured sleeker knobs and dials and a better picture, but he said it was the Belarus II, a few years earlier, that had marked a real breakthrough, combining the television set with a radio and record player.[5]

There was an unspoken divide between the engineers and the metal-lathe operators and metal workers. The engineers were mostly Jewish, and they were much better educated, said Stanislaw Shushkevich, an engineer in the department. Tamara Soroko said it was true that most of the engineers were Jewish, but she added that it was also true that many metal-lathe operators were, too. "The real difference was education," she said. Shushkevich, who is not Jewish, disagreed. He said that tensions between the engineers and the metal-lathe operators and metal workers was camouflaged by an aura of socialist camaraderie. Sometimes, he said, one of the workers would have an idea about how to design a better television, and this could be annoying because you had to listen. Once in a while one of the workers had a good idea, but usually, Shushkevich said, you just nodded, took notes, and said, "This is interesting. I'll see what I can do about it." And then you forgot whatever had just been said.[6]

When Oswald first turned up at the Experimental Department, Lavshuk said, he didn't have any special training and, in fact, didn't even know what the Experimental Department did. "What do they want me to do with him?" Lavshuk recalled thinking. "He can't do anything." Lavshuk gave Oswald two choices—*tokar* (metal-lathe operator) or *sleysar* (metal worker). Oswald chose metal-lathe operator and was assigned to a desk on the second floor, where there were always somewhere between fifty and seventy people welding television sets together. "On the first floor of the department, people worked in two shifts, from eight a.m. to four p.m., and from four p.m. to eleven p.m., but on the second floor, where Oswald worked, they only worked one shift, from eight to four," Lavshuk said.[7]

Vladimir Libezin, a metal worker, became Oswald's "master," instructing the American in the ways of metal-lathing. He found a Russian tutor for Oswald: Stanislaw Shushkevich. Libezin told Oswald where the lavatory was and where people went to smoke. And on Oswald's first day of work, Libezin made sure that some of the other metal-lathe operators took him to lunch at one of the canteens at the factory. Alexandra Lavshuka said Libezin was an excellent master—very patient, very warm. Leonid Botvinik, a senior metal-lathe operator in the department, agreed. Botvinik, who was Jewish, said that even though Libezin was a "typical Russian anti-Semite," he was also a good metal worker. There was no one in the department, he said, who played a more important role in Oswald's life at the factory than Libezin did.[8]

But Libezin's job was not limited to metal-lathing or even the factory. As the most senior Communist Party official in the Experimental Department, he also served as Oswald's ideological supervisor, and no doubt he provided the party with regular updates on the American. Libezin was not a Menchan like Leonid Tsagoiko. He was more of a generic Soviet. It was his view that if Oswald learned about the tenets of Marxism-Leninism and the many things the party had built—such as factories, railroads, collective farms, and power plants—he would see the world the way they did.[9]

In "The Collective," Oswald wrote: "The key person in this shop, as everyone appreciates is . . . Libezin. 45 years old, the party secatary." Libezin, Oswald observed, had been appointed by the Minsk Radio Factory party chief, and he was responsible for "shop disiplen, party meetings, distribution of propaganda and any other odd 'jobs' that might come up including see to it that there are always enough red and white signs and sologan hanging on the walls." It did not take long for him to start grating on Oswald. In his diary Oswald wrote: "I am increasingly aware of the presence, in all thing, of Lebizen . . . fat, fortyish, and Jovial on the outside. He is a no-nonsense party regular." Oswald was learning about the omnipresence, the tentacle-like nature, of the party. It did not jibe with his fervor and expectations. He had thought that he would come to the Soviet Union and start over. But one senses, in his mockery of and irritation with Libezin, the same sense of alienation that he encountered at Atsugi and El Toro and that led him to separate himself from the group, to embrace his Marxism and the label they had assigned him—Oswaldskovich. It would be at least several months until Oswald began to suspect the extent to which the party worked in close consultation with the security organs.[10]

Vladimir Pavlovich Libezin had been born in 1918, one year after the Bolshevik revolution, and he had grown up in the village of Cherem-khovo in eastern Siberia. In 1938, when he was twenty, he met his future wife, Ekaterina Ivanovna Gorelova, who was then seventeen or eighteen, on a railway platform in the town of Alatyr in the heart of European Russia. He was enthralled by her but did not propose immediately. Instead, Libezin returned to Siberia, and Ekaterina Ivanovna went back to Moscow—she had been in Alatyr to complete a *praktika*, or internship, with the local railway authority—and they wrote letters. They were separated by 3,100 miles on the trans-Siberian railway.[11]

After war broke out, according to Libezin's son Oleg, his father was assigned to a tank unit and sent to the front. He was a signaler; his job was to make sure the tanks and soldiers could communicate with each other. He served in the Battle of Moscow and the Battle of Kursk. He was also a proud member of the Communist Party, as Oswald pointed out in "The Collective," suggesting that it was at about this time that Libezin proved his real value to party officials. "During the war," Oswald wrote, "he was for a short time a *tankest* but his talents seemed to have been to good for that job so he was made a military policemen." Oswald echoed a widely held view, that Libezin's job did not entail enforcing military rules but, rather, party loyalty. Libezin, in other words, was a snoop; his job was to report on anyone who said anything deemed traitorous by the party.[12]

During the war, Libezin continued writing letters to Ekaterina. The Red Army soldiers called these letters from the front *treugolnichki*, or triangles, because they were written on open-faced, triangular pieces of paper that could be sent, via internal military post, anywhere in Russia that was not occupied by the Germans. *Treugolnichki* were lifelines that sustained millions of husbands, wives, and lovers. They were short and always of the utmost importance, infused with feeling and an overwhelming sense of urgency. They were the quintessential Soviet love letter, and they could be beautiful and even poetic. But they were not only used in this way. *Treugolnichki* were also used by the army as *pokhoronki*, or death notices. In this way, the corridors of love and death constantly crossed and recrossed each other. To receive a *treugolnik* was to receive great happiness or great pain.

Over the course of the war, Libezin received two Orders of the Red Star, and Ekaterina, who was in Moscow coordinating the transportation of men and matériel across the Ural Mountains, received a statement of commendation. This was a prestigious award, and it came in a handsome, forest-green case. It was signed at the bottom by Lazar Moiseyevich Kaganovich, the minister of railways and a close associate of Josef Stalin.[13]

In 1944, while he was on leave in Moscow, Libezin married Ekaterina. The next year, he marched with his unit all the way to Berlin. His work, rooting out soldiers who had been infected by foreign ways and thinking, would have been particularly important at this time.

After the war, Ekaterina, by then a well-regarded railway administrator, was told by the railway authorities that she could choose from three places to move to: Vilnius, Kiev, or Tashkent. She and Libezin chose Vilnius, in the Lithuanian Soviet Socialist Republic—it was the closest to Moscow, where her family was—and, in 1947, their first son, Oleg Vladimirovich, was born. Then, in 1951, the government reorganized the railway districts, and the family was moved to Minsk, southeast of Vilnius. Libezin, having studied mechanics at Cheremkhovo, was given a job in the Experimental Department at the Minsk Radio Factory. Libezin's boss hung a sign in the entrance of the department announcing that Libezin was a war hero. In 1953, a second son, Alexander Vladimirovich, was born.[14]

In 1960, Libezin and Ekaterina were assigned one of the new *khrushchyovki*. The apartment had a tiny kitchen and bathroom, a living room that was also the boys' room, and a bedroom. The ceilings were low, the walls thin. The corridor that led from the front door to the bathroom was wide enough for one medium-sized person to slip through at a time. But it was a new apartment, and it was theirs. It had walls, doors, locks, and windows that separated them from the rest of the world, and they were grateful.

Also in 1960, in January, something happened that Libezin did not expect: an American named Lee Harvey Oswald arrived at the Experimental Department.

Once, Libezin brought Oswald home to the little apartment. Oleg, who was twelve or thirteen then, recalled Oswald standing in the doorway that separated the corridor from the living room. Oswald leaned against the doorway; he seemed casual. Later, Oleg remembered thinking that it was a very American way to be. He couldn't believe there was an American in their apartment. He remembered his father patting Oswald on the shoulder and thought: my father just put his hand on an American shoulder.

Libezin seemed to like Oswald. At least, this was how some of Oswald's coworkers remembered things. In any event, Libezin probably did not have strong feelings about his new charge. That was not his job. His job was to be Oswald's ideological mentor and, more importantly, to make sure that he did not start saying or believing the wrong things—about communism, the premier, anything that might be considered sensitive or important. That was why it was okay for him to bring Oswald home. Most people would not have dared. That was expected of an *apparatchik* doing what he did, which was what he had done during the war: protecting the party and the state from threats to their security.

At the factory the workers could eat lunch at one of four canteens. Lunch lasted one hour. Usually it would start between twelve and twelve thirty, although sometimes it was later. A bell would ring throughout the factory, signaling that it was time to eat. Workers from the Experimental Department would go in groups of five or six. There would be Skop, Tsagoiko, usually Libezin, sometimes Leonid Botvinik, and two or three other men. Lavshuk, being their boss, never came. They preferred the two canteens in the Administrative Building and usually went to the *stolovaya* on the first floor. Lunch at the *stolovaya* cost about 60 kopeks, but if you added sour cream to your soup or if you had an egg, it would cost a little more—probably between 75 cents and $1 today. Later, the *stolovaya* started charging for bread, even black bread, and everyone at the factory thought this was wrong. Still, lunch was reasonably priced. It consisted of borscht, *solyanka* (a meat and vegetable soup), or mushroom soup (but not with cream); potatoes; beefsteak or "cutlet," which meant pork or beef or some pork-beef combination; fruit juice, or compote, which was called *morz*; tea; and maybe a small wedge of cake that was usually very sweet and a little stale. There were also canteens in the Microwave Electronics Building and the Television Set Building, but they never ate at those.[15]

All of Oswald's coworkers at the Experimental Department could remember one thing very well about lunch at the Minsk Radio Factory: after his first day, they never ate with him again. No one could explain why. No one ever said, "I refuse to eat with the American." This was just the way things were.[16]

Stanislaw Shushkevich said that, despite the friendly reception that Oswald received, he was never a *druyg*, a friend. "He wasn't part of the family" of workers at the Experimental Department, according to Shushkevich. "Absolutely not. The thing was that the family didn't accept him. He was not sufficiently qualified. In the framework of his profession, he was lower than the other people in the department, but he received the same salary as other people." Shushkevich also recalled that "his look, his appearance, was very noticeable, not like the other men in the department. For example, he was always clean, his hair brushed, his buttons buttoned. The other men, and not just the men, were kind of dirty because if you're a worker and your hands are dirty, then you can be proud, because dirt is proof of your work, that you are a real worker." Galina Antonovna Makovskaya, whose desk on the second floor of the department was near Oswald's, assumed that Oswald's failure to fit in, to become a real worker, was what you could expect from Americans and that America, as they had been told, was a very bad place where everyone smiled even though they weren't happy. Also, she was sure there were things about Oswald that they didn't know. "No one could just come here, get an apartment in the center, have a job, get paid good money, and then leave," Makovskaya said. "He rarely spoke. He almost never spoke. And he had a way that he walked."[17]

Tsagoiko agreed with Shushkevich that there was an unspoken distance—he called it "a strange film"—between the American and the

Russians. He also agreed that this had something to do with the way Oswald looked and acted at work, although he insisted that he was never put off by Oswald's lackadaisical attitude toward metal-lathing. It was true that the thickness of the grime under one's fingernails was very important. An inadequate level of dirt meant one wasn't really working. A more abundant filth—which included not only a rich fingernail grit filled with tiny bits of ash and tar but also blackened fingerprints on one's forehead, one's forearms, and the sides of one's neck—was an unofficial symbol of membership in the Experimental Department. "Metal-lathe operators wore boots that came up to the middle of your ankle," he said, "because when you worked with steel there would be some pieces of metal that were red hot. We had changing rooms and showers and, later, a sauna. The whole place was very messy—there was oil, glue, dust."[18]

According to Tamara Soroko, "The department always smelled like it was burning." Tsaguiko explained that "the reason for that was there was a special liquid, an emulsion they used to cool all the details [the knobs and dials] that went into the television sets. The emulsion was made of water, soda, and these chemicals that no one knew anything about." If you walked into the Experimental Department in the middle of the day, Shushkevich said, there would be several miniature, gray-white cumulus clouds of metallic dust hovering over the tabletops and the long fluorescent lamps hanging from the ceiling. Also, Soroko said, it was loud, with the constant grinding of electric saws, the pounding of bolt fasteners, and the colliding of metal cylinders against each other. Shushkevich said the Experimental Department was like the departments of factories where tens of millions of Soviet *rabotniki*, or workers, worked everyday across the country. There was a certain culture. "You see," he said, "workers at the plant had their habits. For example, you're a good worker if you can drink your share of vodka. You're a good worker if you can fight." Referring to Oswald, Shushkevich said, "He wasn't able to do these things."[19]

Complicating things was an unspoken fear: a belief that being too close, or being perceived as being too close, to the American would make other people, and especially the security organs, question one's loyalty. It cannot be a coincidence that most of the people who would spend the most time with Oswald had some institutional protection—parents in the party hierarchy or the military leadership or personal connections to the Interior Ministry. Others were either innocent and probably naïve (Ella German) or, more likely, informing on intimate details of Oswald's life and therefore encouraged to spend as much time with him as possible. But his coworkers at the Experimental Department would not have had these advantages. For them, Oswald would have been fascinating and frightening. Not surprisingly, no one in Oswald's apartment building was known to have ever invited him over for a meal, coffee, or a late-night drink. Nor did Oswald ever invite them—this despite the fact that Oswald entertained other Soviet citizens in Minsk.[20]

Still, Tsagoiko said the American had been welcomed into the department. He recalled that he and some others in the department had taken him hunting once, in the forest outside Minsk. Tsagoiko told me the same thing about Oswald's marksmanship that he had told the KGB: "That whole day, we saw only one hare, and Oswald took a shot at it and missed." Tsagoiko added that after that day, he was told not to take Oswald hunting again. "Someone from the KGB told the head of the department"—Lavshuk or maybe Leonid Botvinik—"and he told us we couldn't take him." Lavshuk told me this wasn't true. He said that no one from the KGB, the party, or anywhere else ever talked to him about Oswald not being allowed to go hunting. Then, he added, somewhat enigmatically, that it was possible that he had discussed Oswald's hunting expedition with someone from the intelligence service and been unaware of it. It was possible, he explained, to be approached by someone—a coworker, a friend, a stranger at the store or on the tram—and to discuss things, directly or indirectly, and to misunderstand what was being asked or said. When I asked Shushkevich what this meant, he laughed. Then he said, "This is the way these things were talked about."[21]

Besides Oswald's work ethic, there was his Russian, which was not good, at least for the first year or so that he was in Minsk. The language barrier made it difficult for Oswald's coworkers to talk to him about anything important, and it meant that, even after spending a long time with Oswald, most people came away not really knowing him. Shushkevich, for instance, said that even though he spent several hours with Oswald tutoring him in Russian, he never felt as if he learned anything about him. There was always, he said, something blank or unknowable about the American. Shushkevich wasn't sure whether this was because of Oswald's Russian or because of Oswald's personality. He thought it was probably both. This disconnect, he added, was not entirely Oswald's fault; there were people who apparently enjoyed spending time with him. It just happened that Shushkevich, who was accustomed to working and socializing with some of the smartest and most ambitious people in Minsk, was not one of them. (By the time the Soviet Union collapsed in 1991, Shushkevich was an accomplished physicist and the speaker of the Belarusian parliament, making him the most powerful man in newly independent Belarus.) Oswald did not have the intellectual heft or the wit to rise to this level. He was mildly interesting, but only to a point and only because he was a novelty. It is not surprising that Shushkevich quickly became bored with him.

Shushkevich said he had been asked to help Oswald. In the Soviet Union, people were expected to do "social work"—digging ditches, planting flowerbeds, cleaning up a patch of forest, attending a class on Marxism-Leninism, or, in his case, tutoring an American defector in Russian.

The tutoring began soon after Oswald arrived at the Experimental Department. Libezin came to Shushkevich's office one day and said he wanted him to teach the newcomer how to speak Russian. Sasha Rubinchik, who was also an engineer, would join them. They met two, three, or four times each week for an hour and twenty minutes or maybe an hour and a half. Class always took place after the workday was over, at about five fifteen, in a little, nondescript room at the factory. They were never disturbed, Shushkevich said, and they were probably listened to.

Teaching Russian to the American was difficult because neither Shushkevich nor Rubinchik knew English. Also, neither engineer was trained to teach Russian grammar or vocabulary. Shushkevich could teach electronics, physics, or advanced mathematics, but he did not know how to explain why it was important to use a certain case or word, or when he should use the perfect or imperfect form of a verb. Libezin was unconcerned: most important, he said, was that Oswald acquire some basic facility in the language. Shushkevich recalled that there were no explicit rules about what the three of them could discuss, but it was understood that they would not touch on anything "interesting"—politics, history, sociology, or even literature. This was made easier by Oswald's limited Russian: he knew very few words, so it was impossible to discuss anything abstract, and he had trouble expressing anything that was not in the present tense.

Their conversations were elementary. They would talk about the weather, the tram, and the factory—the color of the walls, the height of the ceiling, and the numbers of people who worked on each floor of the Experimental Department. It's worth noting that while Oswald was eager to submerge himself in his new life, he found it hard to communicate with his "comrades" in any meaningful way. Once, in the middle of one of his lessons, Oswald mentioned that he planned to attend a concert by Edita Piekha, a famous singer. Piekha had been born into a Polish family in France, but she had moved to Leningrad in the 1950s. Her most famous song was "Moscow Nights," which Oswald almost certainly became familiar with when he was staying at the Metropol. Shushkevich recalled that it would have been impossible for Oswald to understand the lyrics, so they talked about Piekha's voice and looks. When Oswald didn't know a word, Shushkevich added, he would look it up in a Russian-English dictionary and put an X next to it. The problem was, he said, that Oswald never studied the words he didn't know. The words he learned did not come from their lessons, he said. They came from being around Russians.

Oswald annoyed Shushkevich, but Rubinchik was friendlier with him, and they would often engage in lighthearted conversation. Shushkevich resented that he had to spend time with Oswald. He didn't like that the American was unable to talk about anything deep or intelligent—Shushkevich called him "flat"—and that the people in charge at the factory, including Libezin, treated Oswald as if he were important. Most of all, he didn't understand why Oswald had come to Minsk. Shushkevich spent all his time trying to figure out problems, but he could not figure out this one. Oswald, Shushkevich told me, did not make sense. He didn't appear to know a lot. He didn't appear to *want* to know a lot. Shushkevich did not bring any of this up with Libezin—that would only have created difficulties—but he thought about it often, especially when they were in the middle of a lesson and Oswald was trying to pronounce *iy* and *shch*, or to figure out which prefixes to attach to which verbs. He rarely got that right, Shushkevich said. It is unknown to what extent, if any, Oswald's struggles with writing in the English language impeded his effort to learn Russian.

The time Oswald spent with Shushkevich never extended beyond the classroom. When Shushkevich would see Oswald outside the building, where they smoked, or in the hallway between shifts or at the canteen, he would nod at him curtly. Oswald would smile and nod back. Sometimes, they would exchange pleasantries, and Shushkevich would tell him his accent was coming along. Oswald always said thank you after every lesson, and he was always punctual. He was never rude, and he never stayed longer than he was supposed to.

The three of them—Shushkevich, Rubinchik, and Oswald—met for one month, and then it was decided that the American now spoke Russian. Shushkevich told me he did not know who had made this decision. He knew that it had not come from Libezin or Lavshuk. They didn't make any decisions, he said. Their job was to execute. Shushkevich suspected it had come from someone higher up who did not work at the factory, and he said he had no idea how that person had determined that Oswald had made any progress—there were no tests, and he never filed any reports with Libezin or anyone else—but he wasn't sure that was important. All he knew for sure was that one day, unexpectedly, his social work came to an end. One possible explanation was that Shushkevich and Rubinchik's job had not really been to teach Oswald Russian—that neither man had experience teaching Russian backs this up. Their real job, like that of Libezin and any number of people who flitted in and out of Oswald's life, might have been to get information—in this case, to see how much Russian Oswald really knew or with whom he had made contact. But when I asked Shushkevich if there had been any unstated or ulterior reasons for meeting with Oswald, he shook his head.

At about the time that Oswald's Russian lessons ended, his coworkers started calling him "Alik." Before they knew him, they had said "Amerikanets" and then "Ohssvald." Now came "Alik." It marked a progression of sorts, from the general (American) to the formal (Oswald) to the personal (Alik). There was a rumor in the department that they called him Alik because Lee was supposedly a Chinese name. But Sergei Skop and Lavshuk said they hadn't heard that. They said "Alik" was easier to pronounce than "Lee," and definitely "Harvey," which often came out "Garvey." Also, they said, "Alik" was Russian. Botvinik recalled that it was Libezin who started calling Oswald "Alik." He did this because he thought "Lee" and "Alexei" sounded similar. Skop said that sounded right.[22]

Whatever the case, by late summer 1960, Alik was Oswald's new name—unofficially and officially. According to a 1964 CIA report, among Oswald's personal items discovered after the assassination was a membership booklet issued to him on September 1, 1960, by the Electric Power Plant and Electrical Industry Union. The name inside the booklet, the report states, was Alik Harvey Oswald. According to the FBI, Oswald also had an undated hunting license that had been "issued by an organization of the Minsk Radio Plant and reflects membership . . . in a club of hunters and fishermen." The license number was 28231; the name on it was Aliksei Oswald.[23]

By calling him Alik, the Russians seemed to be warming up to him. It made him feel as if he had bridged a gulf. The Russians had given him a hotel room, Dostoevsky, stitches, a train ticket, another hotel room, an apartment, a job, extra cash, coworkers—and now a nickname. They made him feel as if he were slowly moving closer to them. But that was an illusion. He only appeared to be moving. In reality, he was anchored to a frozen foreground set against a shifting background. The scenery evolved, and it seemed as if he and the scene were moving together, in synchronicity, but he was never a part of the scenery, the collective. He couldn't be. He was always on display. He would never be allowed to meld into his new home.[24]

He confused the Russians he met. He was American, and no one knew why he was there. Libezin and Lavshuk never asked where he came from.

Nor did Botvinik, Tsagoiko, Skop, or anyone else at the department. They knew that there were certain things they shouldn't ask about—for example, why the security organs had allowed him to come to Minsk and whether he had any friends or contacts in the government. They also knew that it would be better not to talk about Oswald around certain people, starting with Libezin.[25]

On March 16, two months after he started at the Experimental Department, Oswald was moved from the Hotel Minsk to Apartment 24 at 4 Kalinina Ulitsa, about twenty minutes by foot, or two tram stops, from the hotel. The building was in the center of the city, and it had been designed in the monumental Stalinist style: looming archways, thick columns, oversized windows. It was meant to feel powerful, domineering, even regal. If Oswald walked out of his building and turned right, and then right again, through the narrow driveway, beneath the yellow archway, he would be standing on Kalinina Ulitsa. If he turned left on Kalinina Ulitsa and walked for a minute or two, he would be at Victory Square, which was a traffic circle with an obelisk and eternal flame dedicated to the unknown soldier. If, instead of going to Victory Square, he turned right on Kalinina Ulitsa, he would soon arrive at the military headquarters, shrouded in trees. If he went a little farther, through an oblong patch of forest and up a small hill, he would be at the opera house. Just opposite his window, on the other side of Kalinina Ulitsa and down a short slope, was the river.[26]

Oswald called the apartment on Kalinina Ulitsa "a Russians dream." Apartment 24, at entrance No. 2, encompassed 266 square feet, and it had three rooms: a kitchen, a bathroom with a toilet, and a bedroom-cum-living room. There was also a balcony; a vestibule; a small, built-in wardrobe; and views of the river and opera house. The interior walls, which were made of wood and plaster, were just shy of six inches thick, but the exterior walls, which were brick, were a little more than twenty inches in thickness, which meant it was usually quiet inside the apartment. His neighbors rarely heard him, and he seemed oblivious of them.[27]

The only person in the building he was known to spend any time with was Sergei Skop, who was also a metal-lathe operator at the Experimental

Department. For about a year, three or four times every week, Oswald and Skop walked to the factory together. They never made plans. They just showed up at the same place just beyond the garbage cans and the swing set, about ten or fifteen minutes before the start of the eight a.m. shift. Sometimes, Alla Apalinskaya, a woman who worked at the factory, would join them, Skop said. They would walk up Zakharov, and at the intersection with Krasnaya Ulitsa (Red Street) they would turn right. It took seven or eight minutes, depending on the weather. Skop said they never talked about important things, and even though he liked Oswald, they never became close. Partly, he said, that was a matter of age; Oswald was ten years younger than Skop, and Skop sometimes thought of him as a boy. Skop called him "nice," "decent," and "ordinary." "I'd ask him, 'Why do you live alone? Why don't you get a girl? There are lots of girls at the plant.'" But it never went beyond that. It was very much like Oswald's relationship with Shushkevich—confined to a small place within a limited timeframe—but it was more pleasant. This was the word Skop used repeatedly when he described walking to work with Oswald: "pleasant."[28]

In the two and a half years that they lived in the same building, Skop and his wife never once invited Oswald to their home, and Oswald never invited Skop. Still, Skop said, it was known around the factory that Oswald had what Russians considered a big place. Before Oswald moved into Apartment 24, Skop said, a man who had been a partisan during the war and his family had lived there—and now Oswald was living there alone! In Skop's view, this meant that Apartment 24 only went to people who had done great things or, in Oswald's case, come from the United States. Skop said his apartment was twice as big as Oswald's, but there were six people in it. He, his wife, and their son were living in one room. Another family was living in the other room. The two families shared a kitchen and bathroom.

It is unlikely that Oswald realized he was living in what amounted to a village inside a city. He had been strategically situated within a five- to ten-minute walk of most everywhere he needed to go—the factory, the grocery store, friends, associates, the opera house, the movie theater, the river, the park, and the Foreign Language Institute, where, according to Titovets, there were women who spoke English, listened to jazz, and were more "adventurous." This was clearly illustrated in a 1964 CIA report on Oswald's Soviet period. The report includes a simple street plan of the center of Minsk that shows Oswald's apartment building and other locations that played a role in his everyday life, including the house where his coworker and one-time love interest Ella German lived (just opposite the river); the building where his future wife, Marina Prusakova, lived with her aunt and uncle (three and a half blocks away); the building where the engineer Alexander Ziger, who became friendly with Oswald and served as something of a father figure, lived with his family (on Krasnaya Ulitsa); and the Palace of Culture of the Council of Trade Unions, where he met Marina Prusakova (on the other side of the river, at October Square). It was as if the KGB had constructed a little world just for him.[29]

In fact, said Oleg Nechiporenko, that was common KGB practice. Nechiporenko, the KGB officer who briefly handled Oswald's case when he turned up at the Soviet embassy in Mexico City in the fall of 1963, said the KGB had a name for this sort of "village in a city." They called it a *kolpak*, which means "cover," "dome," or "shroud." They would say that someone was in a *kolpak* or *biyt pod kolpakom*. This meant one was "being under the cover" of the security organs. To make things more convenient, Apartment 24 was on the fourth floor —above the tree line —and it faced the river. From the opposite bank of the Svisloch, the people strolling on the embankment could see the balcony, and, with binoculars, they could certainly get a good look inside through the windows of his bedroom and kitchen, and down the darkened corridor to the vestibule, filled with a bland, yellow light. It was as if his entire life had been reorganized so that other people could watch it.[30]

The *kolpak* accomplished two things: it made it easier for the authorities to watch him, and, more importantly, it put him at ease, which, in turn, made it still easier to watch him. It made him believe he was in a place where he was known and even understood. Here, in this little, invisible village in the middle of Minsk, there were people who worked in the same factory he worked in, spoke the same language he spoke, and liked the same composers he liked. In the coming months, they would go to the movies with him and invite him over for dinner. This feeling of connectivity would have been reinforced daily. Every time he was on the street or at an intersection or on Victory Square, he could expect to run into someone he knew, a friendly acquaintance who would wave and even smile, reminding him that he was somewhere where he could be himself. This was something that Oswald had never had—a sense of belonging. In this way, the security organs anticipated better than Oswald did what he needed. By planting him in this mesh of seemingly thick relations, they oriented and settled him. They made him think that he could do whatever he wanted because he was home now.[31]

It wasn't just atmospherics. There was also, most everyone agrees, extensive monitoring of Oswald. This monitoring almost certainly included listening devices, secret police whose job it was to watch him, and a sprawling network of informants who were recruited by the security organs after he arrived. In fact, nearly everyone who worked with Oswald in Minsk said the same two things over and over: they had never informed on him, and most everyone else had. They didn't like to talk about these things, even fifty years later. But they knew about it. Or, it would be more correct to say, they intuited it. For one thing, Oswald had many bosses—Libezin, Lavshuk, Leonid Botvinik—and each of them seemed to answer to someone else whom no one knew.

"The people who were KGB in the factory would have known perfectly well that if this guy was an American spy, their asses would have been in the sling," said Tennent Bagley, the former head of CIA counterintelligence operations in the Soviet Union. "They were, of course, concerned and had to get coverage on him, as a matter of bureaucratic self-protection. Certainly, they would have put bugs in his apartment. Certainly, they would have used people around him as sources, agents or informants in the formal sense, or people who were just at the factory. This would have absolutely been a requirement of the plant, the radio factory, in Minsk." Jack Tunheim, a federal judge in Minneapolis who chaired the Assassination Records Review Board—which was created by the first Bush administration in 1991, following the release of the movie *JFK*—said the KGB made sure that when Khrushchev visited Minsk, Oswald was out of town. "They were very concerned that he would be purchasing anything that would be used to make a bomb," Tunheim said.[32]

There was another reason why Oswald did not get to know his coworkers better: Ella German. Oswald does not say in his diary when, exactly, he met German. She indicated that it was in April or May 1960. At that time, she was a *montazhnitsa*, or fitter, on the first floor of the Experimental Department. German and several other young women sat at a table and assembled pieces of television sets. Most of the women in her section would work only for a year or two, and then they would go to an institute or university to study. "We were considered, like, the fun department," German said. "The children of party bosses would work in that department, and people would ask you, 'Who is your father? Is he a boss here?'" German was definitely not the daughter of any party boss, but she was capable, intelligent, and, as Oswald observed, beautiful.[33]

Oswald fell for German almost immediately. In his diary he wrote: "Ella Germain—a silky, black haired Jewish beauty with fine dark eyes skin as white as snow a beautiful smile and good but unpredictable nature, her only fault was that at 24 she was still a virgin, and due entirely to her own desire. I met her when she came too work at our factory. I noticed her, and perhaps fell in love with her, the first minute I saw her."[34]

Soon after Oswald met Ella German, they started to eat together most days. "Alik could go at any time," said German, who now lives in Akko, north of Haifa, in Israel. "He was not touched because he was American. He was in a special position, not like all of our workers. He could go earlier, so then I wouldn't have to stand in line, and he could grab two lunches, for himself and me, and we would sit together." German said that, from the moment she met Oswald, she thought he was curious, and she was keenly aware of the differences between them. "He was obviously very different from anyone I had ever met," she said. When she spoke about him in our interviews, she didn't sound as if she missed him; she was more detached. Oswald was an oddity, mostly because she had never expected to meet an American.

She had been born in Minsk in 1937, and like many other Soviet Jews, she stressed that she was "born into a Jewish family," the same way that others said they were born into Russian, Ukrainian, or Armenian families. When the Germans came, in June 1941, Ella was with her grandparents in Mogilev, southeast of Minsk, while her mother was in Minsk. Her grandmother had come to Minsk two weeks before to take Ella, then four, to Mogilev for the summer so her mother could take care of Ella's brother, Vladimir, who was still a baby.

After the Germans occupied Minsk, no one knew where anyone else was. All they knew was that they had to go as far east as they could, so Ella and her grandmother and grandfather went to Tambov and then Saratov, and in Saratov, miraculously, they found her mother and Vladimir. Later, she learned that her mother and Vladimir had been very fortunate. In Minsk, her mother, clutching the baby, had hitched a ride in a truck that was supposed to take twenty or thirty people to Mogilev or somewhere else that was safe. But German bombers were patrolling the skies over the one- and two-lane roads leading in and out of the city, and when they saw the trucks rambling out, they strafed them with their machine guns. Most of the people in the trucks were killed. Those who were not, including Ella's mother and brother, poured out of the truck and into the forest, where they walked for days before they found another truck going east. Eventually, they made their way to Saratov, where a lot of refugees had congregated. But they couldn't stop. As Ella put it, no one knew where Germany ended and Russia began. All they knew was that they had to keep going east. So they found a small space on a *teplushka*, which was a train for transporting horses and cows—*teplo* means "warm"—and that was how the family ended up in Mordovia, which is six or seven hours, by train, southeast of Moscow. Ella's mother's second husband, Pyotr Shapolvalov, did not join them. He was sent to the front when the war broke out and disappeared. Her mother's first husband, Ella's father, had died a few years earlier.

After Minsk was liberated in the summer of 1944, Ella's mother returned alone to Minsk from Mordovia and, after she found a place where the family could live, sent word that they should come. There was a swatch of forest near their home that they called "the burnt place" because it was littered with rubble, and behind them, on a small rise, was the opera house. Near the opera house, on Yanki Kupali Ulitsa, there was another house that was made of stone, and next to that house stood a hospital along with more rubble. Everywhere smelled like tar. On Saturdays, when Ella was in high school, all the students would have a holiday, and they would clear debris (concrete blocks, rubble, shells, pieces of metal). This lasted until 1951 or 1952. By then, they had made enough room for the new buildings that started going up near the Svisloch, on Prospekt Stalina, Kalinina Ulitsa, Krasnaya Ulitsa, and elsewhere.

A few years later, Ella became a *montazhnitsa*, and after that, she started working at the Experimental Department. She said she was unaware at first that Oswald had been seeing other women—she called them "girls"—but she found out later. This was when their relationship became more serious—at least, in Oswald's eyes—in the late summer and fall of 1960. "Probably, like a man, he needed that," German said "I just learned about this at the end of October, at this party, and we spoke about it often, and there were several quarrels about it, of course. I was aggravated that he didn't tell me the truth. I was offended. Right after that, I started not to trust him so much."

The chasm separating Oswald from the Menchani was significant but not unbridgeable. The war, the language gap, a persistent cultural and historical disconnect—all these things made it hard for Oswald to build a new life in Minsk, to understand what kind of place he had been parachuted into and how he might fit into it. Still, it was conceivable that, with time, he might do so. He might have gradually learned the language, the recent history, all the important cultural symbols and signposts, and the assumptions, expectations, and even mannerisms that are part of any community. Alas, the barriers around him—the *kolpak* that had been constructed by the KGB, and the fear and uncertainty of the Menchani who helped to enforce it every day—greatly complicated that effort.

Throughout the first half of 1960, Minsk was still new to him, and it was possible for Oswald to miss or ignore the space that separated him from everyone around him. For several months he would be blissfully unaware of where he was and the ways the Menchani thought. But the KGB would not be able to maintain that farce indefinitely. Eventually Oswald would begin to see through the gaps in the Potemkin village. When this happened, a familiar anger and sense of hopelessness—the same hopelessness he had known as a boy in New York, Louisiana, and Texas, and as a marine at Atsugi and El Toro—would slowly resurface. But that was still a few months away.

7

AN ACCIDENTAL FRIENDSHIP

O SWALD SPENT THE SPRING AND SUMMER OF 1960 SETTLING
into the life that the security organs had concocted for him. There
were signs that Oswald was aware he was being watched—he certainly
thought he was important enough to warrant watching—but he probably had no idea how all-encompassing that surveillance would be. As
it turned out, he couldn't make a cup of coffee, take a shower, or go to
bed with a woman without someone watching or listening to him. It was
during this time that Oswald developed what looks to be the only friendship he had in the Soviet Union that was not arranged by the KGB. It was
this friendship, with Pavel Golovachev, as well as a handful of noteworthy developments, that prompted Oswald to start to reassess his Russian
dream.[1]

He probably thought that he was finally building a life for himself. For the
first time ever, Oswald had a job, an apartment, and a little extra money.
He could go to the opera; he could go to concerts and movies. (*Rhapsody*,
starring Elizabeth Taylor, as well as *The Seventh Voyage of Sinbad* and *War
and Peace*, were showing in local theaters, as well as Soviet films dealing
with the revolution, the war, and the Virgin Lands program.) There were
occasional dinner parties at the apartment, five minutes from his place,
where the engineer Alexander Ziger lived with his wife, Anna, and their

daughters, Anita and Eleonora. And there was Ella German, with whom he would go on walks and take to the movies; he thought they might have a future together. He even enjoyed a degree of what he perceived as celebrity. In October he would be twenty-one. For a young man with no high school diploma, an undesirable discharge from the military (the Marines had downgraded his discharge after they learned of his defection), and limited vocational experience (at some point in early to mid-1960, he was elevated to "level 2" at the Experimental Department), he had done well. To anyone who knew about Oswald's childhood, his time in the Marines, all his scrimping and plotting to defect to the Soviet Union, and the rather tortuous journey he had been on since arriving in Moscow six months earlier, he looked as if he were ready, at long last, to leave behind his adolescence and his many angers and frustrations.[2]

Then, in March 1960, Oswald made his first good friend in Minsk: Pavel Golovachev. At the time, both men were working in the Experimental Department. Oswald had just arrived, and Golovachev would soon be leaving.[3]

There was a warmth that developed between Oswald and Golovachev that Oswald never really felt for any other friends in Minsk. But this was not immediately apparent. In his diary, Oswald, as usual, hewed to the facts, avoiding much in the way of feeling or color. Golovachev, he noted, was a "yonuge man my age friend very intelligent a exalant radio tehniction his father is Gen. Golovacha commander of Northwestenr Siberia. Twice hero of USSR in W. W. 2." More telling are the letters Golovachev would later write to Oswald after Oswald and his wife, Marina, had left the Soviet Union. (Oswald's letters to Golovachev are unavailable.) The letters emphasize the personal: Golovachev conveyed his warmest wishes to Lee and Marina, said he'd be sending some pictures, and needled Oswald for not having written back to him sooner. There are also a handful of instances that suggest a unique closeness between Oswald and Golovachev: Lee and Marina stayed at Golovachev's on their last night in Minsk, and Golovachev was with them at the train station when they left for the United States. Much more important than all this, however, was that Oswald and Golovachev found themselves in similar straits. They were both outsiders. They had both struggled to carve out a niche for themselves. They were both filled with a sense of aimlessness and a great deal of uncertainty about who they were supposed to be. Golovachev had a few big advantages—he was intelligent, and he had a powerful father— and he wasn't as angry as Oswald was. But it must have been apparent to both that they shared a feeling of otherness, and that must have reinforced a certain bond.[4]

Most everyone agrees that Golovachev's father, Pavel Yakovlevich, was the most important influence on his son, Pavel Pavlovich. During the war, Pavel Yakovlevich was a pilot. He served in the Battle of Stalingrad, was in Hungary, and then went on to Berlin. He was injured four times. After his first injury, which involved his head, his left eye was slightly smaller than his right one. He had a meaty look. He had thick digits, pink cheeks, and gray eyes that burrowed deep into his smooth, doughy face. He was an extremely gifted fighter pilot. He had shot down so many Messerschmitts that they had given him the highest award in the land—a gold medal that said he was a Hero of the Soviet Union—twice.[5]

After the war, Pavel Yakovlevich and his wife and children had moved from one post to another: Moscow; Khabarovsk, in the Far East; Tbilisi, in Georgia; Novosibirsk, in the middle of Siberia; and, from 1960 to 1961, Minsk. In Minsk, the air force had given him a driver and a black limousine, and he had a dacha. His family lived in a four-bedroom apartment on Zakharova Ulitsa, near the Foreign Language Institute and Victory Square, with the obelisk and eternal flame. The apartment was a ten-minute walk, at most, from Oswald's apartment at 4 Kalinina Ulitsa. Like Oswald's apartment, the Golovachevs' was in a Stalin-era building, and it was the only one in the building that came with a window in the bathroom. The thickness of the walls, the molding, the doors and doorknobs, the archways, and the wide, capacious hallways made it feel "cozy," said Anna Zhuravskaya, the younger of Pavel Pavlovich's two sisters. Sometimes, in the morning, Pavel Yakovlevich played chess with his driver at the apartment, and they smoked and had tea. In the winter, on weekends, the driver would take the family to a little mountain outside the city to go skiing.

Between father and son there had always been problems. Father, said Zhuravskaya, always knew exactly what had to be done, and he wanted his son to be the same way. In retrospect, she said, it seemed almost inevitable that her brother would befriend someone like Oswald, someone who was bound to upset her father.

Pavel, unlike his father, was never confident. He was kind, and he liked to laugh. But he lacked a sense of himself. "I began to remember my brother when I was six," Zhuravskaya said. One of her first memories involved her riding on his shoulders, near the family dacha, in the summer. The dacha had two rooms; the larger one had a miniature fireplace. The family slept on narrow, dusty beds. Young Pavel was happy at the dacha. He could read or take long walks, and he didn't have to think about the things he wasn't doing with his life.

Pavel Yakovlevich could not understand why his son was not more like him. Pavel Pavlovich liked to play with televisions and radios. Usually he would build things, take them apart, and then put them back together. He loved wires, knobs, dials, springs, coils, and miniature metal plates. He was very good at making things out of nothing. He also loved to take photographs with his Zenit, a Soviet replica of the much vaunted German-made Leica II. At night in his room, Pavel Pavlovich would pore over his images, studying all the buildings and people he had captured. He would play his radio too loud, and his father would become irate.

Pavel Yakovlevich thought his son wasn't serious enough. Most of all, he wanted him to think more about his country, and he thought he should seriously consider a career in the army. When his son started spending a lot of time with Oswald, an American with a slight build and, as Zhuravskaya recalled, a "strange attitude," Pavel Yakovlevich began to worry even more about him. He was not entirely wrong about his son, who jumped from one job to the next without any sense of direction. His *trudnaya knizhka*, or workbook of work, a log of all the jobs he held, makes this clear. On July 29, 1959, per Directive 109, he became an electromechanic at the Minsk Radio Factory's Experimental Department, a little less than six months before Oswald arrived. Then, on April 1, 1960, in accordance with Directive 56, he was transferred to the factory's Department of Devices. Seven months later, on November 18 of that year, he was transferred again (Directive 174), and five months after that, on April 21, 1962, he left the factory for good, having been fired for tampering with some of the machinery in the department. His father tried to save his job but could not. Still, he made sure that Pavel's *trudnaya knizhka* only reported that he had "resigned from factory of his own accord."

The younger Pavel always seemed to be looking for something. Why else would he go to music concerts with the American? Or spend time at parties at his apartment? This was what bothered Pavel Yakovlevich the most—the wandering. And he didn't like his son's constant questioning. He wondered whether Oswald was telling his son bad things—lies—about the Soviet Union. Pavel Yakovlevich had never questioned his country. He did not understand why anyone who knew about history would. It made him angry. It suggested to him that there was something that his son did not approve of. Still, Pavel Yakovlevich loved his son a great deal. His older daughter, Maya Gan, said her father worried about her brother constantly. He wanted him to settle on a career and then pursue it the way he had pursued his own career. The reason why all of Pavel's roaming and picture taking bothered him was not that he was against picture taking per se, Gan said. It was because his son's picture taking suggested that he was unhappy or confused.

Pavel Pavlovich's nephew, Alexei Zhuravsky, agreed that his uncle was unhappy, but he said his grandfather didn't know what to do about it. There was a gap, he explained. It was not simply generational. It encompassed "amazing, terrible events"—meaning the war. An impenetrable wall, philosophical but also spiritual, separated their two worlds, prewar and postwar. Pavel was convinced he and his father would never understand each other. "He would make jokes about himself and grandfather, but you could see that these weren't real jokes, or, maybe, they were meant to be funny, but not many people thought they were funny," Zhuravsky said. Many years later, Zhuravskaya added, when the elder Golovachev was dying and Pavel was rushing home to Minsk to see him one more time, the son hoped that his last conversation with his father would not end in a fight.

Much of Pavel Golovachev's life, from his childhood in postwar Russia to his death in 2002, consisted of a series of minor rebellions. It's not that he openly opposed the system in the same way that Oswald was hostile to the United States. He simply did not fit into it. Nor did he appear to want to. Golovachev wanted something that most people in the Soviet Union did not want: the freedom to construct his own life, from the very start, outside of any framework or institution. He seemed to be constantly slipping through the fissures—of the university, the army, the factory, wherever he happened to find himself—because he didn't want to belong in the first place.[6]

Oswald and Golovachev's friendship marked an important juncture for both men. For Oswald, befriending Golovachev deepened his ties to Minsk. Prior to his meeting Golovachev, there had been few people in his life besides Ella German whom he would have missed had he suddenly left, and there was no one who would have missed him.

For Golovachev, spending time with Oswald amounted to yet another act of rebellion. The friendship could only have compromised his father. True, Oswald and Golovachev faced similar personal challenges, but it was unclear what, exactly, Oswald offered him. Golovachev was not keen on studying English, and his interests (radios, electronics, spacecraft) did not overlap with Oswald's. The truth is, there was something adolescent about his hanging out, as it were, with the American. Anna Zhuravskaya said the friendship was not just adolescent but also dangerous. Golovachev was nineteen, and he was casting about for something to do with his life. He wanted to meet new people and visit foreign countries. He was frustrated and probably depressed, and it was this depression, coupled with his feelings of alienation and rebellion, that may have led him to pursue the friendship. It wasn't that Oswald corrupted Golovachev. Rather, Golovachev, by befriending Oswald, slipped into the field of vision of the security organs and, having done that, would not be able to extricate himself. They would be watching him long after Oswald departed the Soviet Union. They would assume he had a reason for wanting to be friends with an American. In an odd and sadly humorous way, the KGB did not understand friendship.[7]

It's important to note that the KGB had no good or obvious reason for wanting Golovachev to befriend Oswald. Theirs looks to have been a friendship that was not meant to happen. Almost everyone else who met, spoke to, or ran into Oswald on a tram car or street corner, anyone who spent an evening with him at the movie theater or the opera house, the Foreign Language Institute or Alexander Ziger's family's apartment, was supposed to. If it turned out that a genuinely spontaneous crossing of paths had taken place, that meeting would later be turned into something useful—the KGB would derive value from it retroactively. This could be counted on with a nearly mathematical certainty. Golovachev's friendship with Oswald was one the KGB probably would have preferred not to have happened. Golovachev put Oswald two degrees of separation from a high-ranking general in the Soviet air force. Golovachev was also known to harbor anti-Soviet feelings and to talk too much.[8]

Oswald's friend Ernst Titovets described Golovachev as immature, impertinent, overeager, and careless. In "Eleonora Ziger's Concert," Chapter 22 of his memoirs, Titovets recounts a get-together at Apartment 24 that included Golovachev and Anita Ziger, the older of Alexander Ziger's two daughters:

> When I arrived at Oswald's place I found the door unlocked. Anita and Pavel were already present and standing around Lee engaged in a disagreement. Diminutive Pavel was arguing excitedly in his glib manner. Lee seemed to disagree with him. I must have caught them unawares for they all suddenly paused and looked at me, momentarily leading me to suspect that I was the object of their gossip. Anita began humming a tune.

Later in the evening, Titovets recalled that he was alone, peering through a window, when Pavel came up to him.

He began speaking rapidly in his usual agitated manner as if anxious to convince me of something through the sheer volume of his words. Pavel had a penchant for making a big issue of anything, while his compulsory small talk seemed to revolve around his disagreement with certain policies and practices in the USSR. True to this peculiar habit of his, he launched into an excited soliloquy on the Hungarian uprising and the role of the Soviet military in putting it down. He stood looking up into my eyes as if trying to read my mind.

This is probably an unfair (or at least simplistic) portrayal of Golovachev, who comes across here as callow and a little one-dimensional. There was more to him than that. Golovachev was a creative and intelligent young man with a robust curiosity, and he struggled greatly to figure out who he was supposed to be. He was not "glib." He was, if anything, unhappy, wandering, and, to an extent, malleable. Oswald never gave any sign that Golovachev irritated him; he certainly had nothing to say about any "disagreement" he may have had with Golovachev at the small party that night, before Eleonora Ziger's concert. But Titovets found Golovachev insufferable. Referring to his comments about the 1956 Hungarian uprising, Titovets writes, "Pavel ought to have known better than to engage in such a provocative discussion; it was dangerous and had the potential to bring trouble to everyone in the room." As if to silence Golovachev once and for all, Titovets notes: "Anita put an end to Pavel's talk suggesting that it was about time to meet her sister and mother. Pavel obediently shut up."[9]

While we should be skeptical of some of Titovets's criticism, his discussion of that evening and, more generally, Golovachev, tells us something important about the web of relationships between Oswald and Golovachev, Oswald and Titovets, and Oswald and the Ziger sisters, Anita and Eleonora. And it very clearly points to a competition, of sorts, between Titovets and Golovachev. There were, at all times, different forces working on Oswald, shaping his thoughts, coloring his perception of things. His understanding of Minsk, his relationship with the city and his *kolpak*, and the whole idea of socialist utopia and Sovietism were changeable, ill-defined—unfolding.[10]

After several months in Minsk Oswald seems to have imbibed a great deal of Golovachev's disdain for certain aspects of Soviet life and Golovachev's sense of fatigue or helplessness. Whether this is directly attributable to Golovachev is unclear, although it is hard to imagine that Golovachev did not rub off on him. What made his criticisms of the Soviet Union especially potent was that they were mostly more attitudinal than substantive; they had less to do with specific policies, Titovets's story about the suppression of the Hungarian uprising notwithstanding, than they did with a posture or feeling about life in the Soviet Union. This made it harder to reason or argue with Golovachev. His feelings were what they were, and they had the power to influence Oswald simply by being voiced.

Less than six weeks after meeting Golovachev, Oswald wrote in his diary of his first May Day in the Soviet Union: "all factories ect. closed after sptacular military parade all workers parad past reviewing stand waving flags and pictures of Mr. K. ect. I follow the Amer. Custom of marking holiday by sleeping in in the morning." What's most striking about this entry is its uncharacteristic glibness—"Mr. K.," "sleeping in." Also surprising is Oswald's suggestion that he's just following an American custom by getting some extra sleep and skipping what would have been considered his duty as a worker—attending the annual May Day festivities. Seven months before, he had tried to kill himself because the Soviet authorities wouldn't let him stay in the country. Now he was skipping its most cherished holiday. Then, he had marched into the US embassy and told the consular office that he never wanted anything to do with America again. Now, he was joking about America.[11]

The importance of a single diary entry shouldn't be overstated. But it's noteworthy, and it suggests two things that are not mutually exclusive: Oswald's political commitments may have never been as deep as he believed, and Golovachev's arrival had begun to color Oswald's thinking. Oswald does not report on the conversations he had with Golovachev in April, before the May Day holiday. But he certainly was aware of Golovachev's transfer to the Department of Devices—Golovachev had been working in the Experimental Department before he was transferred—and it would not have been surprising for the two men to discuss Golovachev's move, the factory, and possibly politics. Certainly Oswald was not averse to that kind of conversation—nor, if Titovets and Zhuravskaya are correct, was Golovachev.

Also in May, there were at least two other developments that could only have compounded Oswald's worries about or frustrations with his new country. On May 1, a surface-to-air missile near Sverdlovsk, in the Ural Mountains, shot down a U-2 spy plane piloted by Gary Powers. At the much anticipated Paris summit two weeks later, Khrushchev demanded that President Eisenhower apologize. When Eisenhower refused, Khrushchev went home. This put an end to the window of opportunity that had opened in September 1959, when Khrushchev had visited the United States and it seemed as if the two countries might be moving toward the peaceful coexistence that Khrushchev favored. It does not appear that the U-2 incident created any immediate problems for Oswald, although Ella German said he expressed concerns to her about how the incident would affect his coworkers' attitudes toward him. Still, the incident would have given the security organs more reason to fret about the American, and Oswald seems to have felt, or been made to feel, more aware than ever of his outsiderness. The fact that he had once served as a marine at an air base that housed U-2s, and the fact that he had told the Soviets that he could give them information about them, probably exacerbated Oswald's anxieties about life in the Soviet Union and any tensions between Oswald and his hosts.[12]

On the same day as the U-2 incident, May 1, Oswald had a conversation with Alexander Ziger. The conversation took place, according to Oswald's diary, at a party at the Ziger home: "At night I vist with the Zegers daughters at an party throw by them about 40 people come many of Argentine origen we dance and play around and drink until 2 AM. when party breaks up. . . . Opposition I have heard. I respect Zeger, he has seen the world. He says many things, and relats many things I do not know about the U.S.S.R. I begin to feel uneasy inside, its true!" This marks the first time that Oswald recorded any doubts he may have begun having about the Soviet Union. We don't know what Ziger said to

Oswald—he passed away several years ago—but we do know that it left an impression.[13]

By early summer, six months after he had arrived in the Belorussian Soviet Socialist Republic, Oswald was still curious about Minsk and the people he had only recently met, but he also seems to have started to grow bored, despite his friendship with Golovachev and his ongoing pursuit of Ella German. In his "June – July" diary entry, Oswald wrote: "Summer months of green beauty, pine forest very deep. I enjoy many Sundays in the enviorments of Minsk with the Zegers who have a car 'Mosivick.' . . . I have become habituated to a small cafe which is where I dine in the evening the food is generally poor and always eactly the same, menue in any cafe, at any point in the city. The food is cheap and I don't really care about quiality after three years in the U.S.M.C."

His habits made things much easier for the KGB. Not only was Oswald's life circumscribed by an invisible village, but he had also developed daily routines that could be watched and counted on with some confidence. And now, even better from the vantage point of the security organs, they had a spy who could report on all the things that Oswald talked about—politics, literature, Minsk—when he wasn't at the factory: Golovachev, it turned out, was informing on him. He seemed to have been embarrassed or ashamed by this—the truth only came out many years later, after the Soviet collapse, and even a half century after the fact his sisters and nephew vehemently denied that Golovachev had volunteered information about Oswald to the KGB—but he probably had few choices. He had been foolish or myopic in befriending the American, and his father had a great deal at stake, starting with a brilliant career in the air force and a reputation to protect. If his son had not complied with the wishes of the KGB, that could have only created more problems for him. Anna Zhuravskaya became angry when I pressed her about her brother informing on Oswald. She pointed out that he was only nineteen when he met Oswald, and he did not know what he was doing when he started spending time with the American. She said he had been angry with his father, and he had acted the way he always did—recklessly.[14]

Oswald appears not to have had any inkling of Golovachev's double life. But he must have intuited that their friendship had boundaries or limits: in the coming months, new people, new friends, and, eventually, Marina Prusakova, his future wife, would occupy more of his time. Golovachev never disappeared from Oswald's life—the KGB would not have let that happen—but he receded somewhat. He became a semiregular fixture, someone who could be relied on to go places or, as the case might have been, to attend a party.

In his October 18, 1960, diary entry, Oswald wrote: "My 21st birthday sees Rosa, Pavil, Ella at a small party at my place . . . Rosa and Ella are jelous of each other it brings a warm feeling to me. Both are at my place for the first time. Alla and Pavil both give ash-trays (I don't smoke) We have a laugh."[15]

Even though Oswald had embraced the principles of communist revolution, and even though he was determined to make his home in the Soviet Union, he was, by the fall of 1960, beginning to wonder whether he belonged there. Minsk only had so much to offer, and he had heard plenty of criticism of the regime at the Zigers'. But it was Golovachev who really pushed Oswald, however unwittingly, to reassess his attitude toward Russia. Golovachev's frustrations with his homeland probably had a great deal to do with his troubled relationship with his father. (Both of his sisters made the point that Golovachev identified Soviet authority with the general.) But this is not how these frustrations would have been perceived by Oswald. He would not have been able to distinguish between a criticism that was ostensibly about political matters but was really personal in nature from a criticism that was inherently and purely political.

In fact, there is no sign, in Oswald's writings or conversations with friends or associates, that he understood that—let alone how—he was influenced by Golovachev or the relationship between the two Pavels. As always, he had very little insight into his own thinking. What is indisputable is that he had begun to see through the gaps in the wall the organs had built around him, and in the coming months he would start to ponder not only why he had come to Minsk but whether he should leave. This was a haunting proposition. He had traveled to the Soviet Union with the expectation that he would stop traveling once he arrived. Now, one year later, he had reason to doubt that he had escaped the cycle of interloping.

Over the course of the winter of 1960 and 1961, among the loneliest months of Oswald's Soviet period, he would take his first, tentative steps to move once again.

8

A PROPOSAL

T HE LATE FALL AND EARLY WINTER OF 1960 MARKED AN important juncture. Back in the United States, the junior senator from Massachusetts, John F. Kennedy, a symbol of American vitality and idealism, had just been elected president and soon would take office. In the Soviet Union, the unpredictable, start-stop liberalization of the Khrushchev thaw plodded along. The outrage sparked by the U-2 incident had not yet subsided, and in October the Soviet premier had famously turned his shoe into a gavel while addressing the United Nations General Assembly in New York. At the same time, a new generation of young poets, including Yevgeny Yevtushenko, Bella Akhmadulina, and Andrei Voznesensky, were giving voice to the hopeful, doleful, sometimes angry yearnings of a reinvigorated intelligentsia. Oswald, as always, remained cordoned off and mostly unaware of what was taking place in his new country. But he was consumed by a growing turmoil and confusion.

There had been something brilliant about the KGB's decision, in late 1959 or early 1960, to move Oswald to Minsk. They could have built a "village" for him anywhere; almost all the other Americans who defected to the Soviet Union at that time were sent to the Ukraine.[1] But they had chosen a place that was proudly Soviet and conservative—from the collective farms to the rail yards of Brest, the steel mills of Mogilev and the plants and factories churning out refrigerators, automobiles, tractors, televisions, and radios in Minsk. So by the time Oswald was ensconced in Apartment

24 at 4 Kalinina Ulitsa, there were, in fact, not one but two so-called moats, or walls, separating him from the rest of Russia: the "cover" or *kolpak* and, less obviously, the Belorussian Soviet Socialist Republic, which formed a kind of Soviet nimbus around his neighborhood and adopted city. Together, they put a great deal of space—geographic, cultural, and even metaphysical—between Oswald and the many swirling tensions spiraling out of Moscow. Intentionally or not, by keeping him far away from the dissidents and artists who were clamoring to open up Soviet society, the KGB delayed Oswald's own confrontation with communist Russia.

In a way, it was the Menchani, with their ideology and provincialism, who had served as a prophylactic, shielding Oswald from the real Soviet Union—and the real Soviet Union from Oswald. It's not that they believed all the propaganda. In fact, they were troubled by what Khrushchev had told them about Stalin. They were aware that the regime had committed certain "excesses,"[2] but they thought there was something good and noble about their country, which had defeated the fascists and given them apartments and even movie theaters, canteens, and parks where you could stroll and have a cigarette. This was why they were suspicious of anyone, including Khrushchev, who had ideas about changing Russia or who wanted to talk about what had happened under Stalin. "It would be incorrect to call these people proletarians because they were not," Alexandra Lavshuka, Filip Lavshuk's wife, told me of the thousands of metal-lathe operators, fitters, welders, detailers, electrical outfitters, and technicians who filtered in and out of the Minsk Radio Factory every day. "We were free, and that is why it would be right to call us 'workers.' We were a family of workers. When the repressions happened, for instance, before the war, we were not angry or even very surprised, because we knew that the Soviet Union, the workers, had enemies, and would always have enemies, so we knew this was necessary."[3]

But by late 1960, Oswald's understanding of his adopted country was taking on a new aspect, one that would highlight his aloneness. He had begun to peer through the protective cordons and see the Soviet experiment in a more complicated light. This was prompted by a handful of personal and, to an extent, intellectual developments that had started in mid-1960: the arrival of Golovachev; Oswald's conversation, in May, with Alexander Ziger about the true nature of the Soviet regime; and, more generally, a growing weariness with life in Minsk.

In his diary entry from August and September of 1960, Oswald wrote: "As my Russian improves I become increasingly conscious of just what sort of a sociaty I live in. Mass gymnastics, complusory afterwork meeting, usually political—information meeting. Complusory attendance at lectures and the sending of the entire shop collective (except me) to pick potatoes on a Sunday, at a state colletive farm. A 'patriotic duty' to bring in the harvest. The opions of the workers (unvoiced) are that it's a great pain in the neck. They don't seem to be esspicialy enthusiastic about any of the 'collective' duties a natural feeling."[4]

More than anything else, it was the mechanization and programming of daily life that seems to have worn Oswald down, as his writings make clear. In "The Collective," he reported on "the local party man delivering a political sermon to a group of usually robust simple working men, who through some strange process have been turned to stone. Turned to stone all except the hard faced communist with roving eyes looking for any bonus-making catch of inattentioness on the part of any worker. A sad sight to anyone not use to it, but the russians are philisophical." Oswald no longer sounded so committed to "the causc." He added: "The well organized party men mark off the names of the hundreds of workers appoined to arrive at a certain place at a given time. No choice, however, small, is left to the discreation of the Individual."[5]

Nor was his criticism limited to party officials. Oswald was also critical of the state's use of culture, high and low, to further its interests. Of all the books printed in the Soviet Union in 1959, he reported, slightly more than half were "technical" or "industrial" in nature. Twenty-five percent, he informs us, were for "light reading," and "of these, most concerd war stories reflecting the struggle and victory of the Soviet Armed forceses over the Nazis during the 2nd W.W. as well as herioc novels about opening up the virgin lands in Siberia and the wild country East of the Urals . . . Love stories are few and far between with them apt to be 'boy loves tractor, - loves girl' episods or how Ivan increased production at his michine to win the admiration of Natasha, the shop foreman." In one of his "Six Compositions," Oswald decried the Soviets' "prositution of art and culture."[6]

Oswald's initial wondering and skepticism were, by September or October, coalescing into a more serious criticism of his whole Soviet experience. Then Ernst Titovets made his appearance in Oswald's life.

Titovets seemed to be the inverse of Golovachev. He came from an unremarkable family that had moved to Minsk after the war, meaning he had none of the advantages that Golovachev had. But he was an excellent student at the Medical Institute, where he was training to be a neurologist. Besides being highly intelligent, Titovets was focused, diligent, and self-reliant. He spoke fluent English with a British accent, which he claims to have acquired by tuning in to nightly broadcasts of the BBC. He read widely, in Russian and English. And he seemed unbothered by ordinary pains and discomforts. During the course of several interviews, conversations, and email exchanges in 2010 and 2011, he recalled that once, in a laboratory at the Medical Institute, he needed a blood sample for a test they were running, and when it was discovered no samples were available, he simply drew his own blood. During the summer, Titovets liked to travel with a few friends to the Crimea, in the south, and camp out in a tent on the shores of the Black Sea, go scuba diving, and fish. "We lived off whatever we caught," he said.

He seemed unfazed by the rigors of boot camp at an army base in Bobruysk, a little more than a hundred miles southeast of Minsk. "In a way," Titovets wrote in his book *Oswald: Russian Episode*, "the brief extent of our training made it fun with our barracks life not lasting long enough to make it a dreary routine." And he maintained control of his emotions at all times. When I asked Titovets about his family, he mentioned that he had been married twice and that both his wives had died. Then he returned to the subject of Oswald. There was nothing about him that seemed to be wandering. Unlike Golovachev, he knew what he wanted— to do serious research at the institute and, one imagines, achieve a degree of renown—and he had contempt for those, like Golovachev, who did not.[7]

Titovets was intelligent in a practical way. It wouldn't be quite right to call him "street smart," but he was smooth and strategic, and he was careful about the information he shared about himself while learning as much as possible about other people. From the beginning he made it clear that he wanted to meet Oswald so he could practice his English. While he granted Oswald some access to his own life and family, there was always a withholding about Titovets. Oswald, in his diary entries and subsequent letters to Titovets, maintained a jocular formality. The two men spent time together looking for women at the Foreign Language Institute, a five- or ten-minute walk from Oswald's apartment; going to concerts at the conservatory or the opera; and discussing matters political and philosophical. What rarely, if ever, comes through is anything approaching ordinary feelings—disappointments, sadnesses, excitements—on the part of Titovets. There are moments, in Titovets's memoirs, when we glimpse something real or deeply felt in Oswald—for example, a rather nasty exchange that breaks out between Oswald and a security guard at the Foreign Language Institute or, later, his joyful anticipation of fatherhood and his departure from the Soviet Union. Very rarely does Titovets provide much insight into his own state of mind.[8]

Although Titovets does not specify when, exactly, he first met Oswald, it seems to have been in September 1960. He had been angling for a chance to meet the American when, one day, a mutual friend, Albina Shalyakina, informed Titovets that he had been invited to dinner at the Zigers' and that Oswald would be there, too. "Anita [Ziger] opened the door . . . and invited me in," Titovets wrote in his memoirs. "There at the upright piano stood a young man who looked quietly at us as we entered the room. This must be the American called Oswald. And indeed he was. Oswald proferred me his hand in a polite non-committal handshake; his hand was warm and dry." Oswald's blue-gray eyes, he added, were "alert and intelligent." "His brown hair was styled in a half-raised cut. He wore a white shirt unbuttoned at the top, brown trousers and black foreign shoes.

A foreign-looking sand-colored jacket was hanging from the back of a chair. There was something about him reminiscent of a ballet dancer with his long neck, straight bearing and the way he kept his heels together and the toes wide apart."[9]

On the following Wednesday at seven p.m., Titovets wrote, he and Oswald met at Oswald's apartment. There was no plan. They spoke English. Titovets showed Oswald a letter that, he said, came from a British pen pal. Three days later, they saw Tchaikovsky's *The Queen of Spades* at the opera house, a ten-minute walk from 4 Kalinina Ulitsa; Oswald had invited Titovets and bought the tickets. In November, they had dinner at Titovets's apartment and listened to Paul Robeson records; Oswald explained to Titovets that the river in "Ol' Man River" was the Mississippi. Titovets's mother made boiled sausages and stewed cabbage. Oswald borrowed Titovets's copy of Graham Greene's *The Quiet American*, and they had a philosophical dispute, which Oswald would seem to be ill-equipped to take part in, about the nature of reality. Soon the two men were good friends.[10]

For a few months, Oswald was distracted—by Titovets and by a handful of women he had met. This would explain, in part, why none of Oswald's diary entries from September through December contain the same sense of foreboding that some of his earlier entries did. Certainly, they don't signal any looming, ideological shift.

In November, he reported in his diary, "I make the aquiataces of four girls rooming at the For. Ian. domitory in room 212. Nell is very interesting, so is Tomka, Tomis, and Alla. I usually go to the institute domatory with a freend of mind who speaks English very well. Eraich Titov [Ernst Titovets] is in the forth year at the medical insitute. very bright fellow at the domatory we 6 sit and talk for hours in English."[11]

Titovets was impressed by the American—his intelligence, his easygoing manner, his banter. The Russian recalled meeting up with Oswald one night in November. There was a cello concert at the conservatory, a ten- to fifteen-minute walk from 4 Kalinina Ulitsa. After the concert, there was a party. "I spotted Lee standing by the window, away from the crowd, in the company of a strange girl," Titovets writes. "Both seemed to have been deeply engrossed in conversation. Leaning leisurely against the window-sill with his legs crossed, Lee stood looking straight into the girl's eyes. He did most of the talking. The girl seemed to be earnestly considering what Lee was saying. A trace of a triumphal, Machiavellian smile lurked on Lee's face. It might have been his new conquest, as he would put it, so I let him enjoy the moment." Moments later, Oswald glimpsed Titovets walking toward him and the woman, but he didn't want to be disturbed, and he signaled as much by shaking his right foot. "I inwardly smiled at his ingenious use of body language to communicate his message," Titovets wrote, "and slightly nodded my head as I walked past the two."[12]

To Oswald, these women were little more than conquests.[13] He came by them relatively easily because he was an American and a curiosity—there's no sign that he had had it so good with the opposite sex before coming to the Soviet Union—and this encouraged him to think of himself as more desirable than he was. A callousness seeped into his descriptions of women. There was Enna, of whom he wrote: "Enna Ta[unintelligible][14] 23 Blond, frial . . . from Rega Estonia. Studing . . . at conservatorie I met her in 1960 at the Zegers. her family (who sent her to Minsk) apparently well off. Enna loves fancy clothes well made shoes and underthings in Oct. 1960 we began to get very close and clamingating in intercourse on Oct. 21 she was a virgin and very interesting we met in such a fashion on for 5 occiations ending Nov. 4 1960 later upon completion of her last year at the music con. she left Minsk for Rega."

Then, in December, he recorded in his diary: "I am having a light affair with Nell Korobka." Korobka, Oswald related, was "21, large 5 ft. 11 inch 150 lbs, built propertionly, large fruitful breast hips wide . . . from a villige near the polish border of strictly Russian peasent stock." She was, he wrote, "gentle," "kind," "passionate in heat," "stubborn in hate," "plain looking," and "frieghtingly large."[15]

But it was Ella German, throughout these brief entanglements, who remained the focus of Oswald's affections. Ella was the first woman he had fallen for in Minsk—he probably felt more strongly about her than any other woman he ever met, including his wife, in Russia or anywhere else—and it was his break with her that would force him, more than anything else, to reassess his life in the Soviet Union.

On January 1, 1961, Oswald wrote: "New Years I spend at home of Ella Germain. I think I'm in love with her. She has refused my more dishonourable advanis, we drink and eat in the presence of her family in a very hospitable atmosfere. Later I go home drunk and happy. Passing the river homewards, I decide to propose to Ella."[16] Oswald appears to be serious here. He comes across, in his diary, as a little impulsive or, perhaps, taken with himself, but he had known Ella for several months, and it was not uncommon for people at that time to marry in their early twenties.

German had not been expecting Oswald on New Year's Eve. They had made plans to spend the holiday together, but then they had quarreled. At a little past eight in the evening, he turned up at her house with a box of chocolates with a ceramic figurine on top. German asked her mother if he could spend New Year's Eve with them, and her mother said, "Of course." The family lived in a room in a house that had three bedrooms and one kitchen. The house faced the Svisloch River, and it was in a cluster of ten or eleven houses. It had been built before the revolution. Now three families lived there, one family per room. After Ella's family had been there a few years, they carved out a second bedroom and installed a separate entrance, which permitted them to come and go without disturbing the other families. It was unknown how much of the original structure had survived the war. They were always repairing floorboards and cracks in the foundation and piecing together impromptu fixtures, doorknobs, and even windows out of old parts. But there were still inconveniences. For example, there was no plumbing; Ella's family had to walk several blocks each morning to get water. Nor was the house well insulated, and it could feel very small inside. But during the holidays, when the family came together, it was warm and cozy, and there was a smell of soup and cutlets.[17]

That night, New Year's Eve 1961, everyone was there: Ella's mother, her grandmother, her uncles (Boris, Ilya, and Alexander) and each of their wives (Lida, Shura, and Luyba). German's mother sang and played guitar, and everyone danced. Two of her uncles were in the navy, and they had learned to dance the *chechetka*, the folk dance that involves tap-dancing while maintaining a perfectly erect back. "Alik liked it very much," German recalled. "He drank heavily that night, and for the first time ever I saw him drunk." Her mother served meat cutlets with potatoes, cabbage salad, and carrots with sour cream. There was vodka and wine from Bulgaria and a bottle of Riesling. The Riesling was sour, so they had to pour it into a pot, add sugar, and heat it just a bit; when the sugar had dissolved, they cooled it and then poured it back into the bottle. "Then you could drink it for a very long time," German said. It snowed that night, but it was very warm in their house. The little fireplace was blazing, and everyone chanted, "Amerikanets! Amerikanets!"[18]

After the New Year's festivities ended, it took Oswald ten minutes or so to walk from German's house, in a patch of woods next to the military headquarters, to his apartment at 4 Kalinina Ulitsa. It was, as Ella recalled, a perfect winter night: frozen river banks, a snow-filled forest, a handful of Menchani strolling home. There was order and calm, and it was festive. She recalled that Oswald's building, next to the television tower, looked vaguely regal.[19]

The day after New Year's, Oswald saw Ella again. He was still sleeping with Korobka (this continued for another month or so). But Ella was more innocent and, therefore, more beguiling to him. She was also Jewish, which he made note of twice in his diary and, one suspects, found rather exotic.[20]

In his diary Oswald wrote: "After a pleasent hand-in-hand walk to the local cinima we come home, standing on the door step I propose's She hesitates than refuses, my love is real but she has none for me. Her reason besides lack of love: I am american and someday might be arrested simply because of that example Polish Intervention in the 20's. led to arrest of all people in the Soviet Union of polish origen 'You understand the world situation there is too much against you and you don't even know it' I am stunned she snickers at my awkarnes in turning to go (I am too stunned too think!)."[21]

German's fretting about a "Polish Intervention" feels forced, to say the least. Apparently she feared that Oswald, being a foreigner, might be arrested. One can imagine Ella being coached—by her mother, a co-worker, a girlfriend—about what to say in the event that the American proposed to her. The appeal to abstract forces over which neither of them had any control sounds strategic, and not only that: it seems tailored to an outsider. It was the tendency of the outsider, and especially an outsider like Oswald, to impose grand, political-historical causes on local events (for example, the end of a relationship) that had nothing to do with anything beyond what was local and personal. Viewed in this way, the end of their relationship, like the U-2 incident and the election of a young American president, was a function of global forces, not personal ones.

But Ella's contention that she feared for Oswald and that this was why she couldn't be with him was probably a lie. There was no serious cause for concern—especially under Khrushchev—and even though an international crisis involving the United States could have complicated matters for Oswald, there was no indication that Ella paid much attention to politics or foreign affairs. This was, in fact, part of her appeal to Oswald—her innocence and girlishness, her apparent disconnection from the ugliness and moral complexity of the world. It is hard to believe that this was the real reason for rejecting Oswald. The truth is, she did not love him. When I met her, Ella said that, above all, she was surprised and bewildered by Oswald's proposal. She didn't know why he cared about her so deeply.[22]

Oswald seemed to grasp this. As he put it in his diary: "I realize she was never serious with me but only exploited my being an american, in order to get the envy of the other girls who consider me different from the Russian boys. I am misarable!" By the next day, his anger had subsided, but his unhappiness had acquired a more hopeless undertone. In his diary he wrote: "I am misarable about Ella. I love her but what can I do? it is the state of fear which was always in the Soviet Union."[23]

Even though German comes across as dishonest (surely, true love could have overcome fears of a government crackdown on foreigners that there was little reason to fear), there's also a vague kindness that seeps through here. She indicated that she "lacked" love for Oswald but then added that there were complicating variables. He was a foreigner, and foreigners (and not just Poles) were vulnerable. He could be taken away from her at any moment. Then what would she do? She seemed to be implying that he was too important to risk losing, that her happiness was vulnerable, that it was better to preempt the pain of separation than to indulge in the joy of being together. It is perhaps not surprising that Oswald did not see any silver linings in Ella's rejection of him. He may have sensed in her explanation not kindness but calculation: If indeed he were to be expelled from the country, what would she do? How would she care for herself and their children?[24]

Most everyone said it was Ella who rejected Oswald, but she was not sure his love was ever real. "On the fourth of January, he had to change his passport," she said. "He showed me his passport, and it was written in his passport: 'With no citizenship.' He said to me, 'If you agree to marry me, I will request Soviet citizenship. If not, I will not seek citizenship.' There were people, you see, who were telling him not to get citizenship. Remember that it was difficult to live in the Soviet Union at this time, and that's why people were telling him not to get Soviet citizenship, because then it would be more difficult to leave."[25]

On January 4, 1961, Oswald wrote in his diary: "One year after I received the residence document I am called in to the Passport Office and asked if I want citizenship (Russian) I say no simply extend my residental passport to agree and my docciment is extended until Jan 4. 1962." For the first time, Oswald appeared to be moving toward leaving the Soviet Union. In his next diary entry, Oswald reaffirmed this sentiment, acknowledging that it might be time to go. In the entry dated Jan. 4-31, he wrote: "I am stating to reconsider my disire about staying."[26]

The timing here is critical to understanding Oswald's thinking about his life in the Soviet Union and his eventual departure from it. Oswald had first acknowledged some doubt about having moved to the Soviet Union in May 1960, after his conversation with Alexander Ziger. Then, for several months, his criticism of daily life in Minsk mounted; as he neared what he knew would be a long and cold winter, the tone of that criticism sharpened. But for a few months, after he met Titovets and began seeing a few women, he apparently shelved his frustrations and, for a while, immersed himself in the life of the city. But Ella, and her rejection of his marriage proposal, brought him right back to where he had been immediately before he met Titovets—except now he was angrier, more bitter, more alone than he had been before. Now his criticism morphed into a desire to leave the Soviet Union.[27]

This desire suggests that Oswald's ideological fervor was never as intense as he made it out to be. And it points toward Oswald's ideological shift, which began in the first few months of 1961. Titovets, in an interview, said this shift was characteristic of Oswald's intellectual tendency, his interest in learning and growing and, inevitably, reevaluating previous points of view. That seems generous. For one thing, there is little, if anything, in Oswald's past that indicates he was capable of much more than soaking up party dogma. A likelier explanation is that Oswald was now very unhappy in the Soviet Union and that he was inclined to dress up personal motives and behaviors in a bigger-than-life historical or ideological garb. He felt compelled to rationalize his desire to leave the Soviet Union—a desire that comingled with the disappointment, rage, and even humiliation that came with not fitting into this place that he had expected would be his permanent home—by concluding that Soviet "communism," as he would later put it, was not "Marxism." According to this rationalization, Oswald's desire to leave had nothing to do with unhappiness. He had simply arrived at a conclusion, rationally and over several months, that Russia was not the socialist utopia he had imagined it would be. This dichotomy separating that which was real and deeply felt from that which was mere rationalization is reflected in the gap separating his diary, which is shot through with anger and defeat and which he probably did not expect to share with the public, and his compositions and essay, "The Collective," which struck an alternately dispassionate and ideological tone and which he hoped to publish.[28]

In any event, within weeks of German's rejection and Oswald's first acknowledgment privately, in his diary, that he was thinking of leaving, he took his first concrete steps to do so. On February 1, he wrote in his diary:

"Mail my first request to American Embassy, Moscow for reconsidering my position, I stated 'I would like to go back to U.S.'" Oswald failed to note in his diary that, in his letter to the embassy, he also asked for the return of his passport, which he had turned over to Richard Snyder in late October 1959, when he tried to renounce his citizenship.[29]

It was around this time, in late January and early February 1961, that he appears to have begun to reassess the ideological forces—though not the psychological ones—that had led him to Russia in the first place. It was this ideological reassessment that prompted Oswald to distinguish between "communism" and "Marxism.""Marxism," as Oswald understood it, apparently had given rise to his fascination with the Soviet Union, and "communism," which he regarded as the practice of "Marxism" in the Soviet Union, had soured him on Soviet life. All this theorizing reinforced his growing suspicion that the Soviet experiment had been a marvelous promise that had failed to achieve itself. It also seems to have fostered, in Oswald, a view of himself as floating above the partisanship and mindlessness of governments and bureaucracies. As will become clear, he increasingly saw his role as that of synthesizer of world systems—as philosopher-traveler whose job it was to disentangle the seemingly irreconcilable differences between the Soviet Union and the United States.[30]

"We have lived into a dark generation of tenstion and fear," Oswald later wrote in one of his untitled compositions. "But how many of you have tryed to find out the truth behind the cold war clices!! I have lived under both systems, I have sought the answers and although it would be very easy to dupe myself into believing one system is better than the other, I know they are not. I dispise the representatives of both systems weather they be socialist or christan democrates. Weath they be labor conservative they are all products of the two systems."[31]

His thoughts had not exactly matured; they had widened. They had become more expansive, less rigid, and no longer so monochromatic. Now, instead of just memorizing fragments of other people's theories, Oswald wove together those theories with disparate facts and circumstances, making him sound alternately intelligent, illogical, and at times antirational, as if he were trying to force together elements that could not be made to coexist. None of these new thoughts had actually coalesced into a serious argument (they never would). But he thought they had.[32]

Oswald's ideological shift is expressed in the short, poorly thought-through fragments and essays he wrote after he left the Soviet Union in June 1962.[33] It is difficult to trace the precise development of his thought because he wrote retrospectively, squeezing together ideas he arrived at while in Minsk with ideas that came to him after he left. What is known is that his new political speculations began in the first half of 1961, after German had said no to his marriage proposal. These speculations sound less doctrinaire than the diary entries and letters to his brother and mother that came immediately after his arrival in the Soviet Union. At moments, they strike a plaintive tone, as if Oswald was confronting himself. This was not, in fact, what happened. Oswald lacked much insight into his own thinking or behavior. That said, the writings and ruminations that began to take shape during the first few months of 1961 pointed toward a serious reconsideration—of his ideas, if not himself. There is, in all of these writings, a sense of defeat, bitterness, and lamentation.[34]

In the first untitled fragment, for example, he touched on the feeling of ideological homelessness that engulfed him in early 1961. After taking a swipe against "resurgent americanism in the U.S.," which he called, weirdly, "polite" and "pointless," Oswald sounded a more desperate tone. He also hinted at his own system, which he regarded as more balanced and less polarizing than either the American or Soviet system and which he had just started to work through in his head: "To where can I turn? to factional mutants of both systems, to odd-ball Hegelian idealists out of touch with reality too religious groups. to revisenist or the absurd anarchists. no!"[35] Oswald then burrowed a little deeper into the problem, as he saw it:

> Too a person knowing both systens and their factional accessories,
> their can be no mediation between those systems as they exist to-day
> and that person.

> He must be opposed to their basic foundations and represena-
> tives and yet it is imature to the sort of attitude which says 'a curse
> on both your houses!'
>
> there are two great represerative of power in the world, simply
> expressed, the left and right, and their factions and concess.
>
> Any practical attempt at one alternative must have as its nuclus
> the triditionall idealogical best of both systems, and yet be utterly
> opposed to both systems.
>
> for not system can be entirely new, that is where most revolutions
> industrial or political, go astray. And yet the new system must be op-
> posed unequipily too the old that also is where revolutions go astray.[36]

Oswald then set out to reconcile both ways of life and "their factional accessorice" in his fantastical Atheism System (which Titovets and some conspiracy theorists call the Athenian System[37]). Oswald's vision would not be founded on a clearly articulated ethics or politics. It would be not really a philosophy so much as a series of expectations or desires. It would spring from his experiences in the Soviet Union—experiences that he had imbued with a self-important, quasi-religious significance. "I have done a lot of critizing of our system," he wrote at the end of his composition "Speech." "I hope you will take it in the spirit it was given. In going to Russia I followed the old principle 'Thou shall seek the truth and the truth shall make you free.'"[38]

He encapsulated "the truth" in a series of principles that he divided into three groups. The first group was meant to provide a broad outline of the system. The principles in this group are organized by letter, from *A* to *R* (strangely, there is no *F* or *P*). They include items like *B*, which abolishes fascism; *D*, which outlaws racial segregation and discrimination; *I*, which bars the dissemination of war propaganda and the manufacture of weapons of mass destruction; and *N*, which ends the personal income tax. Oswald also voiced support for giving eighteen-year-olds the vote (nearly a decade before the Twenty-Sixth Amendment was adopted in the United States) and a Marxist-styled tax on "surplus profit gains."[39]

In the second group were four principles, also organized by letter. They fall under the subtitle "A system opposed to the communist." Here, Oswald affirmed his support for private property, small business and "speculation on the part of a single individual," and the free exchange of goods and services. The only thing that Oswald came out against was (once again) "surplus value."[40]

The third group encompassed five principles under the predictable rubric "A system opposed to the Capitalist."[41] In this group, Oswald tried to situate all the "anti-communist" or "pro-capitalist" principles of group two in a Marxist framework. He began with principle *A*, which is the central principle of this section, and then moved on to four subprinciples organized according to number. He states:

> A. In that all undertaking of production, distribution or manfator or otherwise the creation of goods must be made on a pure, collective basis under the conditions:
>
>   1. equall shares of investment be made by members.
>
>   2. equal distrubution of profit after taxs, be made to all investers.
>
>   3. that all work or directive or administrative duties connected with the entersprize be done personally by those investers.
>
>   4. that no person not directly working or otherwise directly taking part in the creationial process of any enterprise, have a share of or otherwise recive any part of the resultant profit of it.

He included a "5." after these four subprinciples but provided no description with it.

What is most striking about the Atheism System is its childlike nature. How nice that in the future there will be no "fascism" and "discrimination," that free enterprise will flourish alongside a socialist collective, that anyone not "directly taking part in the creational process of any enterprise" (stockholders, for instance) will be barred from reaping the profits of others' hard work. Oswald seemed not to grasp how many contradictions were built into his system—so much so that it cannot be said to be a self-sustaining program; it cannot be called an argument. One suspects he didn't know how to make an argument. He had feelings, and he taped those feelings onto words and ideas he didn't really understand (German idealism, anarchy, "surplus profit").

This was Oswald's tendency: to explain himself through loosely knit-together abstractions that were supposedly about other things—news events, theories of political organization—but were really about himself. There is, in all this, an obvious grandiosity, a self-importance that, one imagines, people who write big philosophical treatises have. But there is also, possibly, an embarrassment, a feeling that all these other intense feelings about moving to or from the Soviet Union are a sign of weakness. If that is the case, then the interloper was angry not only with the world but with himself, constantly asking himself why he couldn't find a home, wondering what was wrong with him, tearing himself apart.

The process that Oswald embarked on in early 1961—of dislodging himself from his ideological commitments—mirrored, to some extent, a process that many Soviets had begun eight years earlier. Officially, this was called de-Stalinization, but on a more personal level, it came down to extricating oneself from oneself, disconnecting one's original being from the morass of beliefs and dogmas that one had acquired over many years of conditioning and propagandizing. This metamorphosis, starting with Stalin's death in March 1953, had accelerated after Khrushchev's secret speech in 1956, but the real turning point—in Minsk, at least—was the Twenty-Second Party Congress in October 1961. That was when Khrushchev made it clear that Stalinism was no longer to be questioned or reexamined, but rather to be denounced. Oswald did not indicate in his diary that the larger forces gradually penetrating into the Belorussian Soviet Socialist Republic had altered his thinking. But his essay "The Collective" and his untitled compositions show that he was aware of these changes. It's reasonable to assume that, on some level, conscious or unconscious, he was affected by them. Oswald's gradual moving away from his earlier ideas about the Soviet Union coincided not only with the change in his personal feelings about living in Minsk but also with what many Soviet citizens were experiencing.

This was not, for Soviets or for fellow travelers like Oswald, a pain-less process. If nothing else, the garbled ideas and pronouncements that made up Oswald's Atheism System underscored his ambivalence about and lingering affection for the Soviet Union. The process of coming to terms with life in the post-Stalin era was laden with complex realizations and wonderings, speculations about what was to come and who one was supposed to be. It was also about something much bigger than ideology that had a concrete effect on the experience of everyday life across the Soviet Union.

In "The Collective," Oswald recalled the removal, on November 5, 1961, of the thirty-five-foot Stalin statue in the middle of Minsk. The bronze and marble statue was the centerpiece of Stalin Square, and it faced Prospekt Stalina, or the Boulevard of Stalin. If one were facing it, the grand Trade Unions Palace of Culture would have been to the right. Everyday, thousands of Menchani had passed by, in the shadow of the leader. It was a central organizing feature of the city, and it portrayed Stalin the way he was often represented: in an overcoat, with his right arm pressed against his chest, as if he were pledging allegiance to a flag or country. When the statue was removed, it was swift and almost brutal. It was as if he had never existed—which was, as Khrushchev certainly appreciated, a decidedly Stalinist way to handle things. "A force of 100 men desended upon the then Stalin Square (now Lein Square) and with bulldozer and piledriver commenced to tear up (not salvage) the struc-ture," Oswald wrote. "They must have been very enthusiastic because next day they had removed the 10 ton bronze figue of a man revered by the older generation and laughted at by the sarcastic younger generation."[42]

This was a cause not so much for celebration as for uncertainty. A yoke had been lifted, but no one could say what would happen next. Remnants of the old generation feared what would happen to the Soviet Union now that the almighty leader had been jettisoned once and for all. Reformers, on the other hand—dissidents, poets, and members of the intelligentsia—feared a return of the old Stalinist idea. Oswald never stated explicitly where his affinities lay, perhaps because he didn't know. The one indica-tion we have that he may have sided with the reformers, if that's not too much of a stretch, comes at the very end of "The Collective," where he struck an ominous tone when discussing Minsk immediately after the Stalin monument had been done away with. "In full view of all the dignataries and workers going by the destuction of Stalin and the symbolic ending of Stalinism (kprushcheb hopes) was concluded. But Belerussia as in Stalin's native Georgia is still a stronghold of Stalinism. and a revival of Stalinism is a very, very, possible thing in those two republics."[43]

To the reformers, it did not matter where Khrushchev put all the Stalin monuments—or Stalin's body, which had been removed from the mausoleum in Moscow's Red Square, where it had resided next to Lenin's. It was his spirit, with its celebration of the cult of personality and mass violence, that most frightened them. It was the possibility, never remote, that the pendulum would swing back, the people would return to their former selves, and a new dictator, a true leader in the model of Ivan the Terrible or Nicholas I—or Stalin—would emerge, delivering the Russians from their many fears and uncertainties.[44]

9

"HER NAME
IS MARINA"

THE WINTER CHANGED EVERYTHING. HE HAD CLOSED OUT 1960 holding onto some of his early affection for Russia, and, in fact, New Year's Eve at Ella German's house had left him with a warm and romantic feeling, not only for German but also for Russia. It's true that he had grown weary of the Soviet Union and daily life in Minsk, but he had not determined just yet that it was time to go. Indeed, he must have known that, had German agreed to marry him, she would never have agreed to leave Minsk. Her family and friends were there, and she had no intention of saying good-bye to them. By asking for German's hand, Oswald was signaling his willingness to stay. But she had said no, and almost immediately after that, all the doubts and angers that had been coalescing inside his head for the past several months sharpened into a desire to leave.

Sometime in January 1961, Oswald confronted a stark truth: the grand vision that he had laid out after he had arrived in Russia—"I want to, and I shall, live a normal happy and peaceful life here in the Soviet Union *for the rest of my life*," he had written to his brother, Robert—was in a shambles. He had escaped nothing—not his mother, not his country, not his constant fleeing from wherever he was. He was the same person he had been when he arrived in Moscow on the overnight train from Helsinki.

On February 28, according to Oswald's diary, American embassy officials replied to his February 1 letter stating that he wanted to go home. "I recive letter from Embassy," Oswald wrote. "Richard E. Soyeydeck [Snyder] stated 'I could come in for an interview any time I wanted.'" There is no evidence that Oswald was approached by the KGB, the CIA, or any other intelligence agency. We can assume that the Russians opened his mail and certainly knew of his correspondence with the US embassy in Moscow, but they did not do anything about it, one way or the other.[1]

It's unclear how much Oswald knew about the people he spent most of his time with. Were they real friends, or were they befriending him to funnel information to the security organs? There was no way for Oswald to have known for sure, though he surely had suspicions. There are signs that Titovets never gained his full confidence; in his March 1962 diary entry, Oswald noted that he had not informed Titovets of his impending departure from the Soviet Union: "I'm afraid he is too good a young Communist leage member so I'll wait till last min." As for Golovachev, Oswald offered no indication of whether he thought him trustworthy, although Anna Zhuravskaya said that her brother was unaware until shortly before Oswald's departure that he planned to return to the United States. Oswald appears to have learned not to speak freely at work (his coworkers at the Experimental Department said that not only was Oswald lazy and sometimes disagreeable, but that he also did not talk a lot). Alexander Ziger, maybe the only person in Minsk Oswald did trust, cautioned him not to trust anyone else. In the diary entry dated March 6–18, 1961, Oswald wrote: "I now live in a state of expectation about going back to the U.S. I confided with Zeger he supports my judgment but warnes me not to tell any Russians about my desire to reture. I understade now why."[2]

On March 17, 1961, Oswald's life suddenly changed course. That evening, at the Trade Unions Palace of Culture on Stalin Square in the center of Minsk, he attended a lecture on the Fifteenth United Nations General Assembly. The lecture was given by Lydia Cherkasova, the chair of the Department of Biochemistry at Belorussian State University, the head of the Radiation Research Laboratory at the Academy of Sciences of the

Belorussian Soviet Socialist Republic, and a delegate to the recent UN gathering, which had taken place in September. Cherkasova had traveled by sea, from Kaliningrad to New York, with Khrushchev and the other UN delegates on the *Baltika*. She was in the UN General Assembly Hall when the Soviet premier famously removed his shoe and banged it on a table in front of the whole world.[3]

That night, Lydia Cherkasova was accompanied by her son, Yuri Merezhinsky. Like Titovets, Merezhinsky was a student at the Medical Institute. He drove a Volga, which was a very good car in the Soviet Union, and he liked to host dinner parties—with suckling pig, platters of fresh fish, and black caviar—at his parents' apartment in the center of Minsk. He also liked to sleep with women who had wormed their way into the exclusive parties thrown by children of senior party officials.

Merezhinsky always seemed to be in a good mood or drunk. Unlike most of the other people in Oswald's orbit—and especially Oswald's two closest male friends, Golovachev and Titovets—he was not a serious person. "Yuri was my father's younger half brother," Katerina Merezhinsky said, "and, really, he was not even halfway intelligent or accomplished. He was a shithead, not a good student, more interested in women, alcohol, drugs."

Titovets, in his memoirs, did not recall Merezhinsky fondly. "He was some three years younger than me," Titovets wrote. "A tallish fellow with a pretty face, he was his mother's blue-eyed boy. . . . I viewed him as a rather pampered brat who gave many difficulties to his parents because of his loose ways. He kept company with his [kind] and, with pocket money being no problem, went in for girls and was prone to have one too many. He also had health problems, having developed tuberculosis, but continued to smoke."[4]

There were obvious parallels between Yuri Merezhinsky and Pavel Golovachev—above all, their families. Just as Lydia Cherkasova channeled all her ambitions into Yuri, Pavel Yakovlevich sought to steer his son in a more conventional direction. In both cases, there was a strong element of control. To a large degree, this was due to Cherkasova's and Pavel Yakovlevich's status: Neither could afford a son who was an embarrassment.

Both owed their careers, homes, and other comforts to the party, and both had to be careful about how they tread. The result of this control, in both cases, seems to have been sons who never became their own men. In Merezhinsky and in Golovachev, there was a constant, almost pathetic seeking or wandering, just as there appears to have been a great deal of self-hatred. Both men drank heavily, and their drinking contributed to their premature deaths. It is entirely conceivable that it was this restlessness in the two Russians that appealed to Oswald, consciously or not. He may very well have identified with them.[5]

When he arrived at the Palace of Culture that night, Oswald did not know Merezhinsky. By the end of the night, according to Titovets, the two were friends. Oddly, Oswald, in his March 17 diary entry, mentions neither Merezhinsky nor the lecture that his mother gave: "I and Erich went to Trade Union dance," he writes, referring to Titovets. "Boring but at the last hour I am introduced to a girl with a French hair-do and red-dress with white slippers I dance with her. Than ask to show her home I do, along with 5 other admirares Her name is Marina. We like each other right away she gives me her phone number and departs home with an not-so-new freiend in a taxi, I walk home."[6]

There are two details from that evening that Oswald did not share in his diary. The first, which is known, is that it was Yuri Merezhinsky who introduced Oswald to Marina Prusakova. The second, which is unknown, is how Oswald met Merezhinsky. Later, nobody could (or would) say how this happened. It is almost certainly true that Oswald had not met Merezhinsky before March 17. Merezhinsky had not appeared in any of Oswald's diary entries, and, in any event, the two would not have had cause to cross paths. What is unclear is who introduced himself to whom. The answer is very important, according to Titovets. In fact, he said, the "meaning of Marina"—the role she played vis-à-vis Oswald, her feelings for him, and the reason Soviet authorities ultimately allowed her to leave the country—was connected to this seemingly trivial question about who said hello to whom first. Marina, Titovets said, was either who she appeared to be—a pretty woman in a red dress with high cheekbones, painted lips, and a Brigitte Bardot hairdo—or she was a plant deliberately inserted into Oswald's life for the express purpose of reporting intimate details that, presumably, the likes of Pavel Golovachev could not. Is it possible that Soviet agents, for reasons of their own, arranged for Marina to be introduced to Oswald? That question revolves around Lydia Cherkasova's lecture and Yuri Merezhinsky's operation of the slide projector from the orchestra pit in front of the podium.[7]

The Palace of Culture had been built in 1954 in the neoclassical style. Ten unfluted columns with Corinthian capitals adorned the front of the building. The columns were a pale gray with hints of green; the façade, a bold, Prussian yellow, with matching pale-gray trim. Its most distinctive feature was a series of statues built into the pediment. Each statue represented a Soviet archetype, including a worker, an intellectual, and a peasant. Also built into the pediment were a cherub and the words *Slava Truduy*, or "Glory to Work," engraved on top. Inside the palace was an auditorium with seating for six hundred, a stage, an orchestra pit, and a wrap-around balcony. The ceiling was high, and the acoustics were bad, muffling voices and instruments. Six steps separated the wood-plank stage from the rows of seats.[8]

Lydia Cherkasova's speech had been eagerly anticipated. Medical students and faculty crammed into the seats, lined the walls, and spilled over into the aisles. Officials from the party and the ministries of Foreign Affairs and Public Health also attended. But whatever Cherkasova said could not have been that gripping. There are no accounts of her lecture. Titovets did not even bother to show up; he assumed it would be boring. It's unclear what Oswald thought of the speech. Titovets said Oswald had been hungry for news from America, but Oswald didn't make any mention of Cherkasova in his diary or anywhere else. Oswald's Russian, by then, was probably good enough for him to follow Cherkasova's main points. Whether he understood everything is doubtful.[9]

After the lecture, the crowd streamed out of the auditorium through double doors into the ballroom. The walls were peach-colored, and the flooring was parquet. A band began to play a waltz. A golden red light filled up the ballroom, and waiters with platters of champagne flutes pushed through the crowds. The women, in tight dresses and with their hair up, laughed and whispered. The men eyed the women and tried to kiss them. Everyone sipped champagne and danced.

The medical students, especially the men, annoyed Titovets, who had agreed to meet Oswald after the lecture. They "seemed to be uniformly against wearing ties," he wrote. "Most would . . . undo the top shirt buttons and let the collar of the shirt spread over the lapel of their jackets. I did not mind the undone buttons, but I hated the vogue of wearing one's shirt collar over the jacket collar. It was a convention used in Soviet films to denote working-class types and, to me, smacked of conformity and ideological correctness." Oswald, he added, "exhibited his usual, neat, military-style elegance in a gray suit and white tie."[10]

After a few minutes together, Oswald vanished. Titovets did not know where he'd gone and did not really care. He was concentrating on a first-year medical student with blue eyes. She had come with a girlfriend, but her friend had gone somewhere else. Eventually, Titovets wound up dancing with the medical student. The whir of the brushes and blare of the trumpets emanated from the balcony. The party, with its whirlwind of giggles and loud voices, spread through the hall, and the glow of the chandelier streamed through the semicircular windows onto the steps below.

Titovets, dancing with the medical student, felt a little awkward. They were very close, enveloped by a cloud of overlapping perfumes that smelled like jasmine and peaches. He was not a naturally gifted wooer of women—he admitted as much—but he was starting to imagine what might come next. The logistics, he told me, were complicated. He lived with his parents. But he sensed an opportunity.

Then, suddenly, there was Oswald, tugging at his sleeve. Oswald must have known he wasn't wanted there, but he didn't pay attention, or he didn't care. The only thing he said was that he needed Titovets. Oswald turned around—he expected Titovets to follow him, and he did, leaving the medical student on the dance floor—and the two of them pushed through the double doors, into the columned corridor, and up the wide marble staircase to the second floor. Upstairs was another anteroom and then a corridor. They shoved their way through the crowd and another set of double doors into another ballroom. More chandeliers, women, champagne flutes, and trumpets. Titovets told me he was annoyed by the interruption. Maybe he was, but he had allowed himself to be annoyed.[11]

Finally, they arrived. Standing under a stained-glass window were Yuri Merezhinsky; his two friends, Kostya Bandarin and Sasha Peskarev; and Marina Prusakova, the woman in the red dress. Prusakova had a sculpted face and white heels, and she was heavily scented. Her dress was a little too revealing, and she had the famous, slightly disheveled beehive that had been popularized by Brigitte Bardot. As the only woman in the group, she was the axis around which everyone's attention revolved, which she obviously liked. She had a habit that Titovets immediately picked up on: she liked to touch. She would grab your forearm or drag a finger over your wrist. Also, she would stare too long when she was making a point, and she had a tendency to stand too close. After she said something, she would laugh loudly for several seconds.[12]

Marina Prusakova was born in July 1941—a little more than a year after Germany invaded the Soviet Union—near the city of Arkhangelsk, on the White Sea. She was lucky: the Germans were never able to penetrate that far north or east into Soviet territory. The bloodshed and destruction that engulfed the western flank of Soviet Russia never reached her part of the country.[13]

Two things about Marina's childhood were like Oswald's: she never knew her father, and she moved a lot. When she was little, she lived with her maternal grandmother, and then, after the war, she moved in with her mother, Klavdia Vasilyevna Prusakova, and her stepfather, Alexander Ivanovich Medvedev, in Leningrad. By then, Leningrad was a hollowed-out shadow of its former self—it had only been liberated from the Nazi siege a few years earlier—and eventually the family moved to Moldova, where they lived well in a village. Then, later, the family moved back to Leningrad. In 1955 Marina started studying at a pharmaceutical institute, and in 1957 her mother died. Marina recalled that she did not get along with her stepfather: "I was not a good child," she said. After graduating from the institute, she was assigned a job in Leningrad, "but my stepfather didn't want me to remain with him because he thought perhaps he would marry again, and, therefore, I left."[14]

In 1959 Marina moved to Minsk to live with her aunt and uncle; the latter was a member of the Communist Party and a lieutenant colonel at the Ministry of Internal Affairs, or MVD. Marina became a pharmacist at Clinical Hospital No. 3. She worked six days a week, from ten a.m. to four thirty p.m., and earned 45 rubles per month. Like most Russians in their teens and early twenties—Marina turned eighteen that year—she was a member of the Komsomol, or the Communist Party youth league.

People had wildly conflicting views of who Marina was, her character, and the relationship she would have with Oswald. This confusion, like so many supposed confusions surrounding Oswald, was probably, for the most part, imposed on her retrospectively. It was the confusion of outsiders (writers, journalists, government investigators) trying to make sense of this woman who would become the most important person in Oswald's life, and it was compounded by the atmospherics of the apparent mystery that was Oswald and his role, a few years later, in the assassination of the president. Merezhinsky, for his part, contended that Marina had been a prostitute in Leningrad; Mailer, in *Oswald's Tale*, reported Merezhinsky's contention, and Titovets, in *Oswald: Russian Episode*, quoted Merezhinsky as saying the same thing. Merezhinsky was unsparing in his account. "She would now be with one guy, then with another one and another. . . . She had a pretty face and an empty little head," he told Titovets. "Nothing else. She was mostly after men." Priscilla McMillan, the reporter who had interviewed Oswald at the Metropol in Moscow and would later interview Marina, portrayed her in her book *Marina and Lee* as much more innocent and good-natured. McMillan's book opens with a description of Marina methodically and dutifully scrubbing her kitchen floor. In an email McMillan indicated that no one she knew of, including Marina's stepfather, Alexander Medvedev, suggested that she was ever a prostitute.[15]

Whatever the case may be, the question of who Marina was—her past, her sexual mores, her attitudes toward family and Oswald and even housecleaning—was subordinate to a more pressing question that would color the rest of Oswald's time in the Soviet Union: Would she ever inform on Oswald to the KGB? Would she be the woman she portrayed herself as having been in her testimony before the Warren Commission—loving and devoted? Or would she turn out to be a KGB plant who had been artfully inserted into Oswald's life with the express purpose of providing the security organs with even more information about the American?

In her testimony before the Warren Commission, Marina recalled (correctly) that she met Oswald at a party at the Palace of Trade Unions, but she said (incorrectly) that this had taken place on March 4, 1961. She said that Oswald "was very neat, very polite . . . and it seemed that he would be a good family man." She added that Oswald being a metal-lathe operator "was nothing special," adding that "I had a greater choice in the sense that many of my friends were engineers and doctors. But that is not the main thing."[16]

The exact chronology of what happened that night is somewhat convoluted. Apparently, Merezhinsky introduced Oswald to Marina, and then Oswald, unsure of his Russian and Merezhinsky's English, ran downstairs to fetch Titovets. Titovets had been dancing with the medical student but left her on the dance floor and followed Oswald back upstairs to translate for him. It was obvious—to Titovets and probably Merezhinsky and his friends Bandarin and Peskarev—that Oswald was taken with Marina. He kept staring at her, and he wanted to make sure that he would be able to see her again. "Lee listened intently over the dancing pandemonium in the hall to what I interpreted for him," Titovets wrote. "It did not amount to very much. Marina gave Lee her home telephone number and told him where she lived. He asked me to repeat it for him, which I did. That turned out to be all the information that Lee wanted to know for sure. He was satisfied." Titovets noted, more than once, that Marina comported perfectly with Oswald's taste in women: she was overtly sexual, unrefined, girlish. Oswald was transfixed. Titovets found her "repellent."[17]

The critical piece of information missing from Oswald's brief description of that night and Marina's somewhat lengthier discussion of it was how, exactly, Oswald came to meet Merezhinsky. In his memoirs, Titovets offers a long and tortuous explanation—including a behind-the-scenes rendezvous at the Palace of Culture and a late-night party at Lydia Cher-kasova's apartment—that ultimately concludes that Merezhinsky sought out Oswald and introduced him to Marina. According to this line of speculation, Merezhinsky and Marina were both working for the KGB, and they orchestrated the entire evening with an eye toward insinuating Marina into Oswald's life. "Oswald," Titovets wrote, "was unattached at the time. To get him deeply involved with a pretty girl that the KGB must have had control over was a potential way to obtain a string to pull at him. It might serve as a means of obtaining valuable information about the American."[18]

Titovets's theory is plausible only if one ignores Occam's razor and the fact that Marina did not, in fact, meet the profile of a typical KGB agent. People who were KGB agents were usually highly intelligent, well educated, polished, cosmopolitan—and, in the case of those whose job it was to spy on native English speakers, fluent in English. In other words, they were much more like Titovets than Marina.

It is much likelier that Oswald simply met Merezhinsky at the dance, one way or the other, and that Merezhinsky introduced Oswald to Ma-rina, and that Merezhinsky and Marina were *subsequently* recruited by the KGB to inform on Oswald. (In her Warren Commission testimony, Marina would only say that she had gone to the dance with friends from the Medical Institute and that one of them, Merezhinsky, had introduced her to Oswald.)[19] This was the same way the KGB had gone about recruit-ing other people in Oswald's orbit—most notably, Pavel Golovachev. The organs had obvious reasons for wanting to recruit Marina. She could tell them about everything they couldn't see or hear for themselves—about his sleep habits, moods, coworkers, neighbors, the newspapers he read, the cigarettes he smoked, his family, his sexual proclivities, and his opin-ions of everything from the Soviet premier to the new American presi-dent to Jack London, Tchaikovsky, Boris Pasternak, and the poet Yevgeny Yevtushenko. But there was no need for any elaborate scheme that could easily have blown up in their faces. Better to wait and watch and then move in.[20]

This may seem like a distinction without a difference—that of the KGB agent versus the KGB informant—but it was not. Russians empathized with or often took pity on informants, who were frequently backed into corners before sharing information with the security organs. An agent, someone who worked for the organs and actively sought out targets to watch or befriend, was to be feared and sometimes admired, although from afar. To Russians, these were not exactly contemptible people. They were highly capable, devious, often personable. They were special.

Still, Titovets's discussion of the night of March 17 tells us a great deal—especially about Titovets. Indeed, the whole story seems designed to create the impression that everyone but Titovets was in on the plot to watch and choreograph Oswald's every move. And it seems designed to obscure the fact that Titovets was the only person in Oswald's life who had actively made a point of finding and befriending Oswald and that he was the only person who was close to Oswald and did not live inside the little world the KGB had constructed for the American, the *kolpak*. (Titovets's parents' apartment, where he lived, was at least twenty minutes from Oswald's by tram.) When I asked Titovets if he, not Merezhisnsky or Marina, had been working for the KGB, he said only, "I was never in this situation." Then, after a few moments, he added, "From a patriotic point of view, certainly, we were ready to help intelligence, to help whomever, the government, to defend the country. It's our duty." The only reason to suspect that Titovets was not exactly what he appeared to be—a KGB agent who had managed to get closer to Oswald than anyone else in Minsk—was that he resembled a KGB agent too closely. He came across, at moments, as a caricature of the person he said he had never been, and this made him a little absurd and even indecipherable.[21]

Marina soon became a permanent fixture in Oswald's life. In his diary entry dated March 18–31, Oswald wrote: "We walk I talk alittle about myself she talks alot about herself. her name is Marina N. Prosakoba." Oswald did not record that toward the end of March he developed a serious ear infection—he suffered from a chronic case of otitis media, or inflammation of the middle ear—and that he had to be hospitalized at Clinical Hospital No. 4. "Admitted with complaints about suppuration from the right ear and weakening in hearing," Oswald's medical file reported. "The ears have ached since childhood." He spent eleven days in the hospital, where, on April 1, an adenotomy, or incision into one of Oswald's glands, was performed. The file notes that Oswald's physician at the hospital was "Svirnovskaia."[22]

Oswald's hospitalization did not interfere with his burgeoning romance with Marina. "I had arranged to meet with him again," Marina told the Warren Commission. "But he went to a hospital and he called me from there. We had arranged to meet on a Friday, and he called from the hospital and said he couldn't because he was in the hospital and I should come there, if I could." Rankin, the commission's general counsel, asked Marina whether she visited Oswald at Clinical Hospital No. 4 frequently, and she said she had. "I felt sorry for him being there alone," Marina said.[23]

Oswald's relationship with Marina progressed rapidly after he was released from the hospital. According to his diary: "Apr 1-1-30 We are going steady and I decide I must have her, she puts me off so on April 15 I propose, she accepts." It was, perhaps, because he was distracted by Marina and the prospect of getting married that Oswald seems to have missed or ignored the failed Bay of Pigs invasion, which started April 17 and was over two days later—this despite state media organs like *Izvestia* having published prominent articles and *Tass* having issued statements from public officials denouncing the CIA-sponsored attack. In any event, on "April 31," Oswald reported matter-of-factly: "After a 7 day delay at the marriage beaure because of my unusual passport they allow us to registra as man & wife two of Marina's girl friends act as bridesmaids, we are married at her aunts home we have a dinner reception for about 20 friends and neboribos who wish happiness (in spite of my origin and [accent])." The evening was colorful. There was a great deal of eating and drinking, someone whom Oswald identified as "Uncle Wooser" apparently started a fight, and an electrical fuse blew out. In his diary Oswald wrote: "We take our leave and walk the 15 minutes to our home. We lived near each other, at midnight we were home."[24]

The next two entries are among the most revealing in Oswald's diary.

On May 1, 1961, he wrote: "Found us thinking about our future. In spite of fact I married Marina to hurt Ella I found myself in love with Marina."[25]

Then, in the entry marked simply "May," Oswald wrote: "The trasistion of changing full love from Ella to Marina was very painfull esp. as I saw Ella almost every day at the factory but as the days & weeks went by I adjusted more and more my wife mentaly. I still ardent told my wife of my desire to return to U.S. She is maddly in love with me from the very start, boat rides on Lake Minsk walks through the parks evening at home or at Aunt Valia's place [m]ark May." He had found himself a wife, and she, an American, but their love, as it were, had a tenuous feel to it. Ella German remained lodged in his head—a wistful memory of the life he might have had in Minsk.[26]

10

DISENTANGLEMENTS

F OR AWHILE, AFTER MARINA ENTERED LEE'S LIFE, IT SEEMED
as if everything had changed. The downward slope that he had been
on for so many months finally bottomed out, and then, happily, suddenly, he had what looked like stability. It would make sense if all this
had led him to rethink his decision to leave Russia. He now had a wife,
and soon she would be pregnant. They had an apartment (his) that most
everyone they knew envied. And they had jobs. In the United States, it's
unlikely that being a metal-lathe operator had much cachet, but in the
Soviet Union, and especially in the Belorussian Soviet Socialist Republic,
it was something to be proud of. They could easily imagine what the next
several decades might look like.

Oswald would rise from a Level 2 metal-lathe operator all the way to
a Level 6, a "master." Eventually, he would gain Soviet citizenship, and he
would join the party. They would acquire a television set and maybe a
car (probably a Moskvich, which would be perfectly acceptable by Soviet
standards[1]). His Russian would continue to improve, and he would keep
reading Marx, Lenin, and other philosophers and revolutionaries. Their
circle of friends and acquaintances would expand. Their children would
be guaranteed a good education, and if they studied, they would attend
a first-rate institute or university in Minsk. The peripatetic casting about
that had defined Oswald's early adulthood would recede; there would be
no more violent ups and downs. He would be content, and this would be

a good Soviet life. In fact, it would be a much better life than he could have expected in the United States, where neither his apartment nor his job would have been subsidized by the state, he had none of the friends or connections he enjoyed in Minsk, and nobody would have considered him terribly special or important. In the Soviet Union, he was, if not important, at least noteworthy and, of course, far away from his mother.

For a month or two after the wedding, it looked as if Oswald might, in fact, be reassessing his reassessment of the Soviet Union. He seemed happy, and it was now early summer, which meant it was warm and he and Marina could stroll along the Svisloch or through the park. They could enjoy the city. He also had a number of good friends by now—not only Golovachev and Titovets, but Merezhinsky and his crowd, and all of Marina's friends and family. He had a community.

A letter he wrote to his brother less than a week after the wedding hinted at a new maturity. It was the first contact he had with Robert since coming to Minsk more than a year before. It is clear from the letter that he is no longer enamored of Soviet life, but he sounds more content than he did in his earlier letters and diary entries. There are few signs in the letter of the agitation and even desperation that had been building inside him just a few months earlier. Instead, one senses in Oswald a realization that Russia, while not a Bolshevik utopia, might be a place where he could at least build something. He seems more at ease, but he is also more aware: he had had to push through his first pangs of disillusionment with the factory and Minsk, and he had struggled to find a niche. He seemed to have accomplished that, but it had been harder than he had probably expected. He sounds more sober, more connected to reality, than at any other point in his Soviet foray.[2]

In the letter, dated May 5, 1961, he wrote:

Dear Robert.

Its been a long time since I have written you, more than a year, alot has happened in that time.

I am now living in the city of Minsk which is located about 400 miles S-W of Moscow. Minsk is the capital city of the Soviet State of bellerussia.

I shall have been living here already a year and three months. I came to live in Minsk after I wrote my last letter to you. I have been working at the local radio-television plant as a metal-smith.

On April 30 of this year, I got married. My wife is nineteen years old, she was born in the city of Leningrad, which is the second largest city in the U.S.S.R., her parents are dead—and she was living with her aunt and uncle here in Minsk when I first met her.

Not too long ago I recived a letter from mother but I lost the address.

I would like you to send it to me if you write.

We have a small flat near my factory and are living nicely. In general I have found the living conditions here to be good but there is alot of things still to be done.

I hope to send you some things from here if you like. the Soviet Union is one of the most interesting country's I have seen in My travels. You should try to visit us some time I some times meet american tourist here especialy in the summer.

We thats about all for now hope to hear from you soon.

regards to Vatta and Kathy.
Lee

What is most curious about this letter is that not only did Oswald fail to mention that he corresponded, in February, with the US embassy about

leaving the Soviet Union, but he also seemed to be indicating that he intended to stay in Minsk for the foreseeable future. He was "living nicely";
the Soviet Union was "one of the most interesting country's" he'd seen;
and, even better, "you should try to visit us." Far from sounding like a
stranger in a strange land, he comes across as something of a tour guide.[3]

But instead of settling into Minsk, Oswald resumed the course he had
embarked on three months earlier. The wedding, in retrospect, looks not
to have changed anything so much as put on hold a process that had
already been started. Oswald had made up his mind. It was time to go.

By mid to late 1961, Oswald understood that he was being watched constantly. He suspected—correctly—that his apartment was bugged. Alexander Ziger's warning to Oswald, in March, that he shouldn't trust anyone
had sharpened into a more intense worry, or even fear, and by December
he had come to the conclusion that the authorities had started to block
incoming letters from reaching him. Nor was it just a matter of being
watched by the security organs. In the beginning, being a curiosity was
like being a celebrity, and he had enjoyed that, but now it had turned
into a form of segregation. He was at home in Minsk, but he was never
fully integrated. "At times," Titovets wrote in his memoirs, "he felt himself swamped by boredom, enveloped in a kind of dreary inertia. He had
already turned twenty-one and had accomplished nothing yet. . . . He
had doubts that he would get somewhere without compromising what he
believed was right." Oswald became annoyed, more often than before, "by
the propensity of the Russians to treat him as . . . [a] curiosity. His frus-
tration mounted as they would misinterpret his habits as amusing antics
and trivialize him as a clown." When he had first come to Minsk, being a
foreigner had been an advantage. It had set him apart. But he no longer
derived any excitement or pleasure from that. He no longer wanted to be
set apart. Titovets recalled, "He loathed the dubious identity imposed on
him by those around him."[4]

Ella German thought that Oswald might have been persuaded to stay
in the Soviet Union but that Marina Oswald really wanted to move to the
United States. It's true that Oswald had started thinking about returning

home months before he met Marina, but, German said, Oswald was very sensitive to his environment—the buildings, the weather, the people he met on the street. His feelings, she said, could fluctuate wildly. German added that Pavel Golovachev had also thought that it was Marina, more than Oswald, who was determined to leave Russia and that in the Experimental Department they joked that Marina had already thrown away her internal passport.[5]

When I asked German whether she could have persuaded Oswald to stay in the Soviet Union, she was reluctant to answer but then nodded. It was true that, despite what Oswald might have believed, they had never been in love, she said. But she noted (correctly) that she had had a strong influence on him, and she knew that he had married Marina, at least in part, to get over her. She thought that what Oswald really wanted, more than any particular place or person, was to belong somewhere, and she thought that Minsk was that place. She felt that, if he had had the right encouragement, he might have seen this for himself. Going back to the United States, she said, was not a good idea.[6]

There is a great deal of truth to this. The reason that Oswald had defected to the Soviet Union was to find a home, even if this was not the way he might have put it. But it's worth bearing in mind that neither German nor Golovachev was familiar with Oswald's pattern of interloping from one address to another. All they knew was that he was an American who had moved to the Soviet Union. They knew almost nothing about his family and his time in the Marine Corps, and they did not know that he had tried to kill himself in Moscow. They could not have appreciated that Oswald was accustomed to moving often and that his defection to the Soviet Union had been an attempt to put an end to those moves. That German was confused by Oswald's decision to leave the Soviet Union pointed to the intensely psychological—that is, invisible—forces at work in him. More visible factors like the Experimental Department, his apartment, and his neighborhood—which, taken together, made for a rather nice life—could not really explain why Oswald wanted to leave Russia.

There was one complicating variable, as Oswald saw it: his fear that, once back in the United States, he would be prosecuted for having been a traitor and defecting to the Soviet Union. This was a mostly unwarranted concern, but over the next several months, as Oswald and Marina mobilized for their departure, it would grow. He touched on this matter in a May 31 letter to his brother, Robert. In the letter, he indicated that he believed the US government had already begun proceedings against him. "I can't say whether I'll ever get back to the States or not, if I can get the government to drop charges against me, and get the Russians to let me out with my wife, than maybe I'll be seeing you again." The United States had not, in fact, charged Oswald with anything, but he was oblivious to this.[7]

On July 8, Oswald flew to Moscow to inquire at the US embassy about going home. In his diary he struck a melodramatic tone when describing this trip, noting his wife's "tearful and anxious parting." The flight took a little more than two hours, and then he had to catch a bus to the center of the capital. Finally, he arrived at the embassy. "Its Saturday what if they are closed?" Oswald wrote. "Entering I find the offices empty but mange to contact Snyder on the phone (since all embassy personal live in the same building) he comes down to greet me shake my hand after interview he advises me to come in first thing Mon." Snyder, the consular officer with whom Oswald had met in late October 1959, the very same man whom Oswald had so detested at the time, now found himself, weirdly, in the position of having to assuage Oswald's concerns about returning to the United States. According to the Warren Commission Report, "Snyder told [Oswald] informally that he did not know any grounds on which he would be prosecuted but that he could give no assurances in this regard." On July 9 or 10, Oswald's passport, the same passport he had angrily tossed on Snyder's desk in October 1959, was returned to him, and Oswald was informed that Marina would have to come in for an interview so they could start the process involved in obtaining an American visa. She came almost immediately, and on July 14 Oswald and Marina returned to Minsk together.[8]

By late 1961, Oswald was spending most of his time outside the Experimental Department trying to obtain the documents that he and Marina needed to leave the Soviet Union. One problem concerned timing. The Soviets would only grant them exit visas—permission to leave the country—that lasted for a few months, at most. That meant it would be necessary for Marina to have her American visa before moving forward with the Russians. If they didn't take care of the American side of the equation first, there was a chance they might get their Soviet exit visas only to see them expire before the American documents were obtained—and then find it impossible to get new exit visas. Complicating all this was Oswald's looming, annual January 4 date with the Passport Office, which would want to know, yet again, what his plans were. It had been nearly two years since the authorities in the Visa and Registration Department at the Ministry of Internal Affairs had granted him an "identity document" that allowed him to stay in the country and facilitated his move from Moscow to Minsk, and it had been almost a year since they had extended his residency. Now he had to decide whether he planned to stay or go.

On December 1, he composed a handwritten letter to the US embassy in Moscow:

Dear Sirs:

I am writing in regard to a letter which I sent to the Embassy on November 1, in which I asked: 'Does the American Embassy feel that in the light of the fact that my temporary Soviet document for residence in the Soviet Union expires on January 4, 1962, that the deprivation of an exit visa after this date and therefore the foreseeable holding of me against my expressed desires is unlawful?'

I would like a written reply to this question before the expiration date of January 4, 1962 in order to have a basis for my refusal to give my permission for the legal extension on this document.

Sincerely,
Lee H. Oswald[9]

The embassy had been aware since February of that year that Oswald wanted to return to the United States. On December 14, 1961, Joseph B. Norbury, a consular officer at the embassy, replied to Oswald's December 1 letter.

> It is the Embassy's view that, since you are not considered a Soviet citizen by the authorities in this country, you are entitled to receive a Soviet exit visa upon presentation of a valid foreign national passport. Regarding the latter, as we have indicated to you before, we can take up the matter of renewing your expired American passport upon your next personal appearance at the Embassy.[10]

In an interview, Jack Matlock, who was then a US Foreign Service officer at the US embassy in Moscow, said: "The question was, once he wanted to start coming back, whether he had lost his citizenship or not. He had come in . . . and the consular officer, our predecessor there [Richard Snyder], said [to Oswald], 'Sleep on it. This is a serious step that you will not be able to reverse.' And he never came back. The case was put to Washington, and although there was some delay, the State Department ruled that he was still a citizen. Then it turned out he didn't have the money to return. Then he had a wife, a baby. It took a long time. He got very abusive in his communications."[11]

Oswald grew increasingly agitated. He wanted to leave Minsk more than ever. It was as if he were suffocating inside his *kolpak*. He seemed to have forgotten entirely the feelings that had led him to the Soviet Union a little more than two years earlier. He spent most of his time restless, irritated, mercurial, wondering if he would ever be able to go home again.

His state of mind was captured in a recording conducted by Titovets in December. He had taken part in a similar recording session with Titovets one year before, and now he had agreed to a second one. The first time around, Titovets said, he had wanted to study Oswald's English so he could speak more like a native speaker, ironing out his lingering Russifications and mispronunciations. (Titovets called Oswald "an

English-speaking machine.") Now he wanted to do the same thing, and he wanted to compare himself speaking with Oswald in late 1960 and late 1961. He wanted to see if he had made any progress.[12]

Titovets started the second recording session, which took place at his apartment on Leningradskaya Ulitsa, by asking Oswald to read from Ernest Hemingway's short story "Indian Camp." Oswald sounded bored, aloof, as if he were only partly present. He read in a liminal voice, a voice that seemed to hover between places. It was an ideal voice for reciting a short story by Ernest Hemingway. Over the course of several minutes, Oswald's voice slipped in and out of focus. He pronounced a few words with a quiet articulation, and then, unexpectedly, he receded into a veil of muffled sounds: "The Indians rode with quick choppy strokes. It was cold on the water. . . . Uncle George was smoking a cigarette in the dark. . . . They came around a bend and the dog came out barking. . . . More dogs rushed out at them." He sounded oblivious to the characters he was reading about, their states of mind, their feelings. His words sharpened and then turned dull, then quiet, then sharper, then more pronounced.[13]

Oswald moved on to another Hemingway story, "The Killers." "'I don't know,' said Al," Oswald read. "'I don't know what I want to eat.'" Now, his voice was livelier. "Outside, it was getting dark. . . . From the other end of the counter, Nick Adams watched them." ("He's relaxed now," Titovets said of Oswald. "He's not trying to impress anyone, to sound British.") "Two men came in," Oswald continued. "They sat down at the counter. 'What's yours?' George asked them. . . . He had been talking to George when they came in. 'I'll have a roast pork tenderloin with apple sauce and mashed potatoes.'" On the recording, Titovets became annoyed with Oswald for bungling a word. "Fucking idiot," Titovets said on the recording. Oswald read on. His monotone was interspersed with patches of vibrato. He suppressed a laugh.

Oswald and Titovets started to improvise, with Oswald playing the role of a commanding officer in the army and Titovets playing Cadet Titov. Then Titovets pretended to be Senator Titov, and Oswald was a journalist on a radio station interviewing the senator. They discussed the Berlin Wall, which had been built in August, and the heat spell in Texas.

The recording session turned darker. Oswald had been reciting words into Titovets's tape recorder when he decided to be a serial killer named Jack Marr.

OSWALD: Goddamn, fucking machine gun.
   [Then a few words, something indiscernible.]
   Well, it was a young girl under a bridge. She came in carrying a loaf of bread, and I just cut her throat from ear to ear. Well, I wanted the loaf of bread, of course.
TITOVETS: Your most famous killing in your life?
OSWALD: The time I killed eight men on the Bowery sidewalk there. They were just standing there. . . . I didn't like their faces, so I just shot them there with a machine gun. It was very famous. All the newspapers carried this story.
   [More talking.]
   It's all the same to me. They're going to execute me tomorrow.

[We jump to the next day. Oswald is narrating the last moments of his life.]
OSWALD: Here we are in the death cell. They're coming to get me now. I have to go. So long. Here we are in the death cell. Here we are in the death cell. Here we are in the death cell.
TITOVETS: They're strapping him in. . . . They're putting him in the chair now. . . . He's taking the . . .
OSWALD: The switch.
TITOVETS: What is your last word?
OSWALD: Well, don't pull the switch!
[Shrieking, laughter.]
TITOVETS: Well, pull the switch. . . . I can see his body twisting. He's flying around.

It would be a mistake to read too much into a single recording session. The killing spree that Oswald described in it could hardly be said to anticipate his murder of the president, as the PBS program *Frontline* suggested in a 1993 report on Oswald. But it did hint at Oswald's mood, his irritability, his detachment from his surroundings. He had grown weary of Minsk, and he had been gripped by an adolescent quality. When he had arrived in Moscow, and for at least a year after he moved to Minsk, he seemed very serious about his life and what he planned to accomplish in the Soviet Union. Now he sounded spent, punch drunk, as if he wanted to surrender. His energy and his sense of himself, of who he was supposed to be, seemed to have been leeched away by Russia, Minsk, the factory, the *kolpak*.

By the time of the second recording session, in December 1961, Marina was seven months pregnant and Oswald was doing everything possible to leave the Soviet Union—exchanging phone calls with the Foreign Ministry, writing letters to the embassy, arranging for loans to cover their anticipated travel expenses to the United States. A few weeks earlier, on November 20, Oswald had sent a letter to his brother informing him that it would cost about $800 for two people to fly from Moscow to New York. On December 25, the Soviets informed Marina that she would be granted an exit visa. In his diary Oswald wrote: "Its great (I think)." His tentativeness probably had to do with the fact that Marina had yet to receive her US visa, and now they only had a few months to get everything together.[14]

By January 1962, Oswald had grown more impatient and even a little desperate. On January 5 he wrote:

> Dear Sirs:
>
> This letter is to inform the Embassy of the expiring of my former document of residence in the USSR; dlya Lits Bez grazhdanstva N. 311479 expiration date January 4, 1962, and the granting of a new document; vid na zhitelstvo dlya Inostranets AA 549666, expiration date July 5, 1962.
>
> As I have already informed the Embassy, exit visas for myself and my wife have already been granted. I can have mine at anytime, but

will be good for 45 days only. Since I and my wife wish to leave the
USSR together, I shall delay requesting my visa until such time as
documentation from the Ministry of Foreign Affairs of the USSR
and the American Embassy is completed on my wife.

I'd like to be sure we can leave as soon as all documents are finished
since there will be an addition to the family in March.

I would like to make arrangements for a loan from the Embassy or
some organization for part of the plane fares. Please look into this
and notify me.

Yours truly,
Lee H. Oswald[15]

Matlock did not think much of Oswald or Marina. He certainly did not
think the KGB had recruited him. "His wife lied on [her visa application],
gave us some cock and bull story about not being in the Komsomol [the
Communist Party's youth league]," Matlock said. "We considered rank
and file Komsomol memberships, since everybody had to do it, as involuntary. However, lying on the application, if you lie about a material fact,
is also excluding grounds. I noted that I thought she was lying, but, in as
much as there was no evidence her membership would have been anything but involuntary I granted her the visa. . . . Did the KGB send him
back to assassinate the president? Since the KGB was very well informed
about what our visa procedures were, the smart thing would have been
to say that 'Yes, I was a Komsomol member.' Lee had instructed her to lie.
Oswald had not been briefed by the KGB as to how to get out."[16]

But it was not just Matlock or the State Department that was involved.
Soon after Oswald had begun to press his case, writing letters not only to
the embassy but to Senator John Tower of Texas and John B. Connally,
whom Oswald mistakenly thought was still secretary of the navy, the
bureaucratic machine back in the United States began to whir and hiss.

There were people who remembered what he had done, more than two years before, when he'd told Richard Snyder and John McVickar, the consular officers who preceded Matlock at the US embassy in Moscow, how much he hated the United States and never wanted to go back. They had their doubts about letting him go home again.[17]

PART THREE

AFTER MINSK

11

THE GREAT
ESCAPE, REDUX

OSWALD HAD SPENT THE SECOND HALF OF 1961 TRYING TO extricate himself from the Soviet Union. It had proven to be a much more complicated process than he had expected. In the same way he had imagined, before arriving in Moscow in October 1959, that the Soviet authorities would simply grant him citizenship and a new life, Oswald seemed to have thought that the process involved in going back to the United States would not be cumbersome or draining. He was naïve and wrong and, by the end of the year, weary and close to despair. By early 1962, he had his doubts that everything would pan out, and Marina was unhappy: Not only was she in her third trimester, but she was also a Soviet woman known to be seeking, with her American husband, to leave the Soviet Union and move to the United States. There was an air of betrayal about her.

It was in this climate that Oswald plodded through the first half of 1962, securing the documents and, ultimately, the money that would be necessary to leave. His state of mind is hard to characterize. There were competing forces. He definitely wanted to go. So did Marina. Alexander Ziger, as he had noted, supported the move, but it is unclear how Marina's aunt and uncle felt or any of their other friends or acquaintances; most were probably unaware of their plans. Also, there were Oswald's politics and his fears of what might happen to him when he returned home. And there was still Ella German, who had never receded entirely from Oswald's mind. That he saw her most days at the Experimental Department compounded and complicated his feelings; that he avoided her suggests they were still painful.

It is not exactly correct to say that in 1962 Oswald defected back to the United States. Everything he did complied with the rules and procedures of the Soviet and American governments, and, after all, he was still an American citizen—even if he had once sought to break with the United States. At no point during the several months leading up to their departure for the United States did Lee and Marina have to forge any documents or plot any secret escape. Nor did they have to lie. It's true that Marina had lied about belonging to the Komsomol, but that was unnecessary. Nor did they have to place themselves at the mercy of the government of the country to which they hoped to immigrate, as Oswald had done in late 1959 in Moscow. There would be no suicide attempts this time around.

But there was a strong element of defection in Oswald's emigration. To start with, he acted as if it were a secret and as if he were doing something illegal or dangerous. Many of Oswald's and Marina's close friends were unaware they were planning to leave, and Oswald had made a point of trying to keep the Soviet authorities in the dark. He had not asked for official permission to travel to Moscow, in July 1961, and Oswald and Marina had been disturbed to learn, after they had returned from Moscow together, that everyone at the pharmacy where Marina worked knew that she had visited the US embassy. (Presumably the KGB had informed Marina's boss, who had made a point of telling her coworkers—the better to make life more uncomfortable for a would-be traitor.) What's more, there was a general uneasiness and suspicion that coursed through Oswald's letters and diary entries throughout this entire period. He seemed to intuit that he was not just moving. He was moving to America, and moving to America from the Soviet Union (like moving to the Soviet Union from America) was, in spirit, a defection, a rejection of the place one came from as much as an endorsement of the place one went to. No one moved from the one country to the other just to find a better job or a more hospitable climate. Almost always at the heart of that move was an ideological commitment or change of heart, meaning an embrace of one belief system and a rejection of another.[1]

This was not the same kind of defection that he had embarked on in the fall of 1959. When Oswald came to the Soviet Union, he had been propelled by an angry desperation draped in ideology. Everything about him had been geared toward action: He wanted Soviet citizenship now. He wanted to renounce his American citizenship now. He wanted a new life in Moscow now—and, if he couldn't have it, he wanted to end his life now. Back then, he could barely contain his furies. But when it came to leaving the Soviet Union, there was something mournful about it. He did not appear ready to renounce Russia. He seemed far more conflicted.

Certainly this reticence reflected, to a large degree, Oswald's unwillingness to forego the communist fantasy he had embraced while he was in the Marines. That fantasy was not supported by much in the way of reflection or knowledge of history and culture. But it had a strong, emotional pull, and as we will see, after Oswald left the Soviet Union, his affections for it persisted. It seems safe to say that while Oswald's leftist convictions had been weakened or shaken up—or, at least, confronted with a much more complicated and less utopian reality—his idea of himself as someone with leftist convictions had not.

There were also personal considerations. It's important to recall that Oswald's ideas about politics and ideology and his feelings about wherever he happened to be appeared to have been closely intertwined. This had been the case in Texas and Louisiana, before he joined the Marines; it had been the case while he was based at Atsugi and El Toro; and it was the case now, in Minsk. What he believed to be strongly held ideological convictions were usually very personal feelings—about his home, his family, his sense of rootlessness—that had hardened into political viewpoints but, at root, had nothing to do with anything explicitly political. This was why his ideological commitments were so shallow; they weren't, in fact, ideological so much as personal. That Oswald imagined himself to be deeply ideological—that he fashioned himself into a sort of Che Guevara figure—did not mean that he, in fact, was.

The truth was that Oswald, far from embodying the communist ideal, was powerfully affected by the people around him, by all the bourgeois sentiments that the revolutionary was supposed to have steeled himself against. By the time he left Minsk, several people—the Zigers, Golovachev, Titovets, and possibly Merezhinsky and a handful of friendly acquaintances at the factory—were sorry (or said they were sorry) to see him go. By contrast, when Oswald left the United States in 1959, he left behind only his mother and brother—both of whom he instructed, after arriving in Moscow, not to speak with him again. Leaving Russia, and leaving behind all the ideological-cultural baggage that came with Russia, would be much harder than leaving America.

But the most important personal consideration, the one that probably absorbed the most energy and emotion, was Ella German.

In late May, one week before the Oswald family left Minsk, he approached German at the Experimental Department. They had not spoken for almost a year, and she was surprised when he came up to her at the end of her shift and told her he had something important to say. She said they could speak at the factory, but he said it was important. He wanted to go somewhere private. She said no. It would look bad. She added that she was married now. "He asked me if he knew the man I had married, and I nodded, and very abruptly, without saying anything, he just turned around and left," German said in an interview. She didn't have time to tell him her new name—Prokhorchik. "Then, one week later, I heard he had left, and I couldn't believe it."[2]

German told me there was a story behind this. In the spring of 1960, a few months after Oswald had arrived at the Minsk Radio Factory, there was an incident. Oswald had been waiting in line for the mechanical press, which was a machine that the *tokari* used to shape bits of metal into usable parts. Another metal-lathe operator, Maxim Prokhorchik, had been in front of him—he had been working at the press—and then he had stepped away. There was a rule: if a metal-lathe operator stepped away from the press, you had to wait for the metal-lathe operator to come back. You could not start working on your own piece of metal. Oswald probably didn't mean any offense, and he probably wasn't thinking, but he was impatient, and instead of waiting for Prokhorchik, he started welding or refitting some knob or metal plate. When Prokhorchik returned, he was livid. There were rules, and apparently the American did not think he had to follow them. Prokhorchik, Titovets wrote in his memoirs, "was all ready to give Oswald a punch or two when he suddenly realized that he could not hit the man. That damned American offered absolutely no resistance. He stood propped against the steel pillar with his arms dangling limp along the sides of his body looking quietly at Max." Eventually, Libezin (Oswald's master) and two or three other men stepped in. Libezin told Prokhorchik that it was understandable that he had flared up, but that he should forget about it and remember who Oswald was.[3]

Oswald had already acquired a reputation for being lazy. He would put his feet on his desk and complain about work. He was not, as they all knew, one of them. More importantly, Prokhorchik and Oswald were vying for the same woman, and they knew it. German seemed to prefer Oswald, but that was only because he was a novelty: as she said, he was "interesting." After their relationship ended, Prokhorchik resurfaced, and eventually she decided to marry Maxim. The wedding took place in April 1962, about a year after Oswald's own wedding and a few weeks before he approached her at the Experimental Department. When Oswald asked German if he knew the man she'd married, and she nodded, she was sure he knew it was Prokhorchik. "He didn't ask his name," she said. "He just asked, 'Do I know him?'"

German was always ambivalent about Oswald. She said she had never talked to the KGB about him because she cared for him. In fact, if she could have done it over, she said, she would probably have married Oswald. It was a matter of timing. In January 1961, when Oswald proposed to her, she was still not sure about him, and she didn't feel as if she had to get married immediately. By the spring of 1962, her sense of urgency was greater. She said she was tired of not having anything to do on the weekends and going to dances alone, and she wanted a family. If Oswald had proposed to her in April 1962, like Prokhorchik had, she might have said yes. Prokhorchik, she said, was handsome, read books, and knew a lot about art and culture, and he was Jewish (although she insisted that had nothing to do with it). But there was never a great love between them. They married when she was twenty-five, and Prokhorchik moved into her house in the woods, where Oswald had spent one of his happiest nights in the Soviet Union, on New Year's Eve 1961. The couple shared the house with her mother and grandmother; soon, they had their first daughter. German had not forgotten about Oswald, but she had moved beyond him. Still, she never disliked him, and later she sometimes wondered what their life would have been like together.

For several months Lee and Marina had been inching toward their departure. In December they had been informed by the Soviet government that they could leave. Now all they needed was the money to pay for their trip to the United States and, in Marina's case, permission from the Americans to enter the country.

In early January Oswald asked his mother to contact her local branch of the Red Cross—the real Red Cross—and ask them to help him get the $800 he estimated he and Marina would need to travel to the United States. "I would like you to . . . ask them to contact a organization called 'International rescue committee' or any organizations which aids persons from abroad get resettled. . . . Do not, of course, take any loan only a gift and don't send your *own* money."[4]

A month later, Oswald followed up with another letter to his mother that touched on the money issue: "We will probably fly into the U.S. on a airplane and I see no reason for you to come to New York to meet us I want you to understand that although you can aid us in certain, small ways this business about our coming to the U.S., is relatively simple don't make it more complicated than it is." At the time, Marguerite was living in Texas.[5]

What's most noteworthy about Oswald's correspondence with his mother during this period is the bifurcated tone he strikes. Either he's telling his mother how much he and Marina are looking forward to seeing his family—his letters frequently include a postscript that says something to the effect of "Marina sends her love," even though Marina had never met Marguerite—or he's giving Marguerite a list of instructions. Two years later, when she testified before the Warren Commission, Marina would tell J. Lee Rankin, the commission's general counsel, that Marguerite resented her son for not appreciating all the things she had done to help him get out of the Soviet Union. Oswald, Marina said, had not seen things this way. He tended to view his mother, at best, as a hindrance. What Marguerite viewed as her love and devotion to her youngest son Oswald took to be oppressive and controlling. He had never felt truly loved by her—this had been clear since he was a kid in New York—and there is no indication that he felt particularly close to her now. "It seemed peculiar to me and [I] didn't want to believe it," Marina said, "but he did not love his mother, she was not quite a normal woman. Now I know this for sure."[6]

Whatever the case, by mid-February the money issue appeared to have been put to rest. In a letter to his mother, Oswald wrote: "The American Embassy in Moscow sent me an application for a loan (which I requested) so they will make the money available to us as soon as everything is arranged for Marina."[7]

Oswald's more pressing fear, which had been building since the previous spring and now seemed to cast a pall over the forthcoming birth of his daughter, was what would happen to him once he returned to the United States. In a letter dated January 30, 1962, Oswald tells his brother, Robert, that "you once said you asked around about weather or not the U.S. goverment had any charges against me, you said at that time 'no', maybe you should ask around again, its possible now that the goverment knows I'm coming they'll have something waiting." He was especially concerned that his dishonorable discharge (later changed to the less serious "undesirable discharge") from the Marines would complicate matters. In his letter to Robert, he wrote:

> Mother wrote me a letter the other day in which she informed me
> that the Marine Corps had given me a dishonorable discharge in
> Nov. 1959 Did You know this?

Of course, this is not too bad, since It relives me of reserve duty, but
still I should take this into account.

I wrote a letter to John B. Connally Secretary of the Navy who lives
in Ft. Worth asking about my dishonorable discharge maybe you
could ask him to look into the case since I don't know wheater the
Russians will let that letter through.[8]

After dwelling on this fear of prosecution for four paragraphs, Oswald
then pivoted to more mundane affairs: Marina's pregnancy, Robert's farm,
places they might move to (Oswald says he would "sort of like New Orleans"), and the weather. Then, as if to reemphasize the main point of his
letter, he returned to his concern about the things people might be saying
about him in America. "If you find out any information about me, please
let me know," he wrote. "I'd like to be ready on the draw so too speak We'll
keep writing until we get ready to leave so don't quit writing." He signs off:
"Your Brother Lee & Marina."

Oswald had a tendency to think he was more important than he was,
but he was not entirely wrong in this case. While there were no legal
challenges or smear campaigns waiting for him in the United States, there
were government officials who did think that he might pose a national
security threat to the country. Alas, they couldn't do much about him
because, like it or not, Oswald was still an American citizen. That meant
he could say and do what he wanted, and he could go home, and it didn't
matter if this upset anyone. But they could make him not want to leave
the Soviet Union. They could do this by not letting Marina come with
him.[9]

The Oswalds had already provided the US government with what they
thought was the necessary documentation for Marina's visa. Section 205
of the 1952 Immigration and Nationality Act allowed for the admission
into the country of the spouse of an American citizen, and Marina had
shown the Americans her marriage certificate. There was the potential
problem of Section 212(a) (15), which states that no one shall be let into
the country who is likely to end up on the public dole, but there was little

concern about that since Oswald was twenty-two and able to work. And there was the section of the law stating that admission to the United States shall be barred to any foreigner belonging to a communist organization; at the time of her visa application, Marina was a member of the Trade Union for Medical Workers and, as Matlock had noted, the Komsomol, but she was not active in either, and the Americans felt she was not dangerous.

Marina's one vulnerability was her nationality. Section 243(g) of the Immigration and Nationality Act states that citizens of a country that hinders Americans from traveling there are effectively barred from entering the United States. Since the Soviet Union was in that category, Marina could be denied a visa. That said, the Justice Department, which oversees the Immigration and Naturalization Service, could (and did) grant waivers—in the decade since the act's passage, there had been hundreds.

But there was no support for giving Marina a waiver. In a January 30, 1962, memo from J. W. Holland, the San Antonio district director at the Immigration and Naturalization Service, to the service's unnamed deputy associate commissioner of the Travel Control Central Office in Washington, Holland made note of Oswald's petition, on behalf of his wife, for a visa. (Apparently, the San Antonio office had jurisdiction over Oswald's petition because he had told the government that his home in the United States was in Texas.) Holland recalled in the memo that on July 8, 1961, Oswald had turned up at the embassy in Moscow. "He stated at that time that although he had originally declared at the Embassy on October 31, 1959, that he would willingly make available to the Soviet Union such information as he had acquired as a Radar Operator in the United States Marine Corps, he had actually never been questioned by the Soviet authorities regarding his life or experiences prior to entering the Soviet Union and that such information had not been furnished to any organization of that Government," Holland wrote.[10]

In his memo, Holland acknowledged that the government could indeed grant a waiver for Marina. But, he added, he was not about to do that. "Under existing procedures sanctions may be waived in an individual meritorious case for the beneficiary of a petition filed by a reputable relative where no substantial derogatory security information is developed," Holland wrote, lifting language directly from the law. "A substantial amount of derogatory security information has been developed in connection with the petitioner [Oswald], and it is felt that he does not meet the criteria mentioned as to being reputable and considerable doubt has arisen with respect to any meritorious features of this case." Holland went on to note that "it is reported that on his subsequent visit to the Embassy, he stated he had been completely relieved of his illusions about the Soviet Union, and also that much of the bravado and arrogance which characterized his first visit appeared to have left him. These unsupported declarations of the petitioner are not sufficient to relieve the doubts which have arisen regarding his loyalty to the United States. Sanctions will not be waived and the petition will be denied."[11]

Two weeks later, in a February 15 letter to Robert, Oswald reported that "June Marina Oswald, 6 lbs. 2oz." was born at ten a.m. "We are lucky to have a little girl, don't you think? But then you have a head start on me, although I'll try to catch up. Ha. Ha This makes you an Uncle, congratulations!" Oswald then turned to his ongoing effort to leave the Soviet Union. He was unaware that the Immigration and Naturalization Service had already decided to deny Marina a visa. He reported to Robert that he and Marina had received their exit visas from the Soviet authorities and that Marina was still waiting for her US visa. "These are granted by the US. goverment," he wrote, "and they have assured me they are getting all the papers together (they are quite alot) and certified accepted."[12]

Like the January 30 letter, the February 15 letter blended the personal and the political. "I heard over the voice of america that they released Powers the U2 spy plane fellow. Thats big news where you are I suppose. He seemed to be a nice, bright, american-type fellow, when I saw him in Moscow." It's unclear whether this was a lie designed to impress Robert—Oswald never actually saw Powers; by the time the plane was shot down, on May 1, 1960, he was living in Minsk—or whether Oswald meant that he saw Powers on television. This was possible but unlikely. Oswald did not have a television in his apartment.

Then, in his letter, Oswald jumped back to personal matters.

You woulde'nt have any clipping's fromthe Nov. 1959 newspaper of
Ft. Worth, would you.

I am beginning to get interested in just what they *did* say about me
and my trip here.

The information might come in handy when I get back. I would hate
to come back completely unprepared.[13]

The February 15 letter, like all his subsequent letters from Minsk, omitted
almost all the details surrounding his daughter's birth. For more details
about Oswald's personal life, one has to go to his diary or the Warren
Commission Report. On February 15, he reported, Marina woke him at
dawn. "Its her time," he wrote. "At 9:00 we arrive at the hospital I leave her
in care of nurses and leave to go to work. 10:00 Marina has a baby girl.
When I visit the hospital at 500 after work, I am given news. We both
wanted a boy. Marina feels well, baby girl, O.K." His coworkers at the Experimental Department gave them a "summer blanket," six "light diapers,"
four "warm diapers," two "chemises," three "very good, warm chemises,"
four "very nice suits" and two toys for the baby.[14]

He wasn't permitted to see his daughter until February 23, when Marina was discharged from the hospital. Five days later, he had to register
her name with the authorities. "I want her name to be June Marina Oswald," he wrote. "But those Beaurocrats say her middle name must be the
same as my first. A Russian custom support by a law. I refuse to have her
name written as 'June Lee.' They promise to call the city ministry (city
hall) and find out in this case since I do have an U.S. passport." The next
day, February 29 (1962 was a leap year), Oswald was told by the authorities in charge of registering baby names that "nobody knows what to do
exactly, but everyone agrees 'Go ahead and do it. 'Po-Russki'. Name: June
Lee.'"[15]

Meanwhile, back in the United States, the bureaucracy was moving at a
glacial pace. On February 28, Holland sent a letter to the US embassy in

Moscow, stating what he had already decided one month earlier: the Immigration and Naturalization Service would not grant Marina a waiver. And it would be another month before the State Department officially weighed in, urging the Immigration and Naturalization Service to reconsider its denial.[16]

In a March 27 letter from Michael Cieplinski, the acting administrator of the State Department's Bureau of Security and Consular Affairs, to Raymond Farrell, the commissioner of Immigration and Naturalization, Cieplinski offered two reasons for granting the waiver and expediting Oswald's return to the United States. First, there was the question of fairness. Not giving Marina a visa would unfairly punish her for things that Oswald had said. Then there was the bigger and more important political matter.

> If Mrs. Oswald is not issued a visa by the Embassy, the Soviet Government will be in a position to claim that it has done all it can to prevent the separation of the family by issuing Mrs. Oswald the required exit permission, but that this Government has refused to issue her a visa, thus preventing her from accompanying her husband and child. This would weaken the Embassy's attempts to encourage positive action by the Soviet authorities in other cases involving Soviet relatives of United States citizens.

Cieplinski concluded: "Because of these considerations and because I believe it is in the best interests of the United States to have Mr. Oswald depart from the Soviet Union as soon as possible, I request that the Section 243(g) sanction be waived in Mrs. Oswald's case."[17]

Oddly, someone at the Immigration and Naturalization Service appears to have informed Oswald that Marina's visa application had, in fact, been approved—two days before Cieplinski wrote his letter to the agency asking it to reconsider its decision not to grant Marina a waiver. On March 25 Oswald wrote in his diary: "I recive a letter from Immigration & Natur. service at San Antonio, Texas, that Marina has had her visa petition to the U.S. (approved!!) The last document. Now we only have to wait for the U.S. Embassey to recive their copy of the approval so they can officially give the go ahead." Three days later, Oswald recorded in his diary, Marina quit her job at the pharmacy.[18]

It appears that whoever contacted Oswald was mistaken. A little more than two weeks after Oswald was informed that Marina's visa had been approved, he wrote a letter to Robert stating that "the American side" was holding up their departure. No doubt, conspiracy theorists will read into this discrepancy a secret plot. The truth is almost certainly much more banal: bureaucrats and government agencies, as is well known, often fail to communicate with each other, and it is hardly surprising that Oswald learned one thing from one official only to hear something else a few weeks later from someone else.[19]

In any event, it would be almost a month before the Immigration and Naturalization Service replied to Cieplinski's letter. On May 9, Robert H. Robinson, deputy associate commissioner of the Travel Control Central Office, apparently having heard from someone in the commissioner of Immigration and Naturalization's office, wrote to Cieplinski: "In view of the strong representations made in your letter of March 27, 1962, you are hereby advised that sanctions imposed pursuant to Section 243(g) of the Immigration and Nationality Act are hereby waived in behalf of Mrs. Oswald." According to the Warren Commission Report, "On May 10, the Embassy wrote [to Oswald] that everything was in order and suggested that Oswald come to the Embassy with his family to sign the final papers. At his request, he was discharged from the factory on about May 18."[20]

On May 22, the day before Lee and Marina left Minsk, Titovets stopped by their apartment to say good-bye. Marina and June were not there. Oswald was packing. He gave Titovets two books—*The Power of Positive Thinking*, by Norman Vincent Peale, and *As a Man Thinketh*, by James Allen—and offered him a large silver ring that he had bought in Japan and wore constantly. Titovets told Oswald that he was touched but couldn't accept the ring; it was too expensive. Oswald, we're told, complied with his friend's wishes and put the ring back on his finger. Titovets recalled in his memoirs that Oswald "told me the time of their departure and that they would be leaving by train. They would go first to Moscow.

I told him that at about the time of their departure I should be busy at the Medical Institute and might well miss the farewell ceremony at the railway station. It might well turn out that we were seeing each other for the last time. Lee nodded."

Titovets added, "Frankly speaking, even though I was quite busy with my studies, I certainly could still have cut the lectures to see Lee off at the station had he asked me to help him along. But as things stood with him, he could manage without an extra hand. Deep inside I loathed those fussy parting scenes with the exaggerated show of friendly feelings that the situation seemed to call for." He reported that "we simply shook hands. I left holding the two hard-covered religious books under my arm."[21]

On their last night in Minsk, Lee, Marina, and their daughter stayed at Golovachev's apartment.[22] The following evening, May 23, the Zigers escorted them to the train station. A photograph shows Lee and Marina leaning out of a window of a train car, just before they leave the station, Lee smiling weakly and waving. Marina, wrapped in a scarf, looks scared and a little pensive. The profundity of what was about to happen appears to be settling in. He was accustomed to leaving places, and so was she. But this departure was a bit like his departure from New Orleans two and a half years earlier, when he left his home forever.[23]

Oswald's mother, Marguerite, apparently was unaware that her son and her daughter-in-law had secured safe passage out of the Soviet Union. One month before, Oswald had sent his mother a letter in which he brought up the money issue again. The US embassy, Oswald told her, "is apparanitly/trying to get us money from other sourse's than itself for our tickets to the U.S. plobably they'll apporich you for money again don't pay any attention to them." This problem was eventually solved, but Marguerite did not know that. Oswald's letter had whipped her into a frenzy.[24]

Two days after Lee, Marina, and June left Minsk, Marguerite sent two frantic letters to the State Department imploring US officials to send Lee money so he could return to the United States. (She made no mention of Marina or June.) "This is indeed a sad case," she wrote on May 25 to a Mrs. James at the State Department's Office of Soviet Union Affairs. "Here is an American boy wanting to rectify a mistake but the fare is keeping him from doing it. It is amazing how many people know of our need. Not a one has offered to help." She noted that Lee had served in the Marines and that her other two sons had also served in the military. On the same day, she wrote to George H. Haselton, the chief of the Protection and Representation Division of the State Department: "Here is a young man caught in circumstances beyond his control. We certainly preach against communism and such but when we are called upon to help—to do out best—it seems it is not important. Because of a need of the fare, must that boy remain in Russia?"[25]

By then, Lee and Marina were taking care of their final arrangements in Moscow. On May 24, the day the Oswalds arrived in the city, they checked into the Hotel Berlin and went to the US embassy, where Marina was given her American visa. Oswald did not indicate, in his diary or letters, whether they enjoyed Moscow while they were there, but there must have been something vaguely unhappy about the visit: Oswald was now back at the hotel where he had stayed during his first week in the Soviet Union, and his return must have felt like an admission of sorts. In the end, it hadn't mattered that he had tried to kill himself or that he had spent two and a half years in Minsk. The KGB had had its way. He was leaving. As for Marina, she had just left her family and friends in Minsk, and things were not good with Lee: later, on the trip to the United States, she thought he was embarrassed to be seen with her because of her unfashionable clothes.[26]

The US embassy was eager for Oswald to leave the Soviet Union. In a sign of how serious the whole affair had become, on May 31 at four p.m., the American ambassador, Llewellyn Thompson, sent a personal, two-line telegram to the secretary of state, Dean Rusk. "Oswalds leaving here June 1," the telegram declared.[27]

The next day, June 1, Oswald visited the US embassy again and signed a promissory note for a repatriation loan of $435.71. That night, Lee, Marina, and June boarded a train that took them west, back through Minsk and then on to Brest. At Brest, they crossed the Soviet border into Poland, and the next day, they arrived in Holland, where they boarded a ship—not a plane, as Oswald had expected—to the United States.[28]

Also on June 1, Haselton, at the State Department in Washington, sent a "speed letter" to Marguerite:

TO: Mrs. Marguerite Oswald, Box 473, 316 E. Donnell, Crowell, Texas

<u>AIR MAIL</u>

With reference to your letter of May 25, 1962, a telegram was received last night from the American Embassy at Moscow reporting that your son, Lee Harvey Oswald, and his family are leaving there today for Rotterdam where they will board the S.S. "Maasdam," scheduled to arrive at New York on June 13, 1962.

George H. Haselton
Chief
Protection and Representation Division[29]

Six days after that, Robert I. Owen, also at the State Department's Office of Soviet Union Affairs, sent a follow-up letter to Marguerite to inform her that Mrs. James—here she is "Miss James"—had brought to his attention Marguerite's letter of May 25. After telling Marguerite what Haselton has already told her about the Oswalds' voyage from Rotterdam to New York, Owen concluded:

I am sorry you have been caused so much unhappiness as a result of your son's actions. You doubtless realize that his unfortunate situation was the result of his original decision to live in the USSR, and that the American Embassy at Moscow and the Department have made every effort to assist him. As you know, he originally informed the Embassy that he wished to remain permanently in the Soviet Union and never return to the United States. When he changed his mind later, the Embassy, regardless of his earlier actions, advised him regarding the procedure which he should follow to obtain Soviet exit permits for himself, his wife, and child; also the Department granted him a loan to pay for his transportation back to New York. I trust that your son is aware and appreciative of the assistance which has been rendered by the United States Government.[30]

Oswald had succeeded in extricating himself, his wife, and their daughter from the Soviet Union, but it was hardly a success. As the Warren Commission Report would observe, "His return to the United States publicly testified to the utter failure of what had been the most important act of his life." The flight to Russia was Oswald's last serious attempt to escape the series of trespassings that had woven itself through much of his life, and by returning to the United States it was as if he were conceding that that would never happen. There is, about the entire trip to the United States, a sense of loss and lamentation, a looking backward more than a looking forward.[31]

This sense of looking backward is underscored by the fact that Oswald spent much, if not most, of the voyage on the *Maasdam* writing four untitled compositions about the Soviet Union, Marxism, and revolution. (Oddly, the FBI grouped these four fragments together under the heading "Five Untitled Compositions on Political Subjects.")[32] Three of the essays hewed more or less to standard Oswald form; they are about big topics about which he knew little but wrote with great authority. It is the third composition that is the most noteworthy. It is here that Oswald tried to explain himself.

"Where I first went to Russia in the winter of 1959," he wrote

my funds were very limited, so after a certain time, after the Russians had assured themselfs that I was really the naive american who belived in communism they arranged for me to recive a certain amount of money every month Oh it came technically through the Red-cross as fincial help to a poor polical iminegeate but it was arranged by the M.V.D. [or Interior Ministry]. I told myself it was simply because I was broke and everybody knew it. I accepted the money because I was hungry and there was several inches of snow

on the ground in Moscow at that time but what it really was was payment for my denuciation of the U. S. in Moscow in November [1959]
and a clear promise that far as long as I lived in the USSR life would
be very good. I didn't relize all this, of course for almost two years.

As soon as I became completely disgruntled with the Sovit Union
and started negotitions with the American Embassy in Moscow for
my return to the U. S. my 'Red Cross' allotment was cut off.

This was not diffical to understand since all correspondence in
and out of the Embassy is censored as is common knowlege in the
Embassy itself.

I have never mentioned the fact of these monthly payments to
anyone. I do so in order to state that I shall never sell myself inten-
tionly or unintentionly to anyone again.[33]

One can picture Oswald consumed by a barely contained rage as he
wrote this on the *Maasdam*. It appears to have occurred to him only after
he had left Russia and acquired a little more perspective that he had unwittingly prostituted himself to the Soviet cause, and he was determined
to let everyone know that it would never happen again. His bitterness
was raw and unchecked. In the fall of 1959, he had been angry, but his
anger had been fused with hope and expectation. Now, nearly three years
later, he was not only angry but also self-pitying, lost, spent, humiliated.
In Russia he had been stripped of the affections he had once had for the
Soviet Union; he'd been told, obliquely, that he was not really a worker,
a Menchan, that he would never be admitted to the proletarian family
that he had desperately craved. His ideology had been sapped, he'd been
denied the woman who had come closest to being his true love, he'd been
watched and choreographed and forced into a see-through "village," and,
finally, he'd come to the awful conclusion that there was nothing else to
do, so he left.

12

AMERICA

THE MISSING FACTOR IN OSWALD'S THINKING ABOUT GOING back to America was America. The country he was returning to was not the same one that he had left two and a half years earlier. There is no indication that he understood this. He couldn't have.

With limited access to Western media in the Soviet Union, he had known very little about what was going on at home. It was not at all strange, Titovets told me, for example, that the good people of Minsk had had to rely on Lydia Cherkasova to learn what had happened at the UN General Assembly in New York five months after the fact. Also, people in Minsk, fearful of the security organs, had not been inclined to discuss the news or to voice opinions about politics or international affairs. This had been true of Oswald's fellow metal-lathe operators and people who attended a university or an institute for scientific or medical training such as Stanislaw Shushkevich or Titovets. It was wiser to have conversations about theoretical matters or culture, which traditionally took the place of open political discourse.[1]

Maybe the most important change that had taken place in the United States since Oswald had left was that the great Cold War tension of the late 1950s, the fear of American inaction and "softness," had abated. Before he left, there had been real, if unfounded, suspicions that the United States was falling behind the Soviet Union in science and military power; these were greatly exacerbated by the 1957 launch of *Sputnik*, and they were reflected in Senator John F. Kennedy's mostly baseless claim, during the 1960 presidential campaign, that there was a missile gap between the two superpowers. Those suspicions had ebbed. President Kennedy, exuding confidence and charm and a conviction that America could (and would) achieve its greatest ambitions, had, temporarily at least, assuaged many Americans' anxieties.[2]

This conviction had been suggested from the very start, at Kennedy's inauguration. What was atypical of this inauguration was the theme—not exactly central, but recurrent—of breaking with the past. Certainly, the Kennedy inauguration, like earlier ones, paid homage to that which had come before. But it returned, again and again, to the newness and boldness of the incoming administration. Robert Frost signaled this theme in the poem he had composed in honor of Kennedy—"Dedication," which called the 1960 election "the greatest vote a people ever cast." (In fact, Frost did not recite "Dedication" but "The Gift Outright," which he had composed decades earlier; the glare of the sun during the ceremony is believed to have made it hard to read the new poem, but he knew the old one by heart.) Nevertheless, the poem Frost intended to read was the one he had only recently written, and it came much closer than "The Gift Outright" did to capturing that particular moment.[3]

It was Kennedy himself who was the boldest voice at a very bold moment, forcefully if somewhat indirectly calling for a historic break from the America of old. In the second minute of his slightly more than fourteen-minute inaugural address, the president famously declared that the "torch has been passed" and that "a new generation" of Americans born in the twentieth century would be running the country from now on. Then, compounding the sense of historical consequence, Kennedy recalled that "in the long history of the world, only a few generations have been granted the role of defending freedom in its hour of national danger." While this might cause some to fear for the future—particularly given that the new leadership would comprise young, relatively inexperienced men—it seemed to excite Kennedy. "I do not shrink from this responsibility," he said. "I welcome it. I do not believe that any of us would exchange places with any other people or any other generation. The energy, the faith, the devotion which we bring to this endeavor will light our country and all who serve it, and the glow from that fire can truly light the world." He ended with a somewhat utopian call to arms that, in a different context, would have sounded vaguely radical. "Here on Earth," the new president announced, "God's work must truly be our own."[4]

The speech also sounded the two signature themes of the administration. Eloquently and with an almost uncontainable idealism, the president challenged America to achieve a new greatness. And he confronted the Soviet Union in a "twilight struggle" that was remarkable for its combativeness, daring, and, in retrospect, recklessness. Later the president would be remembered, accurately or inaccurately, as a pursuer of peace: he stood up to his own military advisers when they wanted to take more aggressive measures than he did in Laos, Vietnam, and Cuba, and when it came to the Berlin Wall. He sought and signed the Nuclear Test-Ban Treaty, and in 1963 at American University, in one of his best-known speeches, he sounded support for "peaceful coexistence" with the Soviet Union. But that was not the tone he struck on his inauguration day in January 1961, and it was not the tenor of his administration's rhetoric throughout much of 1962, in the months before his most dangerous confrontation of all, the Cuban Missile Crisis.

Oswald could not have been more disconnected from this new America, and from the moment he and his family arrived at the dock in Hoboken, New Jersey, on June 13, 1962, he was despondent and irascible. While there would be lighthearted moments during Oswald's post-Soviet period, mostly his mood and outlook did not change. Unhappiness, fury, a permanent and deepening sense of alienation—this was Oswald's new default position. It was the natural state, the nearly unavoidable state of mind of a twenty-two-year-old man who was now confronted with a life of inescapable rootlessness. "I would say that immediately after coming to the United States Lee changed," Marina would later tell the Warren Commission. "I did not know him as such a man in Russia."[5]

The clearest sign of this rootlessness was the immediate resumption of his interloping. With an even greater intensity than ever before, Oswald would spend the next seventeen months—from June 1962 to November

1963—jumping from one address to the next. Not counting brief stays at the YMCA in Dallas, his trip to Mexico City, and weekends at the Irving, Texas, house of Ruth Paine, a woman whom Marina would befriend at a dinner party, Oswald would live at nine addresses after returning from Russia—on average, a little less than two months per address. Marina was sucked into the shifting blur of apartments, cities, jobs, and neighbors. He was unable, as always, to build a life anywhere—to hold onto a job, pay his rent or bills, make friends, or tend to the chores and duties of daily life. It did not matter whether he was living in a Marine Corps barracks in Japan, an apartment in Minsk, or a boarding house in Dallas. The problem was Oswald.

They were met in Hoboken by Spas T. Raikin from the Traveler's Aid Society. It was twelve days after they had left Moscow on the nighttime train heading west. A State Department official had contacted the society. Raikin "had the impression that Oswald was trying to avoid meeting anyone." Raikin shepherded the Oswald family through customs, and then they were referred to the New York City Department of Welfare, which found them a room at the Times Square Hotel. Oswald told Raikin and the people at the Welfare Department several lies and half-truths—that he had been a marine stationed at the US embassy in Moscow; that he had renounced his citizenship; that it had taken two years to get exit visas from the Soviets; and that he had paid for their travel expenses. He didn't mention the trouble they had had getting Marina an American visa. He also told them he had only $63 to get to Texas.[6]

The people at the Welfare Department called Robert Oswald's house in Fort Worth, and his wife, Vada, answered. When Robert learned that his younger brother had arrived in New York, he wired $200 to him, but Oswald refused, at first, to accept the money. He felt the Welfare Department should pay his family's way to Texas. He said if they didn't, the three of them—Lee, Marina, and June—would go as far as they could with the little money they had, and then they would rely on local authorities to help. After much commotion, Oswald accepted the money his brother had sent them, and the next day, June 14, the Oswald family flew from New York to Texas. Waiting for them at Love Field in Dallas were Robert, Vada, and their two children. Robert told the Warren Commission that "the most noticeable change in his brother's appearance was that he had become rather bald; he seemed also to be somewhat thinner than he had been in 1959," and, he thought, "his brother had picked up 'something of an accent.'" Lee noticed that there were no newspaper reporters waiting to interview him, and he seemed disappointed.

He had, in fact, been thinking about what he might say to the press. The fifth of his six ostensibly nonpolitical "compositions"—the same series of fragments in which he discusses his Atheism System—is a series of questions and answers he jotted down in anticipation of a press conference he planned to give after arriving in the United States. The questions are, in fact, what one might expect from reporters; for example, "Why did you go to the USSR?" and "Why did you remain in the USSR for so long?" More telling are Oswald's prepared answers, which underscore his persistent fear of being deemed a traitor and facing prosecution at home. In response to the question "Are you a communist? Have you ever know a Communist?," Oswald wrote: "No of course not. I have never even know a Communist, outside of the ones in the USSR but you can't help that." As for the question "What are the outstanding differences between the USA and USSR?," he answered, "Freedom of speech travel outspoken opposition to unpopular policies freeom to belive in god"—this from a man who had voiced no interest in religion, a man who appeared to have no spiritual aspect.[7]

And then the constant movement started again. For a while, Lee, Marina, and June stayed at Robert's house, and everything was fine, but about a month later they moved in with Marguerite, who had moved back to Fort Worth from Crowell, Texas, to be closer to Lee. This was a bad idea, as Oswald should have known.

Marguerite had harbored suspicions (or, one imagines, hopes) that her son had been an American agent secretly spying in Russia. While Lee, Marina, and June were staying with her, she decided to ask him about this, albeit obliquely. "I said, 'Lee, I want to know one thing,'" she recalled in her testimony before the Warren Commission. "'Why is it you came back to the United States when you had a job and you were married to a Russian girl?'" She thought that Oswald—just maybe—had married Marina because he had been ordered to, that it had been part of his cover, or mission. We don't know what Oswald told his mother—Marguerite never said—but she did suggest, in her testimony, that she had not only doubts about her son's feelings for her daughter-in-law but also doubts about her daughter-in-law's feelings for her son. "I believe that Marina loved him in a way," Marguerite told the commission. "But I believe that Marina wanted to come to America." It is not known exactly what was said between Lee, Marina, and Marguerite, but it did not take long for Oswald to regret that he had moved in with his mother.[8]

After a few weeks, Lee, Marina, and June moved out of Marguerite's place and into their own apartment in Fort Worth. It was on Mercedes Street, had one bedroom, was furnished, and cost $59.50 per month. "Mrs. Oswald visited her son and his family at their apartment and tried to help them get settled," the Warren Commission Report noted, referring to Marguerite. "She testified that she bought some clothes for Marina and a highchair for the baby but that Oswald told her that he did not want her to buy 'things for his wife that he himself could not buy.' Finally, Oswald apparently decided that he did not want his mother to visit the apartment anymore and he became incensed when his wife permitted her to visit despite his instructions. After he moved to Dallas in October, Oswald did not see his mother or communicate with her in any way until she came to see him after the assassination." Marina, testifying before the commission, said Oswald did not want Marguerite to know the address of their new home. She said she felt sorry for Marguerite.[9]

By the late summer of 1962, Lee and Marina's relationship began to disintegrate. It had been strained since they had come to the United States, but by early August, things were falling apart. First, Marina said, Lee talked about wanting to go back to Russia. Then he thought it would be best if Marina went by herself. "I told him that if he wanted me to go then that meant that he didn't love me, and that in that case what was the idea of coming to the United States in the first place. Lee would say that it would be better for me if I went to Russia. I did not know why. I did not know what he had in mind. He said he loved me but that it would be better for me if I went to Russia, and what he had in mind I don't know."[10]

Also, the FBI wanted to talk to him. They knew, of course, that he'd just returned from the Soviet Union, and they wanted to know about his experiences there and, more importantly, whether he had been approached by anyone he thought might be a Soviet agent. They questioned him twice. The first time, June 26, appears not to have had much of an effect on Oswald. The second time, in the back of a car in front of his house, took place on August 16, and it upset him a great deal. He had been back in the United States barely two months, and the fear he had harbored in Minsk, that he would be prosecuted for having defected to the Soviet Union, seemed to have been prescient. Marina would later tell the Warren Commission that, during this time, Lee was always filled with great tension and irritability.[11]

At a dinner party in late August, the Oswalds met George Bouhe, a well-known member of the Russian expatriate community in the Dallas–Fort Worth area. Soon they met other people in that community, many of whom had non-Russian surnames because they had married Americans. Bouhe estimated that there were no more than fifty people in the community, and they came not only from Russia but from all over the Soviet Union. They included Anna Meller, Elena Hall, Alexander Kleinlerer, Katya Ford, and George and Jeanne De Mohrenschildt, and they took a liking to Marina because she came from their country, she was far from home and couldn't speak English, and the Oswalds didn't have money. Oswald they were less enthusiastic about. For one thing, there was Oswald's politics. He was an avowed Marxist, whereas the Russian-expatriate community was filled with people whose families had fled Soviet communism and were mostly patriotic Americans. There were also cultural differences. The Russians were descended from the old, prerevolutionary Russia, where educated people spoke French and had governesses and a nineteenth-century gentility. They were disgusted by the Soviet regime, which they thought was violent and godless, and which they blamed (not unreasonably) for destroying the place they came from.

Finally, there was something deeper, more instinctual or elemental, about Oswald that they did not like—and that made him not like them. George Bouhe, testifying before the Warren Commission, called Oswald "a rebel against society." He said Oswald never seemed to settle down, to think, to plan. "I got dizzy following his movements," Bouhe said. The Russians tried to help the Oswalds—they bought them groceries and gave them old furniture and clothes, and they tried to find work for Lee—but he resented this.[12]

It was in September that the Russians noticed Marina's black eye, and then another. Eventually, it came out that Lee was beating her. Soon Marina moved into Elena Hall's house, and Lee cleared out of the apartment on Mercedes Street. He spent October 15–19, the first few days of the Cuban Missile Crisis, in a room at the YMCA, and then he rented a room or an apartment—the address is unknown. Then he moved into another apartment on Elsbeth Street. Neither the Warren Commission Report nor Marina's testimony indicates that Oswald had any thoughts about Cuba or was even aware of what was going on. He was apparently too busy figuring out where to live and how to make ends meet.

The last year of Oswald's life, from November 1962 to November 1963, was more chaotic, frenzied, hapless, and desperate than any other time he had known. There had been dark moments—his suicide attempt in Moscow, the first few months of 1961 in Minsk—but there had never been such a long period of continuous unraveling. He had fallen out of touch with Robert. He had severed ties with his mother. He was estranged from his wife. He had no factory he was compelled to work at or political party he was compelled to pledge allegiance to. Life had been much easier inside his *kolpak* in Apartment 24. Now the flurry of short-term jobs, apartments, and pathetic, mindless efforts to escape the unhappiness he found himself in would ratchet up dramatically. When it became too much for him to hold together, violence would result.

In March 1963, Oswald began to cobble together a small arsenal. First, he ordered a Smith & Wesson .38 revolver from a store in Los Angeles. He used the name A. J. Hidell, and he dated the sales form January 27, but the revolver wasn't shipped until March 20. On the same day, a 6.5 milli-meter Carcano bolt-action rifle that he had ordered from Klein's Sporting Goods in Chicago under the name A. Hidell was also shipped. He told Marina, with whom he was living again—this time in an apartment on Neely Street, in Dallas—that he planned to hunt. She took two photos of him posing with his rifle and revolver and copies of the newspapers *The Daily Worker*, which was published by the Communist Party of the United States, and *The Militant*, which was published by the Socialist Workers Party. In the photographs Oswald looks absurd and out of place. He is dressed in black, and he is serious and apparently ready to do battle, yet he is framed by a quintessentially American backdrop: a backyard with a patch of grass and a white picket fence. It had felt strange to be a revolutionary in Moscow in 1959. Now he was in Texas, and he wasn't ironic or passé; he was isolated.

Oswald appeared to be mobilizing for something, and in fact for a month he had been preparing to kill Edwin Walker, a former general who had been reprimanded by President Dwight Eisenhower and, ulti-mately, forced to resign by President Kennedy for his outspoken, hard-right views. Oswald had photographed the alley behind Walker's home in Dallas, and he had plotted when and where he would attack. He had even postponed the murder by a few days so that it would coincide with a nearby church function—the better to have a diversion when it came time to flee. But on the night of the planned assassination, April 10, Os-wald shot once and narrowly missed Walker. After that, he quickly left the alleyway and took the bus home.

The Walker incident was a critical juncture. There was the obvious, anticipatory element, with all the superficial but not unimportant par-allels between the attempted assassination of Walker and the successful assassination of Kennedy. In both cases, Oswald did not give any sign in advance that he had been thinking about killing, let alone planning to kill, anyone in particular. In both case, he targeted a well-known polit-ical figure. In both cases, the execution of his crime hewed to a simple, three-step process, with Oswald taking his shot, stowing his rifle away in a nearby hiding place, and then departing the scene on foot. In both cases he either denied committing, or was appalled to learn that others might think he had committed, the crime. And there was the fact that Oswald used the same rifle in both instances.

But the more important issue here is not political or criminal or logistical, but psychological. The Walker assassination attempt marked the first time since his suicide attempt that Oswald had sought to resolve his mounting furies with a powerful and culminating violence. He had left Russia ten months earlier, and it had been disastrous and humiliating. That left him with only two alternatives: to try to escape his constant lurching and trespassing, which he had failed to do in the Soviet Union and which he probably intuited would be impossible, or to kill himself once and for all. For several months, he had tried to make something of his new situation in the United States, to postpone his destruction. He had sidestepped that fate in Moscow in late 1959—either because he was lucky or, more likely, because he didn't really want to die just yet—and he must have thought for awhile in Minsk that he had escaped it. But now, in Texas, in the same place from which he had started out, after trying to no avail to carve out a home for himself, he was confronted with the uselessness and inanity of pushing on.

In Oswald's mind, assassinating Walker would be a triumph and a conclusion. It would elevate him to what he believed was his rightful place, alongside other heroes of the revolution—Oswald told Marina that killing Walker would be analogous to killing Hitler—and it would end the miserable spiraling. He may have thought that he would escape, but he must have known that nothing would be the same afterward. Killing someone, and especially killing someone important, would change everything. His previous life would be over. Walker's death would be a grand finale to a long unhappiness.

Oswald never put it this way. As far as we know, he never wrote about the Walker incident, and even though he admitted to Marina what he had done, he didn't share with her anything beyond a few facts. But it's noteworthy that, after the attempt on Walker's life, the frantic moving about would become even more harried. Oswald should have been more settled by now. He had a little girl, and Marina was pregnant again; she was due in the fall. But during the last seven months of his life, from April to November 1963, instead of planning for the baby and the future, his lurching would reach a white-hot climax.

Oswald would move to New Orleans and take to the streets and air-waves to defend Fidel Castro; he would travel to Mexico City with the goal of traveling on to Havana or Moscow; he would return to Dallas a little more than two weeks before his second daughter, Rachel, was born; and, a few weeks after that, he would learn about President Kennedy's upcoming trip to Dallas and figure out how he might pull off a successful assassination. At no point in this last, awful stretch did Oswald ever spend much time on the future. He looked for jobs, but the jobs were menial and meant to insure he could get by for the time being.

It appears as if Oswald had been absorbed and even taken over by an unending series of trespasses and escapes. Most, if not all, hope of build-ing a life had been jettisoned. All he could do now was to keep leaving the place he was in and go somewhere else. The only way to end that, as he already seemed to grasp, was death.

On April 24, two weeks after the attempt on Walker's life, Oswald took a bus to New Orleans. When he arrived at the terminal, he called his aunt, Lillian Murret. Marguerite's sister had always been fond of Oswald—in the winter and spring of 1942, when he was still a toddler, she had taken care of him when Marguerite could not—and she was happy to hear from him. She hadn't known he had returned from Russia. Oswald told her he was in New Orleans to find a job. Marina thought it was a good idea for him to go to New Orleans, with the police still looking for Walker's assailant. She also probably didn't mind the space. They had been fight-ing—as usual.

But there was another reason for the trip to Louisiana, and it was as telling and predictive as the attempt on Walker's life. Soon after Oswald

arrived in New Orleans, he did something he had never done before: he
visited his father's grave. Then he found a local telephone book and called
every Oswald in it. He tracked down only one relative: Hazel Oswald, the
widow of William Stout Oswald Sr., who was the brother of Lee Oswald
Sr., Oswald's father. According to the FBI report, Lee told Hazel, who was
living in Metairie, just outside New Orleans proper, that he was in New
Orleans and wanted to ask some questions about his father's relatives.
"Lee came to her residence and arrived alone by bus," according to the report. "They talked about his father's folks and she gave him a photograph
of his father. During her conversation with Lee he said he left his wife and
child in Texas until he could find some employment in New Orleans and
that he wanted to find employment as a photographer."[13]

Oswald had never talked much about his father. There had been other
father figures in his life—Edwin Ekdahl, who had been married to Marguerite for a while; Alexander Ziger; and even Vladimir Libezin—and he
had looked up to his brothers, but he had never had an older man in his
life who was always there and looking out for him. In "The Collective" he
acknowledged that this lack had left a scar. In a short autobiographical
statement that appears before the essay, Oswald wrote: "Lee Harvey Oswald was born in Oct. 1939, in New Orleans, La., the son of an Insurance
Salesman, whose early death left a mean streak of independence brought
on by neglect." It was a rare moment of clarity and insight. Oswald then
drew a link between this "mean streak of independence" and his enlist-
ment in the Marines and his journey to the Soviet Union. "Immediately
after serving out his 3 years in the USMC, he abandons his American life
to seek a new life in the USSR," he wrote. "Full of optimism and hope he
stood in red square in the fall of 1959 vowing to see his chosen course
through."[14]

Now, in the spring of 1963, Oswald was hopeless, and he had nowhere
else to go. He had come back to New Orleans, in part, one imagines, because he associated it most closely with his father, guidance, structure—
all the things missing from his life. The trip to Hazel Oswald's home must
have been poignant, even emotional, but unsatisfying. His father was descended from General Robert E. Lee—that was how his brother, Robert,

got his name, and it was how Lee got his—and Oswald seems to have wondered, perhaps more than he intimated, what his life would have been like had his father not died before he was born. He seems to have wanted a father now, more than before, with everything in a state of disarray. Russia had come close to giving him something like that, but in Russia they made him feel as if he did not belong. And now he wanted to leave again.

In May 1963, Oswald took up the cause of Fidel Castro. He was receiving unemployment benefits from the state of Texas despite the fact that on May 10 he had started working at the William B. Reily Company, which roasted, bagged, and sold coffee in New Orleans. Toward the end of the month, he opened a local branch of the revolutionary organization known as Fair Play for Cuba Committee, and he handed out leaflets, scuffled with anti-Castro demonstrators, and took part in a debate on a radio show hosted by William Stuckey called *Latin Listening Post*, on WDSU in New Orleans (Oswald fared poorly, but Stuckey was impressed with his intelligence). Oswald probably wanted to go to Cuba to join the cause, and it has been suggested that the whole point of taking part in the Fair Play for Cuba Committee was to help him get a visa. But there has also been speculation that Oswald really wanted to return to the Soviet Union His ultimate goal or motivation is unimportant. What is important is that Oswald desperately wanted to flee the United States, and what is just as important is that neither the Cuban nor the Soviet authorities complied.

On September 17, just over a month before Marina would give birth, Oswald obtained a tourist card from the Mexican consulate in New Orleans that was good for one trip to Mexico lasting no more than fifteen days. Eight days later, he left New Orleans with about $200 on a bus that would take him to Houston. At 2:35 the next morning, Oswald boarded another bus, in Houston, that took him to Laredo, on the border. He crossed into Mexico in the early afternoon and reached Mexico City the next morning, on September 27. He visited the Cuban and Soviet embassies in Mexico City, requested visas at both, and was denied at both.

While he was in Mexico City, Oswald visited museums, bought postcards, and saw a bullfight. He seems to have enjoyed himself. What's odd was that he left. Surely he could have found work and eked out a living there. But as always, he didn't know what he wanted so much as what he did not want. He never knew how to stay. So at 8:30 a.m. on October 2, he left Mexico City on a bus headed north. It should not come as a surprise that, on the way back, he encountered some problems with the Mexican authorities. There were questions about his documents. At the border, they detained him for a while, and then they let him go. He arrived in Dallas at 2:20 p.m. on October 3, spent that night at the YMCA, and called Marina the next day.

He had tried one more time to run away, and he had failed. Now he was emptied out, resigned, and this was reflected in what was a surprisingly quiet period in October and November. Oswald applied for a job but did not get it (they checked his references, and they were not good). Then he landed a position at the Texas School Book Depository; Ruth Paine helped him get it. He and Marina were happy. They were not living together—Marina was staying with Ruth Paine in Irving, and Oswald had rented a room in Dallas—but he had a job, and there was a modicum of stability in his life again. When Marina gave birth to their second daughter, Rachel, on October 20, two days after his twenty-fourth birthday, he wept.[15]

That month, the Oswalds received a letter, dated September 29, from Pavel Golovachev. "Hello, Lee, Marina and June!" Golovachev wrote. "I think that this letter will arrive ahead of the new member of your family. I congratulate both of you and especially you, Marina. I, too, wish that this would be a son, because if it would be a girl, you would become a whole primary organization within the family and would be always able to 'crush' Lee by a majority vote. I am joking." Golovachev knew the Oswalds had had trouble settling into life in Texas—they had been corresponding with him for a year—and he advised: "If you get permission, come to Minsk—first, you both know it; and, second, it is one of the best cities in the Union. Marina, do not worry; everything will be all right. As the saying goes, 'The world is not lacking in kind people.' Try to encourage Lee. I remember him before his departure from the Union."[16]

Lee and Marina's relationship was still troubled, but there was a warmth between them. "I felt that she and Lee had a troubled relationship but did care about each other," Ruth Paine told me. "Lee was affectionate at times when he visited at my house, putting his arm around her shoulder as they watched television, or at one time patting his lap as an invitation to her, which she accepted, to sit there. They argued, bickered, some at my house. This tended to be over matters related to how Lee wanted things: how she cooked fried potatoes, or how she ironed his shirts." She never saw Lee hit Marina. It appeared as if things might be getting better. There was a new tenderness and an excitement surrounding the baby, and for a few weeks, or even a month, it did not feel as though everything were about to collapse on itself.[17]

Oswald did not have a special hatred for John F. Kennedy. Marina Oswald told the Warren Commission: "From Lee's behavior I cannot conclude that he was against the President, and therefore the thing is incomprehensible to me." According to an FBI report, his aunt, Lillian Murret, recalled that during one of Oswald's visits to the Murret home in the summer or fall of 1963, Oswald said "something in praise of President Kennedy and Jacqueline Kennedy but it was during a casual conversation and not in connection with any political discussion." But it was important that Oswald found America so inhospitable—he couldn't hold down a job; he couldn't live with his wife or maintain a relationship with his mother or brother; he couldn't find a place for himself. And it was just as important that Kennedy embodied something essential and unique about America at that particular moment. He had captured—he *was*—the national zeitgeist. This country was confident, bold, unwavering; it knew exactly what it was, and that certainty was central not only to America but to Kennedy's persona. It was also as different from Oswald as could be. It was a taunt, of sorts, and it greatly exacerbated the sense of dislocation and alienation he had experienced before he left for the Soviet Union.

New From the moment he returned, Oswald was in a state of constant motion, but really, he had been in a state of motion, fleeing, interloping since infancy. Now he had arrived at a point of homicidal and suicidal destruction. Did he plan to kill the president—this president—months or even years before he did? No. But his angers and disappointments put him at odds with America, and he would have been open to the idea of killing an American head of state. He would not have been inhibited. The assassination would elevate him to world-historical status, and it would end all his pains and furies.[18]

There have been speculations that the Lee Harvey Oswald who returned from the Soviet Union to the United States was not the same person who left. This is not meant metaphorically. There is a subset of the conspiracy-theorizing universe that is convinced that a different person, an Oswald double, an evil doppelganger, took the place of the real Oswald and that this person, a Russian agent posing as a one-time American defector, assassinated President Kennedy. The most notorious exponent of the evil-doppelganger theory was Michael Eddowes, the author of a self-published book, *Khrushchev Killed Kennedy*, that claimed that the Oswald who returned to the United States from the Soviet Union was actually a KGB assassin named Alek whose job was to kill the president.

To quell these suspicions, the House Select Committee on Assassinations, during its investigation of the Kennedy assassination in 1978, commissioned a study of photographs of Oswald before and after his Soviet foray. William K. Hartmann, a photo consultant who took part, noted that it was Oswald's right ear—the same ear that had given him trouble for years—that put to rest, or should have put to rest, these suspicions.

> A peculiar characteristic of Oswald's ear structure was noticed in examination of these photos, which carries through in a precisely recognizable way from the 1956 [M]arine photo to the photo moments before Oswald's death. On Oswald's right ear, the helix or upper rim has a smooth curvature as photographed from the front. But the left ear helix is made up of more linear segments which define a rather pointed region at the top. This appears clearly visible in all four 8 x 10 prints supplied by HSCA, as mentioned above. If a second individual ever replaced the Marine Oswald photographed in 1956, the facial characteristics were the same even down to this level of detail.

Ellis Kerley, a forensic anthropologist at the University of Maryland who also examined the photographs, agreed. "The hairline, if one makes appropriate allowance for the passage of time, is quite compatible in all photographs examined," he wrote. Alas, this was not enough to quash the evil-doppelganger theory. In 1981, Eddowes, with Marina's support, had Oswald's body exhumed only to discover that the person buried in Oswald's coffin was Oswald.[19]

The conspiracy theorists notwithstanding, the Lee Harvey Oswald who came home to America in the summer of 1962, the same Lee Harvey Oswald who had left in the fall of 1959, was not programmed by the KGB or any other intelligence agency. He simply failed to accomplish what he had set out to do, and this failure was monumental and devastating. When he stepped off the boat in Hoboken, he must have known it. Something quasi-metabolic had happened, and now it would be nearly impossible to undo the wreckage of his Soviet adventure. Something ca lamitous was almost inevitable.

EPILOGUE: A CONJECTURE

After the assassination, the KGB was afraid the American government would think they had done it. The FBI's report on its meeting with Yuri Nosenko, the KGB officer who claimed to have overseen the Oswald case in Moscow, makes this clear. About two hours after the assassination—close to midnight in Moscow—Nosenko was summoned to KGB head quarters. Since headquarters could not find its Oswald file, Nosenko said, he was ordered to call Minsk to get a telephone summary of Oswald's life in the Belorussian Soviet Socialist Republic. When Nosenko did this, he discovered, much to his dismay, that the KGB officers in Minsk had, in fact, "endeavored 'to influence Oswald in the right direction.'" This was a cause of great concern to KGB higher-ups, including General Oleg M. Gribanov, head of the Second Directorate, which oversaw internal security.

According to the FBI report, "the KGB in Minsk had been instructed to take no action concerning Oswald. General Gribanov ordered all records at Minsk pertaining to Oswald be forwarded by warplane to Moscow with an explanation." This was an unfortunate and misleading remark, Nosenko indicated. The KGB had never actually attempted to "influence Oswald in the right direction," he said, and it had not had anything to do with whatever Oswald did after returning to the United States. The KGB officer in Minsk who made this comment was simply alluding to Marina's uncle, a lieutenant colonel in the local militia, who had apparently suggested to Oswald at one point or another that he not be too critical of the Soviet Union once he went back to the United States. Nosenko added that

KGB officers in Minsk did not appreciate "the international significance" of Oswald's Soviet period when he had called them a few hours after the assassination. The Second Directorate believed the comments that the KGB officer in Minsk had made about trying to "influence" Oswald were "a self-serving effort to impress the KGB center."[1]

Once the KGB in Minsk had been made aware of Oswald's "international significance," it moved fast. On or about November 23, 1963, agents showed up at the apartment on Zakharov Street where Pavel Golovachev lived with his family. The KGB agents wanted to talk with Golovachev about his friendship with Lee Harvey Oswald. They wanted to know everything that Golovachev had ever talked about with Oswald; they wanted to know where they had gone together and what they had done. The KGB agents took a long time. They asked the same questions over and over, but in different ways. They rifled through everything he owned—radio parts, old books, magazines, and, finally, his photographs. Anna Zhuravskaya said, "They took all the photos that they thought shouldn't have been taken in the first place." Her son, Alexei Zhuravsky, explained, "That would be any photographs of buildings or people. They left images of nature—fields, snow." The most important thing, the KGB agents told Golovachev, was that he never talk again about Oswald. "They forbade him to speak about this for twenty-five years," said Alexei Zhuravsky.[2]

The security organs also visited everyone at the Experimental Department. They were told the same thing: do not utter the words "Lee Harvey Oswald" for twenty-five years. "I asked them what happens after twenty-five years," Sergei Skop told me. "They said, 'We'll discuss that then.'" When I told Skop that some of the people at the department had told me that the KGB never told people they couldn't say certain things, he laughed and said, "Of course, they said that."[3]

Yuri Merezhinsky didn't need to be told what he shouldn't talk about. Nor did the Zigers or Ella German, who later claimed no one from the organs ever approached her (a claim that almost no one believes).

Titovets was in Moscow when the assassination happened. On November 19 he had left Minsk on the overnight train, and on the morning of November 20 he had checked in at the Hotel of the Russian Medical

Academy, on Baltiyskaya Ulitsa, near the Sokol metro station (and not far from Botkinskaya Hospital, where Oswald had been rushed to after he tried to kill himself four years earlier). Titovets had come to Moscow to visit some researchers at the Biochemistry Department at Moscow State University and to buy some hard-to-find supplies at the university's Central Chemical Reagents Store. He was also looking forward to visiting the All-Russia State Library for Foreign Literature, otherwise known as the Foreign Languages Library, where he could find English-language books that were unavailable in Minsk.[4]

Titovets said he heard about the assassination while listening to the radio in his hotel room.[5] It was the evening. "I sat alone in my hotel room," he wrote. "I decided to make a call home to Minsk and went downstairs for the public phone in the lobby. As there was no telephone in our flat, I dialed our neighbors next door, asking them to invite anyone from my family to the phone. After an endless wait with only weak high-pitched wailing coming from the receiver, I finally heard the voice of my sister Emma. She told me they had already heard the news. They were sorry for Lee. Nobody believed he had done it." Titovets said he did not learn that Oswald had been killed by Jack Ruby on November 24 until after he returned to Minsk.[6]

A few days after he returned from Moscow, Titovets said, he was questioned by officials at the university and by the KGB. He said that it was hard to recall many details about Oswald's life in Minsk because he had had no idea, when Oswald was living there, that he would have to remember these things. Soon after that, a Captain Nikolaev from the KGB came to Titovets's apartment. "I handed him a packet with Oswald's letters. He took the packet saying something to the effect that the letters would be quite safe in the KGB's keeping and they would return them to me later if I wanted them back. He went out. I have not seen those letters since."[7]

Meantime, all across Minsk, Titovets wrote in his memoirs, "the KGB continued an extensive mopping up operation with the objective of debriefing those who knew Oswald and removing all material evidence about him from their possession." The Russian authorities wanted to airbrush Oswald out of Russia. They knew it was public knowledge that Oswald had lived in the Soviet Union, but they did not want the CIA to connect his life there with Kennedy's assassination.[8]

Tennent Bagley, the former head of CIA counterintelligence operations in the Soviet Union, said the case of Yuri Nosenko illustrated how important this was to Moscow. When Nosenko defected to the West in February 1964, it was Bagley he came to, in Geneva. Nosenko had established contact with Bagley a year earlier, and he had been a double agent since then. The Americans were unhappy that Nosenko now wanted to defect—that meant he could no longer feed them information—but they believed he was in danger, and Nosenko was secreted out of Switzerland to West Germany and on to CIA headquarters in Langley, Virginia. Eventually, Bagley and other senior CIA officials came to believe that Nosenko was not a defector but a mole. There were many reasons for thinking this, but there was one thing in particular that Bagley remembered. Nosenko knew very little about a lot of things, but he knew a great deal about one thing—Lee Harvey Oswald—and the message he kept repeating to his CIA debriefers was simple and very important: the KGB was not involved in Kennedy's murder.

In an interview Bagley told me, "I believe the KGB used Nosenko's contact with CIA as part of their frantic efforts to reassure the United States government that they had nothing to do with the killing of JFK by their former guest in the USSR." Bagley said he doubted that Nosenko actually knew many details about the Oswald case, but he thought that Nosenko had been dispatched by the KGB to make sure the CIA did not think Oswald was working for the Soviet Union. "It is far more likely that Nosenko told, and was able to tell, only what the KGB briefed and instructed him to tell," Bagley said. If the United States thought the Russians had killed the American president, there would be a war. The point of Nosenko's defection, Bagley said, was to stop that from happening.[9]

The KGB was understandably worried, but there was probably no need to be. The FBI and the CIA quickly determined that Oswald had fatally shot the president from the sixth floor of the Texas School Book Depository.

There was no good reason to think that he was a secret agent or a "patsy." The only reason for the Warren Commission was Ruby's murder of Oswald and a fear that people would think there had been a cover-up. The commission's investigation was meant to dispel the conspiracy theorizing. Obviously, it did not succeed. Although the commission examined all the angles of the assassination, it did not leave the nation feeling as if the matter had been put to rest. Doubts were not limited to people on the margins; they seeped through the whole country. There was—there is—always a question: Who really killed John F. Kennedy?

But the question we should be asking, the question raised in the introduction of this book, is: Why did Oswald kill the president? And what was the culture or place that produced him? Oswald was his own man, but he was also the product of larger forces, and those forces can tell us a great deal about the United States in the middle of the twentieth century and, perhaps more importantly, today.

Oswald was an ordinary man, but he was also exceptional, and not just because he killed a president. On January 7, 1960, the day the Soviets sent him to Minsk, he was made into—and this is not meant to sound dramatic or overly literary—an antihero. Once they capitulated to his demand that he be allowed to stay in the Soviet Union, he was elevated, almost magically, with a great and sudden force. For the first time, he had done something that most other men could not have imagined doing: he had convinced the KGB to let him stay in their country, and he had gone to great lengths to persuade them—trying to kill himself and then waiting them out in a somber and lonely hotel room. He was not a sympathetic character, but he had admirable traits—perseverance, concentration—and these traits had enabled him to push through the ports, planes, railroads, bureaucracies, and intelligence agencies that separated Dallas and Minsk. He had done something profound.

His anti-heroism was unmistakably American. Oswald achieved this status in the Soviet Union in late 1959 and early 1960, but the seed of that transformation had been planted and nourished in New York, Louisiana, and Texas in the early 1950s. It was this very early, underdeveloped feeling of dislocation and disenchantment that had propelled him to leave the United States—and to go to the Soviet Union—in the first place. Oswald's fury, naïveté, narcissism, and even indifference to whatever place he had parachuted himself into—all these things were reflections of an uncontainable rage that felt and sounded American. That is, they were expressions of a classically American individuality, a desire to be free of external forces and to achieve a wholly separate self that had not been shaped by other people, clans, or institutions.

This was a yearning that would have been entirely unfamiliar to the Menchani he would encounter at the Experimental Department in Minsk. The Menchani craved order and calm, and they were members of classes and genera that had been created for them by other people. But in America there was a growing anxiety about the standardization and mechanization of a massive, hyper-industrial, government-corporate complex that seemed to eclipse and suffocate the old ways of thinking and being—the individuality, the uncharted wildness of the country, the sense that anything that people imagined could be made real. There was a deepening suspicion that there was something inauthentic in the new postwar America, which seemed so detached from its earlier self—its real self. More than ever, the United States rallied governments and peoples around the world to the cause of "democracy" and "freedom," and more than ever those words seemed sullied by the realpolitik of empire management. There was, in certain quarters, a suspicion of and even a hostility toward order and calm, and this had begun to make itself felt in the early 1950s, but it had been boiling up out of the deep folds of the republic for ages. Oswald qua antihero was a product of the new era. He was an expression of the place he came from.[10]

Alas, there is nothing in his diaries or the handful of essays or fragments that he penned that indicates Oswald had any insight into this larger context. Nor did anyone who knew him, in the United States or the Soviet Union, ever indicate that he was particularly wise or deep—a hipster à la Norman Mailer or, better yet, Rousseau's existential wanderer. Oswald was not a teller of truths. He did not see things that other people did not see. His antiheroism was not exactly achieved by his own efforts.

It was a manifestation of larger forces about which he knew almost nothing. It was automatic and passive.

In any event, it is hard to imagine any other type of American besides the would-be antihero venturing to the Soviet Union in 1959 and mustering the will to stay there for as long as Oswald did. This was the quintessential antiheroic experience of the period, the bridge that the loner or rebel would have had to cross in order to detach himself fully from his beginnings and become the full-fledged antihero he was predisposed to be. For the Soviet Union was not just *a* country. It was *the* country. It occupied a singular, almost religious place in the American consciousness. It represented the refutation of everything Oswald had come from. Its very existence challenged the existence of the United States, and implicit in this challenge was the moral indignation and nihilist rage of the radical.

Ironically, Oswald's antiheroism appears to have contributed to his feelings of estrangement not only from America but also, eventually, from the Soviet Union. That was because his status, his cultural dislocation, made him odd to Russians—not just an unknown but an unknowable quantity. He looked and sounded like an American, but he did not seem quite right. There was something askew. It was as if he were a copy of someone who was a real American. This perceived out-of-placeness was reflected in the question the Russians he would meet came back to over and over: Why did you come here? It wasn't that they were unable to imagine that an American might oppose or question something about America or its government; they were not that enamored of the United States. What they could not understand was that someone could be in a *permanent* state of opposition, that Oswald's opposition had less to do with specific issues or policies and more to do with a state of mind. They did not—they could not—understand that his antiheroism was a natural byproduct of the new postwar America, that it was, in its striving for a real and impregnable individuality, deeply American. This idea was irreconcilable with the Mechani experience. Collectivization, the war, Stalin, the very idea of the state as it had always been understood in Russia: these were phenomena, political and cultural and even spiritual forces, that defined a separate universe. They could not be squared with an unbridled,

New World individuality. That individuality, like Oswald himself, was alien and confusing. Most of them had not known that people like him existed.[11]

It was not just the Russians who found Oswald mystifying. Many Americans could hardly relate to his feelings of alienation and detachment.

That was the bigger, mainstream America—the America that took part in the political process, held down jobs, and had mortgages—and it had been casting about for many years in search of a figurehead to assuage its fears and articulate its aspirations. These Americans did not have to travel to Russia to find a home. They felt at home in America, but they worried that the country was turning weak, and they saw in it great wells of potential energy. Even though they had great respect for Dwight Eisenhower, they fretted that his moment had passed. That Eisenhower had suffered a heart attack in 1955 and a stroke in 1957, that he had undergone abdominal surgery in 1956, and that he was the first president whose spokesmen openly discussed his health while he was in office may have compounded these fears. The Cold War demanded a more vibrant, or active, government.[12]

This America finally found its voice in John F. Kennedy, and for a few years, starting in the early 1960s, there was a new optimism. This optimism was felt most everywhere in the country, and it was very intense, so much so that it bordered on a previously unknown sense of invincibility. This sense of invincibility was reflected in the popular culture, journalism, intellectual life, and the actions and policies of the new administration. It seemed to overtake the fears and doubts, the alienation, the dissonance and atomization that were embodied by Oswald and had been building for so many years before Kennedy's rise to power. Ben Bradlee—the *Newsweek* correspondent and, later, editor of the *Washington Post* who was a friend and neighbor of the junior senator from Massachusetts before he became president—spoke for the Washington establishment when he called Kennedy "this remarkable man who lit the skies of this land bright with hope and promise as no other political man has done in this century."[13]

Nor was it just fawning journalists who were enamored of the new president. In California, which was Nixon's home state and had backed the Republican in 1960, 63 percent of voters said Kennedy was doing a good job in a Field Poll released October 25, 1961. In fact, twenty-four Gallup polls taken from March 1961 to December 1962 show Kennedy's nationwide approval numbers averaging 73.3 percent. (His ratings dipped into the low 60s as the 1962 congressional elections neared, flatlined during the Cuban Missile Crisis in October 1962, and then picked up in late November and December.)[14]

It was only after Kennedy had been sworn in that this feeling of optimism and invincibility deepened and then spread. That was when a mythological aura seemed to envelope the White House. The president was not just a president but a *hero*. To his supporters, he seemed to hover between man and god—to be half man, half deity, and a conduit connecting them with something eternal and deep. Americans had rarely, if ever, experienced this feeling with their presidents. The nation's democratic ethos had imprinted on the electorate a distrust of anyone who sought its approval. There had always been a tension that held the compact together. The ruler presided over the ruled only because he was required; in an ideal world, in a world in which the Hobbesian state of nature did not prevail, there would not have been a ruler. The president existed because he had to. But with Kennedy's election, a Rubicon of sorts seemed to have been crossed. Suddenly the affection or sympathy that many Americans had at one time or another felt for a president morphed into a kind of love. Other presidents had come close—Abraham Lincoln, Theodore Roosevelt, Franklin Roosevelt. But it was Kennedy, more than any of the thirty-four who preceded him, who crossed into the magical realm.

This is not to say that the new politics was immune to reason or criticism. The American voter had not been rendered a zombie by Kennedy's ascension to power. But a change had taken place. Expectations had shifted. With Kennedy's election, the American idea of leadership became something else entirely. It was no longer enough to be persuaded or even inspired. Voters wanted an emotional connection with their president.

The idea of a mythological White House encouraged, however subtly or tentatively, the idea of a mythological America, an America that was capable of things it had never imagined doing in the past. This new America, popularized and widely subscribed to in the media and the public discourse, conveyed a sense of supreme sure-footedness. The president's men were crisp, punctual, clean-shaven, and inclined to precise, almost rectilinear definitions (David Halberstam famously dubbed the Kennedy men "the best and the brightest," whereas Theodore Sorensen, Kennedy's speechwriter and a member of the inner circle, alternately celebrated and pooh-poohed the "Kennedy style"). Their manners, gait, expression, vocabulary, and even the narrow emotional range within which they operated (at least publicly) all suggested a well-honed sense of purpose.

In many respects, this style was not all that different from the style of the preceding decade, except that now there was an even greater boldness: race relations could be mended; regimes (in Cuba and Vietnam) could be replaced; men could be sent to the Moon. Kennedy was not the first president to lead the country in this direction—the US-British overthrow of a democratically elected Iranian leader in 1953 and Eisenhower's support for civil rights legislation in 1957 and 1960 and his use of force to integrate a Little Rock High School, also in 1957, offered key precedents. And Kennedy was not nearly as committed to implementing a transformative agenda as his supporters like to believe (his administration was far more conservative than that of later Democratic presidents). But transformation was the message the new president conveyed. While the Eisenhower era was widely perceived as one of standing still, that of Kennedy was about moving forward.[15]

The fear that America had been falling behind for so many years was answered with an overpowering activity that was idealistic and, at times, bellicose. Not surprisingly, Oswald saw in this a grave danger. Soon, he predicted, the "two world systems" would be forced into a Manichean showdown, and out of the wreckage would emerge a more lasting peace. "The mass of survivors . . . will be too disallusioned too support either the communits or capitalist parties in their respective counties." In one of his more hard-to-comprehend sentences, Oswald added that "after the atomic catorahf they shall seek a alturnative to those systems which brough them misery." He was not, as mentioned, a great seer of hidden truths; he seemed to point toward a churning, mounting violence.[16]

These two forces—the new optimism symbolized by Kennedy and the skepticism and antiheroism of a darker, more unsettled America symbolized by Oswald—had historical antecedents that stretched all the way to the nation's founding, but they emerged out of World War II and the sharpening confrontation with the Soviet Union.[17] They constituted something of a double helix, and from this double helix emanated a series of debates and conversations, books and articles about modernity, mass communication, the regulation and ordering of daily life, suburbanization, race, and freedom. Each of these debates or lines of inquiry spawned a wave of movements, and the intensity and velocity of these movements reflected the turbid wanderings of a people trying to make sense of its new identity in a bifurcated, capitalist-communist universe.

William Barrett, the philosopher at New York University who helped popularize existentialism in the United States, recalled in his memoirs, *The Truants: Adventures Among the Intellectuals*, the rapid succession of mini-schools popping up in the New York art scene in the mid-1950s: op art, pop art, minimal art, conceptual art. "One style did not emerge as the inevitable and necessary way of painting in this time," Barrett wrote. "Instead, the *Zeitgeist* was to find its expression in a riotous proliferation of new schools, often tendentious and in conflict with each other."[18]

To some extent, these stirrings were confined to a small world of self-appointed *penseurs*, but it would be incorrect to think that they did not point to broader arguments and discontents. The new jazz sound, with its dissonance and rejection of traditional structures; abstract expressionism; Tennessee Williams's *Cat on a Hot Tin Roof*, Arthur Miller's *Death of a Salesman* and *The Crucible*, and Leonard Bernstein's "The Age of Anxiety"; the emergence of the Camus-like rebel and the rise of "cool"—all of these cultural representations were not simply the voices of a self-contained coterie of poets. They were the causes and effects of bigger tensions.

Oswald gave no sign that he was aware of the new forces sweeping America, and he certainly did not see where he fit in. But he was not

exactly ignorant: he knew about current events. And he had strong opinions, but his opinions always had an ethereal quality, a remoteness that
seemed to parallel Oswald's feeling of disconnectedness. His writings
were mostly devoid of journalistic details or specifics. When Oswald
talked about the United States, he never talked about it as if it were a
place, in terms of topographies or landscapes. He sounded, weirdly, like
a Russian, a foreigner who had been told that America was bad but had
never seen it, walked it, talked to its people, lived there. It was not as if he
lacked things to write or think about. There had been plenty. It was just
that none of his experiences—sitting on a bus in eastern Texas, wandering
through the French Quarter, navigating the tenements of Spanish Harlem, arriving in San Francisco from Japan on the USNS *Barbet*—seemed
to engage him. None of the vistas, rooms, lights, whiffs, howls, scrapes, or
textures he encountered ever came up in his thoughts or conversations.
It was as if there were an impermeable membrane separating him from
the external world. Everything was theoretical, ideational—detached.[19]

But for all his detachment and weirdness, there was a vaguely predictable cadence to Oswald's interloping. He shot himself, accidentally or not,
in the arm when he was at Atsugi, a little more than a year after he had
enlisted with the Marines. He first gave voice to his growing frustrations
with the Soviet Union in his diary in the fall of 1960, a little less than a
year after he had arrived in Moscow. And after hopping around Dallas–
Fort Worth and Louisiana in search of a job and a place to live, in September 1963 Oswald took the bus from New Orleans to Houston to Mexico
City, hoping to travel on to Cuba or the Soviet Union—a little more than
a year after returning to the United States. In all three phases we see the
same impulse to escape or trespass and, roughly, the same period of time
separating the start of the phase and the first sign Oswald wanted it to
end. Three examples does not a meaningful statistical sample make, but
they do point to a pattern or rhythm—a rhythm that was established
when he was still a child, when he and his mother averaged, incidentally,
a little less than one year (10.2 months) per address.

The critical difference between each escape or trespass was that, with
each failure to fit in, the intensity and anger and violence grew. It began

when he hit his mother in New York. Then he wounded himself in Japan. Then he attempted to kill himself in Moscow. Then, in the United States, he attempted to kill Edwin Walker, and finally he killed John F. Kennedy, and this murder accomplished what he had failed to do before, which was to bring about his own death. Did he know that Jack Ruby would shoot him? Of course not. But he must have known that, after he shot the president of the United States, his old life would be over.

In this sense, the murder of the president was also a suicide, and it was a suicide that was anticipated many years before by an awful childhood that could not be corrected for by schools or social workers and could not be overcome in the Marines or the Soviet Union. Oswald's interloping was a process that was nearly destined to end spectacularly. There have been, no doubt, thousands of other interlopers, but we don't care about them because they didn't kill the president. What distinguished Oswald as an interloper was that he possessed a remarkable force of will. Other interlopers, like other defectors to the Soviet Union, had elements of antiheroism, but their antiheroism was often mitigated by family or friends, jobs, commitments. They were not prepared to go to the same lengths that Oswald went to. Oswald's interloping was unchecked. There were a few moments when it might have been curbed—his visit to John Pic's apartment in New York, his proposal to Ella German—but the odds were never good. The trajectory he had been placed on many years before, when he was an infant, did not lead ineluctably to violence, but it pointed him in that direction.

None of this makes sense if we fixate on the so-called mystery of the Kennedy assassination. But if we pull back a bit, if we take into account Oswald's history, and if we look most carefully at his Soviet period, the whole terrible rhythm and pattern, the interloping, is exposed. Then, suddenly, he makes a little more sense, and the mystery is no longer a mystery but a tragedy, for which the contemporary human, with his rationalist pretensions and his obsessions with technology and himself, is ill-suited.

The plethora of conspiracy theories surrounding the Kennedy assassination is nonetheless understandable in light of Oswald's own murder, his past, the checkered and violent histories of the many people tied, directly and tangentially, to the assassination, and the political and geopolitical climate. Also, the intense hatred directed at the president and, in fact, the whole Kennedy clan by anti-Castro Cubans, segregationists, the mafia, and extreme elements on the American right contributed to an air of hostility and violence. That Kennedy was murdered in Dallas, where he was thought to be particularly unwelcome, did not help. On top of this, it's hard to accept that Oswald was the lone gunman acting of his own volition because it's hard to document, with absolute clarity, a state of mind, a desire, an impassioned lurch. The conspiracy theorizers would like to attribute the president's murder to a complex series of secret moves and deliberations, and they assume that all of these discrete operations can be fitted into a single organization, or web of organizations, that defines the parameters of the conspiracy—the mob, the CIA, the Kremlin, Fidel Castro. But that assumes a perfect rationality, a computerlike order and process that cannot take into account the vicissitudes or strivings of a man and his ideas. Explaining that man, not as a bit part in a complex organization but as a self-contained entity with fears and inclinations and a tortuous history, is more complicated than fitting him into a machine.

Oswald cannot be explained by looking at discrete operations. He was not part of a detective story. He was simply himself, and at noon on November 22, 1963, he took possession of history for just a few moments. He reordered it forever.

In this sense, his crime is twofold. First, he killed a man. Second, in killing him, he elevated him—he mythologized a president who was already a myth, and not just him but his title, the presidency. Mindlessly, America has been seeking a way back to the Kennedy feeling for fifty years because it once tasted that feeling briefly and it was addictive, and because the country possesses a very truncated vision of Kennedy, one that ends the way most movies and middle brow novels end—simply.

The point of the conspiracy theorizers, of course, is not to figure out who killed John F. Kennedy. It is to justify and perpetuate a conviction that there is something deeply and characterologically dark about the United States. It is to unearth the military industrial complex, or the evil collusions between organized crime and local law enforcement, or the machinations of foreign intelligence agencies working in concert with the CIA (certainly, the thinking goes, Langley was well aware that the KGB killed Kennedy). Most important, it is not to get to the bottom of anything. It is to pursue, endlessly, a web of supposedly interconnected interests that does not exist, fueling the belief that beneath all the wealth and pomp and talk about "democracy" and "freedom," there is something about America that is a sham.

All of this is somehow, ominously, vaguely believable unless we take into account Oswald. It is not enough to say that Oswald was the lone gunman. That description is inherently superficial and inadequate. It fixates on action, on that which can be seen, and it leaves open the possibility that Oswald was the lone gunman who was also working for someone else who was, in turn, working for someone else. His psychology and all the interior forces that preyed on him remain a secret, and that secret provides the theorizers with the tiniest of openings.

It would be more accurate to say that Oswald was his own agent, that he was moved to act by dint of his own inclination. That inclination was born of a fragmented and peripatetic youth, adolescence, and early adulthood, but ultimately Oswald was self-propelled. The mysterious and fictional heart of darkness residing somewhere in America did not murder the mythical hero-president. Oswald did.

NOTES

INTRODUCTION

1. *Report of the President's Commission on the Assassination of President Kennedy* (Warren Commission Report), Chap. 7, 395, US National Archives.

CHAPTER 1

1. *Report of the President's Commission on the Assassination of President Kennedy* (Warren Commission Report; hereafter WCR), Appendix 13, "Early Years," 669–681, US National Archives, traces most of the important places and dates that comprise Oswald's childhood and adolescence.

2. See, for example, ibid., Chap. 7, 377–383, and the testimony before the Warren Commission of Renatus Hartogs, a psychiatrist who evaluated Lee in 1953, in New York (April 16, 1964, vol. 8, 222–224, US National Archives). Also, Marguerite Oswald's Warren Commission testimony is revealing (February 10–12, 1964, vol. 1, 126–264, US National Archives), as is her essay on Oswald's funeral, which she titled "Aftermath of an Execution: The Burial and Final Rites of Lee Harvey Oswald, as Told by His Mother Marguerite" (House Select Committee on Assassinations, August 7, 1978, record no. 1801007710085, US National Archives).

3. Author's interview with Ernst Titovets, one of Oswald's closest friends in Minsk in 2010. The impression one gets of this early period of Lee's life is that of a permanent disconnectedness and, increasingly, anger. This is backed up by the adults who supervised him at Youth House in New York: Dr. Hartogs; the social worker, Evelyn D. Siegel; and a probation officer, John Carro. Oswald was sent to Youth House on April 16, 1953, after being declared a truant. In his report, Dr. Hartogs observed: "Lee has to be diagnosed as 'personality pattern disturbance with schizoid features and passive-aggressive tendencies.' Lee has to be seen as an emotionally, quite disturbed youngster who suffers under the impact of really existing emotional isolation and deprivation, lack of affection, absence of family life and rejection by a self-involved and conflicted mother" (WCR, Chap. 7, 379–380).

4. Important details about Marguerite and Lee's stay with John Pic are found in WCR, Appendix 13, 675–676. Even more revealing is John Pic's testimony before

the Warren Commission, the source of most of the information in this section ("Testimony of John Edward Pic," May 15, 1964, Warren Commission Hearings, vol. 11, 1–82, US National Archives). Also helpful is the testimony of John Pic's father; see "Testimony of Edward John Pic Jr.," April 7, 1964, Warren Commission Hearings, vol. 8, 197, US National Archives.

5. According to the Bureau of Census Current Population Survey of April 1953, the median family income in the United States in 1952 was $3,900 (Bureau of the Census and US Department of Commerce, "Current Population Reports Consumer Income," press release, April 27, 1954). Pic's yearly salary of $1,800 may have been somewhat supplemented by his mother-in-law's Social Security benefits, but it's unknown if she was receiving benefits and, if so, how much those came to. Peter Martin, an expert in Social Security law at Cornell Law School, noted, in an interview, that in 1951 the average retired woman received $30 per month in Social Security. Amendments to the Social Security law in 1950 boosted payments considerably. Still, the most that Mrs. Fuhrman could have been expected to contribute to the yearly household income in 1952 would have been $360 to $420—meaning the family would have had no more than $2,220, well below the national average.

6. "Testimony of Mrs. Marguerite Oswald," February 12, 1964, Warren Commission Hearings, vol. 1, 226–227, US National Archives; "Testimony of John Edward Pic," 38.

7. WCR, Chap. 7, 380.

8. For more on Lee's state of mind, see ibid., 378–385. See also Frank Meyer's discussion of the psychology of communist indoctrination, in *The Moulding of Communists: The Training of the Communist Cadre* (New York: Harcourt, Brace, 1961), esp. part 5 ("Psychological Pressure").

9. WCR, Chap. 7, 388. "Oswald Correspondence in Russia to His Mother and Brother, Robert Oswald," FBI, letter no. 6, p. 8, record no. 124-10086-10419, US National Archives.

10. Beauregard Junior High School records, House Select Committee on Assassinations, record no. 1801004310182, US National Archives. (More legible copies of the school records can be found under record no. 124-10158-10058.) Also, see WCR, Chap. 7, 383. Later, in the Marines and in the Soviet Union, Oswald read a good bit. "Interview with John Neumeyer," conducted by FBI, November 27, 1963, Senate Select Committee on Intelligence, record no. 157-10003-10379, US National Archives.

11. WCR, Appendix 13, 680.

12. Ibid., 680–681.

13. Handwritten note from Lee Harvey Oswald to Socialist Party of America dated October 3, 1953, FBI (report filed December 18, 1963, by Special Agent Richard L. Kessler), record no. 124-10011-10323, US National Archives.

14. Former marines Ray Elliott, John Laccinole, and Daniel Powers offered insights and memories that were helpful in writing this section. Former marine David Puckett, who served in later decades, also provided important perspective, as did retired navy captain Daniel Appleton.

15. WCR, Appendix 13, 675.

16. Author's interview with Ray Elliott, in February 2012.

17. James Engelken, who served as a radio seaman apprentice with the navy on the *Bexar* from 1956 to 1958, provided a copy of the ship's cruise log from those years. Engelken says he never met Oswald.

18. Author's interviews with Daniel Powers in 2011. Like many people who met Oswald, Powers has vague memories of him. Oswald rarely left vivid first impressions but gradually would convey a certain sense of himself. Also, like that of so many people who met Oswald, Powers's idea, or composite memory, of Oswald seems to consist of three, broadly construed layers of recollection—from his initial meeting or meetings with Oswald; the moment when he learned that Oswald had been arrested for killing President Kennedy; and the many Oswald-related moments, or interactions, that have accumulated over the years, e.g., testifying in front of the Warren Commission, speaking with family members and journalists, reading a particular book, visiting Dallas, etc. Almost invariably, the second layer of recollections (those having to do with Oswald's arrest) are the clearest and most detailed. Powers, for instance, recalled: "I was coaching wrestling at a high school in Wisconsin. I think we had heard about [the assassination] late in the afternoon, and there was some talk we'd postpone some events, and then we went forward anyway. I saw Oswald's face on television that night. Immediately, when I saw him coming down the hallway [on television], I recognized him. I remember the conversation that my wife, Toni, and I had, and I got the footlocker out and showed her these old photographs [from the Marines]."

19. See WCR, Appendix 13, 682–689, for a more comprehensive report on Oswald's Marine Corps experience, including discussion of his aloofness and scrapes with authority, and a physical description of Oswald. Powers believed Oswald had a girlfriend while he was stationed at Atsugi, Japan, but this was never confirmed. As the WCR suggests, Oswald's sense of isolation, as a child and adolescent, seems to have evolved into a somewhat high-level conversation with himself about Marxism and the Soviet Union. As these ideological commitments sharpened, Oswald grew more willing to state his position, openly and robustly, in conversation with fellow marines. This tendency was still rather nascent when he first enlisted in the Marine Corps, in October 1956. By the time he arrived at the Marine Corps Air Station at El Toro, in California, a little more than two years later, it had intensified.

20. WCR, Appendix 13, 683. I am greatly indebted to Rear Admiral Ronald Tucker (ret.) for helping facilitate my trip to Atsugi in the summer of 2010 and to Timothy McGough, the then public affairs officer at the base, for giving me a lengthy tour of the base (including those sites where Oswald's barracks are believed to have stood), discussing the history of the base, and providing me with old photographs of Atsugi, including an image of Oswald's barracks.

21. WCR, Appendix 13, 693. Author's interviews, in 2011, with Gene Poteat and Robert Stephan, who teaches at the Institute of World Politics and formerly specialized in Soviet and Russian counterintelligence at the CIA. See also CIA director Richard Helms's letter to the FBI director, in which Helms voices doubt that

Oswald had access to classified information related to the U-2 while he was based at Atsugi ("Lee Harvey Oswald's Access to Classified Information About the U-2," May 13, 1964, CIA, Record No. 104-10003-10086, US National Archives).

22. WCR, Appendix 13, 683–684.

23. Ibid., 684; "Compositions on 'The Collective' and Minsk, Russia, with Foreword and Autobiographical Sketch of Oswald," pp. 3–4, FBI, record no. 124-10086-10419, US National Archives. (Also grouped together in this record are Oswald's diary, his "Six Compositions," and his "Five Untitled Compositions on Political Subjects," which are quoted at length below and should not be confused with "The Collective." Dallas police found all the writings at two locations after his arrest: the Irving, Texas, house where Oswald's wife was living at the time of his arrest and the room in Dallas that Oswald had been renting before the assassination.)

24. For Oswald's letter to Robert, see "Oswald Correspondence in Russia," letter no. 6. One of the many signs of the triteness of Oswald's rhetoric is the weird similarity between his characterization of US forces in the Pacific and Soviet authorities' characterization of those same US forces. See, for example, the undated letter, from the Presidium of the Supreme Soviet to the Communist Party's Central Committee, that was written soon after Oswald arrived in Moscow and makes reference to his military service. Description of Corregidor from author's interview with Powers.

25. WCR, Appendix 13, 683–684.

26. Ibid., 684. For more context, see John Pic's Warren Commission testimony.

27. For a more comprehensive discussion of Oswald's defection plan—and the degree to which he lied or bent the truth in the service of this plan—see ibid., 685–690. Also, see Oswald's November 8, 1959, letter to his brother for a brief discussion of his preparations leading up to his departure for Russia ("Oswald Correspondence in Russia," letter no. 5). *Oswald: Russian Episode* (Minsk: Mon Litera, 2010), a memoir written by Oswald's close friend Ernst Titovets, in Minsk, provides insight, esp. 115, 129, and 325.

28. WCR, Appendix 13, 686–687.

29. Ibid., 686–687.

30. "Testimony of Kerry Wendell Thornley," May 18, 1964, Warren Commission Hearings, vol. 11, 87, US National Archives.

31. WCR, Appendix 13, 688–689.

CHAPTER 2

1. "Affidavit of Billy Joe Lord," June 26, 1964, Warren Commission Hearings, vol. 11, 117–118, US National Archives.

2. "Affidavit of George B. Church Jr.," June 27, 1964, Warren Commission Hearings, vol. 11, 115–116; "Affidavit of Mrs. George B. Church, Jr.," June 27, 1964, Warren Commission Hearings, vol. 11, 117; *Report of the President's Commission on the Assassination of President Kennedy* (Warren Commission Report; hereafter WCR), Appendix 13, 690, US National Archives. I have quoted Oswald, from the WCR and his various writings, verbatim. I have done this because I feared that, in the

process of cleaning up Oswald's at times atrocious English, I would misconstrue his meaning. Also, it is important to convey his many struggles with spelling and grammar, which illustrate his background and lack of education as well as his frame of mind and his inability, at times, to make himself understood. These problems, as will be seen, are scattered throughout his diary, compositions, fragments, and letters.

3. WCR, Appendix 13, 690. Pauli Jokinen, a meteorologist at the Finnish Meteorological Institute, provided weather data for Helsinki and the Finnish coastline all the way to the Russian border, October 9–15, 1959.

4. WCR, Appendix 13, 690. See also "Official and Private Documents and Correspondence of Lee Harvey Oswald," 2, FBI, record no. 124-10086-10419, US National Archives.

5. WCR, Appendix 13, 690. This section relies, in part, on my observation of present-day Vainikkala, the Finnish border town through which Oswald's train passed. Rossiyskie Zheleznye Dorogi (Russian Railways) would not confirm which buildings on the Russian side of the border were standing in October 1959, but it was possible to rule out certain structures and to rule in others, given eyewitness accounts, building materials, wear and tear, and so forth. Those structures that I could not confirm were standing at the time that Oswald traveled across the Finnish-Soviet border have been left out of my description of the station and surrounding area. Sakari K. Salo, a researcher at the Finnish Railway Museum in Helsinki, provided helpful information about Finnish-Soviet train traffic in May 1959, including departure and arrival schedules, ticket prices, train-car configurations, and the kinds of engines and sleeper cars used by Finnish and Soviet authorities.

6. See George Kish, "Railroad Passenger Transport in the Soviet Union," in *Geographical Review* 53, no. 3 (July 1963): 363–376. J. H. Price, "Russian Railway Journey," *Railway World* (December 1957), offers useful information on the train schedule from Helsinki to Moscow in the late 1950s, the train's interior configuration, first (soft) class versus second (hard) class, and other details.

7. Among the best accounts of this period is William Taubman's *Khrushchev: The Man and His Era* (New York: Norton, 2003), esp. Chaps. 11–13. Roy Medvedev and Zhores Medvedev, *Khrushchev: The Years in Power*, trans. Andrew R. Durkin (New York: Norton, 1978), is one of the best portraits by Russians of the Soviet leader. Despite their sympathies, the Medvedevs offer useful insight into Russian Marxists' conception of Khrushchev as a necessary counterpoint to Stalin and a redeemer of the revolution. John Lewis Gaddis offers a thoughtful discussion of peaceful coexistence in *We Now Know: Rethinking Cold War History* (New York: Oxford University Press, 1998).

8. See Taubman, *Khrushchev*, Chap. 15.

9. Author's interviews, in 2010 and 2011, with Priscilla McMillan and, in 2011, with Rimantas Pleikys, Lithuania's former minister of communications and information technology, author of the self-published book *Jamming*, and a co-producer of *Empire of Noise*, a documentary on Soviet jamming of the Voice of America, BBC, and other Western radio signals broadcast into the Soviet Union.

10. True, there was good reason to question the Soviet leadership's ideological commitments. But the nature and strategic posture of the Soviet state, no matter how reform-minded the Soviet premier may have been, pointed to an eventual showdown.

11. WCR, Appendix 13, 690.

12. The bear now stands in the hotel restaurant (author's interview with Irina Gavrilova, in 2012).

13. WCR, Appendix 13, 690.

14. Yuri Nosenko's interview with the FBI, February 26–27, 1964, 23, "Collection of Documents Supporting the Warren Commission Report," CIA, record no. 104-10085-10010, US National Archives.

15. Oswald mentioned his conversation with Shirokova about seeking Soviet citizenship on the third line of his first diary entry, dated October 16, 1959; see "Oswald Diary in Russia," p. 1, record no. 124-10086-10419, US National Archives. The diary, which is sometimes referred to as the "Historic Diary," was discovered among Oswald's writings after his arrest. In several entries in the diary, Oswald does not include the complete date. Adding to the confusion is the fact that it is not clear when the diary was written. The Warren Commission notes that the "earlier entries," presumably those recording Oswald's time in Moscow, in the fall and early winter of 1959, were written after the fact but that the Minsk entries were written contemporaneously. Whatever the case, the diary remains an important source of information about Oswald's daily activities, travels, and moods, as well as the people he met. See also WCR, Appendix 13, 690–691.

16. Author's interviews with former KGB officers Oleg Kalugin, in January 2010, and Oleg Nechiporenko in March 2010. In late 1963, the latter briefly handled Oswald's visa application while posted at the Soviet embassy in Mexico City. Jack Tunheim, a federal judge in Minneapolis who chaired the Assassination Records Review Board, which was created by the federal government in the early 1990s to investigate, once again, the JFK assassination, said of the KGB, "They just didn't know what to make of [Oswald]. They didn't know if he was someone who would be useful to them. He had been in the Marine Corps, but at the same time his sort of boastful nature, they were really concerned that he was either acting up and he might be a spy sent by the Americans, or that he might just be an unstable individual. My recollection is that they eventually concluded that he was an unstable individual" (author's interview with Tunheim in 2010).

17. "Oswald Diary in Russia," 1.

18. I was alerted to this letter by Peter Vronsky, a Canadian filmmaker who has done extensive research into Oswald's time in the Soviet Union. Mary Kay Schmidt, an archivist at the US National Archives , provided me with a copy.

19. WCR, Appendix 13, 691–692.

20. The dates and timelines are a little confusing. According to the Presidium letter, Oswald's visa was set to expire on October 21, but the visa in his passport (visa #403339, issued on October 14) was said to have been valid until October 20

and to have been extended until October 22. Any discrepancies probably had to do with interagency miscommunication. It should also be noted that some portions of the Soviet Ministry of Health records pertaining to Oswald's stay at Botkinskaya conflicted with Oswald's account of his suicide attempt. According to a CIA summary of the Soviet records, "Oswald was discovered unconscious in his room, room 320 of the Hotel Berlin, suffering from a slashed left wrist, and taken to the Botkina [Botkinskaya] Hospital at 1600 hours" (Memo from CIA deputy director for plans to J. Lee Rankin, April 21, 1964, House Select Committee on Assassinations, record no. 180-10092-10354, US National Archives). But in his diary Oswald wrote that he didn't decide "to end it" until seven p.m.—three hours after the Soviet Ministry of Health records indicated he was admitted to Botkinskaya. "The Defector Study," commissioned by the House Select Committee on Assassinations, raised questions about the accuracy of the Health Ministry's records (453), pointing out that an incorrect date appears at the bottom of a document with an analysis of Oswald's blood. That said, Peter Vronsky contended that the Health Ministry timeline was correct and that Oswald had his dates wrong. (This happens more than once in Oswald's diary.) Citing former KGB officer Oleg Nechiporenko, Vronsky claimed that the meeting Oswald said he had on October 21 with the "balding stout" man at the Visa and Registration Department actually took place on October 20, and that Oswald learned, from Rima Shirokova, on the morning of October 21 that he would have to leave that day. See Nechiporenko's *Passport to Assassination: The Never-Before-Told Story of Lee Harvey Oswald by the KGB Colonel Who Knew Him*, trans. Todd Bludeau (New York: Birch Lane, 1993). Nechiporenko cited a KGB document, which allegedly stated that at noon, after Oswald learned the devastating news from Shirokova, hotel officials told Oswald that he had to be at the Visa and Registration Department at 3 p.m., and that a train ticket to Helsinki had been secured for him. Vronsky said that Rosa Agafonova, the translator who had been assigned to Oswald at the Hotel Berlin, confirmed this timeline, adding that she had ordered a car to pick up Oswald at the hotel at 2:40 p.m.—just in time for him to arrive at the Visa and Registration Department by 3, as Nechiporenko said. See "The Defector Study," March 1979, House Select Committee on Assassinations, record no. 180-10147-10238, US National Archives, and Vronsky's online report on Oswald's Soviet period, "Lee Harvey Oswald in Russia: An Unauthorized History from the Kennedy Assassination," www.russianbooks.org/oswald-in-russia.htm.

21. In some records, Dr. Mikhailina is reported to have the first name Lydia. Oswald medical file from Botkinskaya Hospital, Ministry of Health of USSR, Department of State, record no. 179-40002-10409, US National Archives.

22. "Oswald Diary in Russia," 2. Interview with Gavrilova.

23. Yuri Nosenko's interview with the FBI, 24, February 26–27, 1964.

24. The most recent, and most provocative, of these titles is Ion Mihai Pacepa's *Programmed to Kill: Lee Harvey Oswald, the Soviet KGB and the Kennedy Assassination* (Lanham, MD: Ivan R. Dee, 2007). Other works that have made the case that the Soviets steered Oswald toward killing the president include Robert Holmes,

A Spy Like No Other: The Cuban Missile Crisis and the KGB Links to the Kennedy Assassination (London: Biteback, 2012), and, more famously, Edward Jay Epstein, *Legend: The Secret World of Lee Harvey Oswald* (New York: McGraw Hill, 1978).

CHAPTER 3

1. Harvey Klehr, the historian of American communists at Emory University, noted, in an interview, that American leftists, from the October 1917 revolution on, were "fixated on the Soviet Union." "By the 1930s," Klehr said, "one could not be a member of the American Communist Party without understanding that it had very strong emotional bonds to Russia." Klehr identified three factors, in the mid-fifties, that forced American leftists to reconsider their attachments to the Soviet experiment: reports in Polish communist newspapers that Stalin had murdered numerous Jews; Khrushchev's "secret speech" in February 1956; and the Soviets' violent suppression of the Hungarian uprising later that year. See also Paul Hollander, *Political Pilgrims: Western Intellectuals in Search of the Good Society*, 4th ed. (Piscataway, NJ: Transaction Publishers, 1997). For a comprehensive report on the eleven Americans who defected to the Soviet Union from 1958 to 1964, see "The Defector Study," March 1979, House Select Committee on Assassinations, record no. 180-10147-10238, US National Archives.

2. Author's interview with John McVickar in 2010. McVickar recalled that "there was one case of an American mathematician who came to a conference of mathematicians in Russia, and he met and fell in love with a Russian lady mathematician and wanted to return to the States with her, but we couldn't give her a visa, so he decided to stay there." This appears to be a reference to Martin Greendlinger; see "The Defector Study."

3. "Oswald Correspondence in Russia to His Mother and Brother, Robert Oswald," FBI, letter no. 6, record no. 124-10086-10419, US National Archives.

4. Ibid.; the emphasis is Oswald's. McVickar called Oswald an "ambitious defector" who was propelled by a powerful rage and poorly thought-through ideology.

5. "The Defector Study." See esp. the discussions of Morris and Mollie Block (439–441), Nicholas Petrulli (445–446), Libero Ricciardelli (446–448), and Robert Webster (449–451).

6. Author's interview with Priscilla McMillan in 2010. For a brief history of the Metropol, see William Craft Brumfield, *The Origins of Modernism in Russian Architecture* (Berkeley: University of California Press, 1991), Chap. 3.

7. Interview with McMillan; "Oswald Diary in Russia," p. 3, record no. 124-10086-10419, US National Archives.

8. *Report of the President's Commission on the Assassination of President Kennedy* (Warren Commission Report), US National Archives (hereafter WCR), Appendix 13, 693; "Oswald Diary in Russia," 3–4. During his time at the Metropol, Oswald appears to have changed rooms at least once. Here he states that he was in Room 214; later, he indicated that he was in Room 233 (see "Oswald Correspondence in Russia," letter no. 5). It's possible that Oswald recorded the wrong room number,

but it's just as possible that, over the course of a protracted stay at the hotel, he was moved from one room to another to make way for new guests.

9. WCR, Appendix 13, 693; "Oswald Diary in Russia," 3–4.

10. John McVickar, "Remembered Vignettes of a U.S. Consul in Moscow in the Early 1960s," an unpublished essay on McVickar's time in the Soviet Union. McVickar gave me a copy of the essay. The Warren Commission Report incorrectly calls McVickar Snyder's subordinate. McMillan, in an email dated April 22, 2010, wrote: "In 1959, I mistakenly thought that Snyder & McVickar were no. 1 and no. 2 respectively in the consular office, but actually they were of the same rank."

11. "Oswald Diary in Russia," 4; WCR, Appendix 13, 693. McVickar's recollection of the meeting with Snyder at the embassy more or less comports with Oswald's. "At this time I shared the same office with Mr. Snyder and was present in the room during his interview with Oswald," McVickar wrote in a memo. "As I recall their interview may have lasted an hour or so. Oswald was extremely arrogant, truculent and unfriendly to America and Americans in general. He wanted to divest himself of his citizenship forthwith. His reasons were not too clear, but he gave the impression of being very angry about something or things which had happened to him during his childhood or during his duty in the Marine Corps. He said, however, that he was a 'Marxist' and that he had become disgusted with American 'imperialism' as he had observed it in operation in the Far East while in the Marines. He gave evidence of some education in the rudiments of Communist dogma and he apparently had some knowledge of the legalities involved in the renunciation of citizenship" (Memo from Foreign Service Officer John A. McVickar to Mr. Thomas Ehrlich, November 27, 1963, p. 2, SSCIA, record no. 157-10006-10160, US National Archives)

12. "Incoming Telegram to Department of State from Freers," October/November 1959, CIA, Record No. 104-10067-10163, US National Archives. The date of the cable has been blocked out. Presumably, it was sent soon after Oswald's appearance at the US embassy on October 31, 1959.

13. "Oswald Diary in Russia," 4; WCR, Appendix 13, 693–694. McVickar indicated, in a memo written a little more than two weeks after the embassy meeting, that consular officials viewed the Oswald case very seriously, and that they considered Oswald an adolescent who, reasonably enough, was a danger to himself (John McVickar, Memo, November 17, 1959, State Department, record no. 119-10021-1009, US National Archives).

14. "Oswald Diary in Russia," 4; WCR, Appendix 13, 694.

15. Telegram from Robert Oswald to Lee Harvey Oswald (c/o US Embassy), November 1, 1959, State Department, record no. 179-10002-10000, US National Archives.

16. Marie Cheatham, Memo, November 2, 1959, CIA, record no. 104-10007-10116, US National Archives.

17. Telegram from John Pic to Lee Harvey Oswald (c/o US Embassy), November 9, 1959, CIA, record no. 104-10054-10169, US National Archives.

18. McVickar was apparently referring to a *dzhurnaya*, the older woman whose job it was to take the keys of outgoing guests. There were *dzhurnayas* on each floor.

19. John McVickar, Confidential Note to Secretary of State, November 9, 1959, CIA, record no. 104-10007-10059, US National Archives.

20. "Oswald Diary in Russia," 4. Oswald incorrectly stated, in his diary, that the interview with Mosby took place November 15. This cannot be since her story ("Fort Worth Defector Confirms Red Beliefs") appeared November 14 (see Warren Commission Hearings, vol. 26, 90, US National Archives). The correct date is probably the one found in the Warren Commission Report, November 13 (WCR, Appendix 13, 695).

21. Interview with McMillan; WCR, Appendix 13, 696.

22. Interview with McMillan.

23. Johnson was McMillan's maiden name.

24. McVickar, Memo, November 17, 1959.

25. "Oswald Diary in Russia," 4.

26. Ibid., 5; see esp. the November 17–December 30 entry. "Documentary Record of Contacts with the US Department of State and the Immigration and Naturalization Service," p. 10, from a memo from William T. Coleman to J. Lee Rankin, March 6, 1964, Warren Commission, record no. 104-10085-10008. Marina Oswald's discussion of Oswald's relationship with his mother is particularly revealing here. See "Testimony of Mrs. Lee Harvey Oswald," Warren Commission Hearings, February 6, 1964, vol. 1, 94–95, US National Archives.

27. Interviews with McMillan, Oleg Libezin, Sergei Skop, Filip Lavshuk, and Leonid Tsagoiko, in 2010; email from Ruth Paine, January 19, 2010.

28. "Oswald Diary in Russia," 3; interview with McMillan; interviews with former KGB officer Oleg Kalugin in January 2010, and former CIA counterintelligence director Tennent Bagley in January 2010 and December 2011. Oswald's diary entries from November and much of December 1959 paint a robot-like existence that consisted of waiting, studying Russian, and occasionally eating.

29. Former KGB officers Oleg Nechiporenko, in a March 2010 interview, and Kalugin were helpful here. So, too, was Stanislaw Shushkevich, who tutored Oswald in Russian and later became the most senior Communist Party official in the Belarusian Soviet Socialist Republic.

30. See, for instance, Priscilla McMillan's comments in the WCR: "[Oswald] liked to create the pretense, the impression that he was attracted to abstract discussion and was capable of engaging in it, and was drawn to it. But it was like pricking a balloon. I had the feeling that if you really did engage him on this ground, you very quickly would discover that he didn't have the capacity for a logical sustained argument about an abstract point on economics or on noneconomic, political matters or any matter, philosophical" (Chapter 6, 262). Also, Oswald's appearance on William Stuckey's radio show, *Latin Listening Post*, on WDSU in New Orleans, during which Fidel Castro's Cuba was discussed, was telling. This took place in the summer of 1963, one year after Oswald had left the Soviet Union. "They have said that they are a Marxist country," Oswald told Stuckey.

On the one hand, so is Ghana. So are several other countries in Africa. Every country which emerges from a sort of a feudal state, as Cuba did, experiments usually in socialism, in Marxism. For that matter, Great Britain has socialized medicine. You cannot say that Castro is a communist at this time because he has not developed his country, his system, so far. He has not had the chance to become a communist. He is an experimenter, a person who is trying to find a best way for his country. If he chooses a socialist or a Marxist or a communist way of life, that is something upon which only the Cuban people can pass. We do not have the right to pass on that. We can have our opinions, naturally, but we cannot exploit that system and say it is a bad one, it is a threat to our existence and then go in and try to destroy it.

Cuba, Oswald continued, "may go the way of Czechoslovakia, Yugoslavia, or it may go the way to the other extreme, the way of China, in other words, a dogmatic, communist system. That depends on how we handle the matter here in the United States." Oswald's distinction between the Novotny and Tito regimes, in Czechoslovakia and Yugoslavia, respectively, and that of Mao's China suggested he had acquired a somewhat nuanced understanding of leftist developments. But his knowledge of day-to-day superficialities could not compensate for his ignorance of the historical processes that had given rise to this or that political configuration. This ignorance was reflected in his truncated interpretation of Marx's theory of dialectics. Oswald seems to have believed that he could squeeze the whole of human affairs, from uprisings in sub-Saharan Africa to the overthrow of the Castro regime in Havana to social democracy in Britain, into a single, Procrustean bed. (For more on this, see "Testimony of William Kirk Stuckey," June 6, 1964, Warren Commission Hearings, vol. 11, pp. 156–178, US National Archives.)

31. Norman Mailer, *Oswald's Tale: An American Mystery* (New York: Random House, 1995), 791. One suspects that in Oswald Mailer found a case study—*the* case study—of the so-called hipster, whom Mailer introduced in his 1957 essay "The White Negro: Superficial Reflections on the Hipster." (Gary Gilmore, the focus of Mailer's much better work, *The Executioner's Song*, more neatly fits into this role.) See Mailer's *Advertisements for Myself* (Cambridge, MA: Harvard University Press, 1992).

32. The opposing view favored by most conspiracy theorists—that Oswald was a simpleton who was used by far more sophisticated people or organizations to kill the president—is similarly unfounded. These conspiracy theorists include an array of investigators and writers, from the 1960s to the present, including Jim Garrison, the district attorney of Orleans Parish; James Douglass, author of *JFK and the Unspeakable*; David Lifton, author of *Best Evidence: Disguise and Deception in the Assassination of John F. Kennedy*; and, more recently, Barr McClellan, author of *Blood, Money & Power: How LBJ Killed JFK*. Oswald, no doubt, possessed a certain intelligence, and he had a fairly impressive, if skewed, knowledge of current events. What's more, he was prone to bouts of irritability and even fury. In short, he hardly resembles the hapless vehicle that those who have made him into a pawn (of the KGB or Cuban intelligence, or the CIA or the mafia) imagine him being.

33. "Oswald Correspondence in Russia," letter no. 6, pp. 8–9.

34. Ibid., 9.

35. Ibid., 10–11.

36. Ibid., 11.

37. Ibid., 8.

CHAPTER 4

1. "Oswald Correspondence in Russia to His Mother and Brother, Robert Oswald," FBI, letter no. 7, record no. 124-10086-10419, US National Archives. Ray Elliott, the former marine, suggested that Oswald's "hyper-concentration" on the task at hand may have come from his military experience. He noted that the skills and mind-set that were ironed into all marines—assessing a problem, coming up with a plan to solve the problem, and then executing that plan as expeditiously as possible, with minimal resources—would have served Oswald well during his voyage to the Soviet Union and his time in Moscow. That Oswald seemed unaware of, or even indifferent to, changing circumstances in the Soviet Union was due not so much to a lack of interest in his surroundings as to an "over-interest" in executing his plan and, ironically, building a life there (author's interview with Ray Elliott, February 2012).

2. For a complete, recent history of the city, see Timothy J. Colton, *Moscow: Governing the Socialist Metropolis* (Cambridge, MA: Belknap Press of Harvard University Press, 1995). Carl Mydans, the well-known photographer for *Life*, took a series of images of the Russian capital in December 1959, including the famous ice swimmers (*morzhi*, or walruses), children sledding or playing on a slide, ice-skaters and cross-country skiers, street vendors, couples and old women trundling through the snow, and the Kremlin and Red Square. The images do not offer much in the way of political or cultural context, but they do give some sense of day-to-day life in Moscow at this time. Walter Benjamin's classic account of Moscow in the 1920s provides a very good basis of comparison with postwar and especially post-Stalinist Moscow (*Moscow Diary*, ed. Gary Smith, trans. Richard Sieburth [Cambridge, MA: Harvard University Press, 1986]).

3. Robert Tucker touches on this point about the two thaws in his essay "The Image of Dual Russia," in *The Soviet Political Mind: Stalinism and Post-Stalin Change*, revised ed. (New York: Norton, 1971), 121. Certainly other national literatures make abundant use of winter as metaphor or symbol, but Russian writers elevated the symbol from an allusion or a motif to a state of mind. A very cursory survey of such works would have to include Pushkin's "The Snowstorm," Gogol's "The Overcoat," Tolstoy's "Master and Man," Ilya Ilf and Yevgeny Petrov's "Wicked Cold," and, of course, Pasternak's *Dr. Zhivago*, for which the author was awarded the Nobel Prize a year before Oswald arrived in Moscow.

4. Tucker, "The Politics of De-Stalinization," in *The Soviet Political Mind*.

5. Colton, *Moscow*, 796.

6. "The Collective," in "Compositions on 'The Collective' and Minsk, Russia, with Foreword and Autobiographical Sketch of Oswald," p. 29, FBI, record no.

124-10086-10419, US National Archives; Colton, *Moscow*, chap. 6. See also Ksenia Choate, "From 'Stalinkas' to 'Khrushchevkas': The Transition to Minimalism in Urban Residential Interiors in the Soviet Union from 1953 to 1964," master's thesis, Department of Interior Design, Utah State University, 2010.

7. Author's December 2010 interviews with Ellen Mickiewicz, a political scientist who has studied Soviet television programming, at Duke University, and George Michael Snyder, whose master's thesis ("The Blue Screen in Black and White," Department of History, University of North Carolina–Chapel Hill, 1994) explores the role of television in the age of Khrushchev. See also Ellen Mickiewicz, *Split Signals: Television and Politics in the Soviet Union* (New York: Oxford University Press, 1988), 3. Oswald discussed the new television culture in "The Collective," 43. On weekdays, he informs us, programs aired from six p.m. to eleven p.m., "so that all workers can get enough sleep." On weekends, television started earlier and ended later. "Programs," he wrote, "are varied but include as all ways more than 33 percent pure Soviet politics but there are often good films, re-runs of movies and cartoon for the kids the best programs however are the ballet preformaces from the Moscow and Leingrad Bolshowi teaters also smyphonic music concerts are often used to break the monoonus run of politics and dry facts and figures." (Note on pagination: For reasons unknown, the FBI file designates pages 1–35 of "The Collective" in numerical form, and then begins anew, in a different font, with pages 1–21 in capital letters. The forty-third page, for example, is designated "PAGE EIGHT." For simplicity's sake, I designate all pages numerically.)

8. Interview with Snyder. It's worth considering that the Soviet Union did not launch its first communications satellites until 1965 and that mass penetration of television sets did not start until a few years later, meaning that before this time relatively small numbers of people tuned into any given broadcast. In addition to the general openness of the late fifties and early sixties, this may have encouraged, in television producers, a somewhat more creative or adventurous spirit. For more on the development of the Soviet television-viewing audience, see Mickiewicz, *Split Signals*, Chap. 1.

9. Interview with Snyder. Of course, the live broadcast was not limited to Soviet airwaves. Maybe the best-known live broadcast of the era came a few years later, on November 24, 1963, when the nightclub owner Jack Ruby, in front of television cameras in a garage at the Dallas Police Department, shot Lee Harvey Oswald.

10. Gretchen Simms, "The 1959 American National Exhibition in Moscow and the Soviet Artistic Reaction to Abstract Art," D.Phil. diss., University of Vienna, 2007, 103. For a lengthier discussion of the political-cultural context within which the National Exhibition took place, see Yale Richmond, *Cultural Exchange and the Cold War: Raising the Iron Curtain* (University Park: Pennsylvania State University Press, 2000). Particularly helpful is Chap. 2, in which Richmond describes in some detail the Sixth World Youth Festival. Held in 1957 in Moscow, the festival, which drew thirty-four thousand people from other socialist countries and sixty thousand Soviet delegates (plus a large British delegation and a smaller American one), anticipated the National Exhibition held two years later.

11. John McVickar, echoing press reports in the United States, noted in a June 2010 interview that there was usually a handful of Russians at each exhibit at Sokolniki who would ask provocative questions that were meant to make the United States look bad. Soviet propagandists were fond of overstating the levels of racial violence in the United States and, in fact, seem to have affected Oswald, who may have been sensitive to these charges because of his Southern roots. In one of his writings, he praised the Soviets' racial harmony, understating the degree to which that was imposed from the top, while criticizing Americans for allowing the "segregationist minority" and "indifferent people in the South" to tarnish the nation's image ("Speech," from "Six Compositions," p. 2, FBI, record no. 124-10086-10419, US National Archives).

12. Simms, "The 1959 American National Exhibition," Chapter 2C, interviews with Lucia DeRespinis and Michael Ben Eli, a protégé of the futurist and senior designer of the American exhibition, Buckminster Fuller; Greg Castillo, *Cold War on the Home Front: The Soft Power of Midcentury Design* (Minneapolis: University of Minnesota Press, 2010); Richmond, *Cultural Exchange and the Cold War*, Chap. 12. See also Michael L. Krenn, *Fall-Out Shelters for the Human Spirit: American Art and the Cold War* (Chapel Hill: University of North Carolina Press, 2005), 166–173.

13. Oswald, in his November 26, 1959, letter to his brother, Robert, dismissed this sort of "exploitation," accusing the US government of imposing a credit-based system on workers that traps them in an endless cycle of depression, inflation, speculation, and war ("Oswald Correspondence in Russia," letter no. 6, p. 7). Author's November 2010 interview with Jake Gorst, grandson of Andrew Geller, from the architecture firm Raymond Loewy/William Snaith Inc. Geller was brought in to make the final changes to Splitnik. Gorst, a documentary filmmaker, has done extensive research on his grandfather's work in connection with his documentary *Leisurama*. Andrew Wulf, *Moscow '59: The Sokolniki Summit Revisited* (Los Angeles: Figueroa, 2010), provides a thorough discussion of the politics and geopolitics of cultural exchange in the late 1950s.

14. Castillo, *Cold War on the Home Front*, x. A June 29, 2011, roundtable discussion of the National Exhibition (hosted by the National Archives and Records Administration, moderated by Timothy Naftali, and broadcast by C-SPAN) was also helpful. The discussion included Ambassador Gilbert Robinson, who was the coordinator of the National Exhibition, and tour guides Tatiana Sochurek and George Feifer. The C-SPAN discussion also included a previously taped interview with William Safire, who died in 2009. "I got the picture of Nixon arguing with Khrushchev, and there was a pushy Russian trying to get into the middle of the picture and I kept trying to get him out, but I couldn't get him out," Safire said. "That was Brezhnev."

15. The website Watergate.info includes a transcript of the kitchen debate.

16. Safire's account, in the C-SPAN discussion, was particularly useful. See also Castillo, *Cold War on the Home Front*, ix–x.

17. "Oswald Correspondence in Russia," letter no. 6, p. 7. The emphasis is Oswald's.

18. Simms, "The 1959 American National Exhibition," 45–47.

19. In a December 2010 interview, Elizabeth Frank, an American studies professor at Bard College who has written on Pollock, said of *Cathedral* and other artworks displayed at Sokolniki: "This work was chosen as an example of, 'Look, we have people who do this sort of thing, and we don't send them to Siberia because they paint this awful stuff.'" See also Krenn, *Fall-Out Shelters for the Human Spirit*, 166–173. It should be noted that the selection process behind the artworks at the National Exhibition was filled with ironies. Many of the artists on display had communist sympathies, and a few members of Congress, offended by the artists' politics or the artworks themselves, demanded that they be cut from the show. President Eisenhower, not wanting an "American Pasternak" scandal in the lead-up to the National Exhibition, overruled these objections and gave organizers authority to choose those artworks they deemed appropriate (see Krenn, *Fall-Out Shelters for the Human Spirit*, 159–166).

20. This is, in fact, exactly how Marilyn Kushner describes the National Exhibition in her article "Exhibiting Art at the American National Exhibition in Moscow, 1959," *Journal of Cold War Studies* 4, no. 1 (Winter 2002): 6.

21. Krenn, *Fall-Out Shelters for the Human Spirit*, 169.

22. Ibid. See also Matthew Jesse Jackson, *The Experimental Group: Ilya Kabakov, Moscow Conceptualism, Soviet Avant-Gardes* (Chicago. University of Chicago, 2010), 53. Elizabeth Frank said in the December 2010 interview, "Russian avant-garde art was as avant-garde as you could be, and then, after the revolution, it was condemned, ignored. It wasn't a part of their history. . . . If socialist realism and the canons of socialist art hadn't been erected as the dominant art style, there is no telling what role Russia would have had in twentieth-century art. It could easily have outclassed the West because it got there earlier than the West."

23. "Oswald Diary in Russia," p. 5, record no. 124-10086-10419, US National Archives.

24. Ibid.

25. Ibid. See also Oswald's third composition in "Five Untitled Compositions on Political Subjects," p. 11, FBI, record no. 124-10086-10419, US National Archives.

26. "Oswald Diary in Russia," 5. The second to last single quote in this entry is confusing; it appears to have been included mistakenly.

27. "Documentary Record of Contacts with the United States Department of State and the Immigration and Naturalization Service," pp. 11–12, March 6, 1964, Warren Commission, record no. 104-10085-10008.

CHAPTER 5

1. The most comprehensive discussion of the Jewish experience in Minsk during the war is Barbara Epstein, *The Minsk Ghetto 1941–1943: Jewish Resistance and Soviet Internationalism* (Berkeley: University of California Press, 2008).

2. Oswald does not state when, exactly, he arrived in Minsk. But his diary indicates that he left Moscow and arrived in Minsk on the same day—January 7, 1960 ("Oswald Diary in Russia," pp. 5–6, record no. 124-10086-10419, US National

Archives). *Report of the President's Commission on the Assassination of President Kennedy* (Warren Commission Report) does not specify when Oswald left Moscow, but it does say that he arrived in Minsk on January 7. The train trip from Moscow to Minsk is seven to eight hours; trains depart in the morning (arriving in the early evening) and at night (arriving in the early morning).

3. It's true that Oswald wrote, in his January 7, 1960, diary entry, that he was leaving Moscow for "Minsk, Belorussia," but this was almost certainly written after he arrived there.

4. The consensus of officials in the former Soviet Union and the United States is that Oswald was sent to Minsk because it was a provincial city far from anyone important. Oleg Nechiporenko, the former KGB officer, pointed out in a March 2010 interview that other American defectors to the Soviet Union had been sent to provincial cities, and he said that it was entirely in keeping with KGB policy for the security organs to keep some distance between Oswald and anyone—at the Kremlin, the Defense Ministry, or the intelligence services—who might have been of interest to the CIA. Other defectors' experiences in the Soviet Union at this time seem to bear this out. According to "The Defector Study" (March 1979, House Select Committee on Assassinations, record no. 180-10147-10238, US National Archives), Morris and Mollie Block were moved to an apartment in Odessa; Harold Citrynell, Kharkov; Bruce Frederick Davis, Kiev; Joseph Dutkanicz, Lvov; Libero Ricciardelli, Kiev. (Ricciardelli apparently asked to be moved to a climate that better suited his health.) It's curious that all these defectors were sent to the Ukraine and that Oswald was the only one in this group who went to the Belorussian Soviet Socialist Republic. Why he was not sent to the Ukraine is unknown. That said, the central point—that Oswald was consigned to the provinces to limit his contact with important people—is buttressed by the cases of his fellow defectors.

5. "Oswald Diary in Russia," 6. "The Collective" in "Compositions on 'The Collective' and Minsk, Russia, with Foreword and Autobiographical Sketch of Oswald," pp. 32–33, FBI, record no. 124-10086-10419, US National Archives.

6. "The Collective," 24–26.

7. Oswald first mentions Detkov in his January 8, 1960, diary entry, spelling his last name "Detkof." A correct transliteration calls for either Detkoff or Detkov.

8. Author's interviews with Barbara Epstein in April 2010 and Igor Kuznetsov in March 2010.

9. "The Collective," 15.

10. There is a rich cache of humorous, iconoclastic, and otherwise subversive literature, samizdat (underground literature), and photography that came from *outside* Belorussia. But there is a striking dearth of this sort of expression from Minsk, Vitebsk, Pinsk, Brest, or any of the other cities in the republic. See Emil Draitser, *Forbidden Laughter: Soviet Underground Jokes*, English and Russian ed. (Los Angeles: Almanac, 1980), and Diane Neumaier, *Beyond Memory: Soviet Nonconformist Photography and Photo-Related Works of Art* (Piscataway, NJ: Rutgers University Press, 2004).

11. "The Collective," 24.

12. Author's interviews with Tamara Pavlovna Soroko, in February and March of 2010, provided information used extensively throughout this chapter.

13. Author's interviews with Sergei Skop, Ernst Titovets, and Anna Zhuravskaya, a sister of Oswald's friend Pavel Golovachev, conducted throughout 2010. See also Titovets's description of Marina in *Oswald: Russian Episode* (Minsk: Mon Litera, 2010), 231. Stanislaw Shushkevich, who was from Minsk, was atypical of Menchani, with his superior education and much more cosmopolitan worldview.

14. Author's interviews with Leonid Tsagoiko, in February and March 2010, provided critical information (especially on the war, day-to-day life in Minsk, the Minsk Radio Factory's Experimental Department, and Oswald) that is used extensively throughout this chapter.

15. "Oswald Correspondence in Russia to His Mother and Brother, Robert Oswald," letter no. 7, FBI, record no. 124-10086-10419, US National Archives.

16. See, for instance, "The Collective," 31–32, 51.

17. Author's interviews with Tamara Soroko; Alexandra Lavshuka, the wife of Oswald's boss, Filip Lavshuk; and Galina Makovskaya and Sergei Skop, both co-workers, throughout the winter and spring of 2010.

18. "The Collective," 24; interview with Titovets.

19. Interview with Skop.

CHAPTER 6

1. Yuri Nosenko's interview with the FBI, February 26–27, 1964, p. 24, in "Collection of Documents Supporting the Warren Commission Report," CIA, record no. 104-10085-10010, US National Archives.

2. There is a discrepancy with regard to the date of Oswald's first day of work at the Minsk Radio Factory. In his diary, Oswald stated that he visited the factory for the first time on January 13 ("Oswald Diary in Russia," p. 6, record no. 124-10086-10419, US National Archives). But according to what appears to be his *trudnaya knizhka*, or "workbook of work," a state-issued booklet that includes a detailed record of one's work life, Oswald started one day earlier. The FBI description of the workbook, found among Oswald's personal effects after his arrest, reads: "A worker's book written in Russian, issued to Lee Harvey Oswald, born 1939, who has received a middle (high school) education, and with job classification as 'regulator'. His past experience is shown as none prior to work in the Minsk Plant. The booklet shows he began work in the experimental section as a regulator first class on January 12, 1960" ("Official and Private Documents and Correspondence of Lee Harvey Oswald," p. 3, sec. 6, FBI, record no. 124-10086-10419, US National Archives).

3. A book published by the factory to commemorate its fiftieth anniversary provided useful details here as well as an overview of the factory's growth during the 1950s and early 1960s. See *Zolotoi Yubiley: 1950–2000* (Minsk: FUA Inform, 2000). Oswald quotation from "Compositions on 'The Collective' and Minsk, Russia, with Foreword and Autobiographical Sketch of Oswald," pp. 5–7, FBI, record no. 124-10086-10419, US National Archives.

4. Author's March 2010 interview with Filip Lavshuk. "The Collective," 14, in "Compositions on 'The Collective.'" In a March 2010 interview, Alexandra Lavshuka, Lavshuk's wife, said Oswald's characterization of her husband was "mostly correct."

5. Author's interviews, in February and March 2010, with Sergei Skop, Lavshuk, and Lavshuka.

6. Author's interview with Stanislaw Shushkevich in February and April 2010. He recalled that in the 1940s "the factory was reconfigured in such a way as to produce military goods and weapons and things along these lines in addition to televisions, and they didn't want the Jews to work there—Jews were thought to be spies—which was a problem because a majority of the specialists who had worked there were, in fact, Jewish. So the Jews had to build televisions and radios, which is where I worked."

7. Interview with Lavshuk.

8. Author's interviews with Shushkevich, Lavshuka, and Leonid Botvinik in December 2011.

9. Lavshuk shared this sentiment.

10. "The Collective," 10; "Oswald Diary in Russia," 7.

11. This section relies on information from several interviews in February 2010 with Oleg Libezin, the older of Vladimir Libezin's two sons. Oleg also provided photographs and letters that corroborate details of his story about his father.

12. "The Collective," 10; the emphasis is Oswald's. Galina Makovskaya, in an interview in February 2010, said it was dangerous to speak freely around Vladimir Libezin.

13. Oleg Libezin showed me the commendation (including Kaganovich's signature), which he keeps in a box full of documents, medals, photographs, and other materials that trace his parents' careers and personal lives.

14. "The Collective," 10. Oswald suggests that it was Libezin's party ties that landed him the job more so than any skills or training he might have had.

15. Author's interviews with Ella German in February and March 2011, Leonid Tsagoiko in March 2010, and Skop. Skop and Tsagoiko could not recall the full names of the other men who sometimes ate lunch with them but did note that their surnames were Generalov, Shestilovskiy, and Baranchik. For several reasons it is difficult to translate Soviet rubles into US dollars, and all approximations are just that—approximations. That said, it's safe to say that the value of whatever goods and services Oswald bought while in the Soviet Union was substantially lower than comparable goods and services would have been in the United States. See University of Michigan economist Morris Bornstein's congressional testimony comparing the two currencies ("Comparisons of the U.S. and Soviet Economies," part 2, 377–395, Joint Economic Committee of Congress, 1959).

16. Interviews with Skop, Tsagoiko, German, and Oleg Libezin.

17. Interviews with Shushkevich and Makovskaya.

18. Interview with Tsagoiko.

19. Interviews with Tamara Soroko (March 2010) and Shushkevich.

20. Skop, who lived in the same building as Oswald, was particularly helpful here.

21. Interview with Shushkevich, who provided information used throughout this section.

22. Interviews with Botvinik, Lavshuk, and Skop.

23. Memo from CIA deputy director for plans to Rankin, J. Lee, April 21, 1964, House Select Committee on Assassinations, record no. 180-10092-10354, US National Archives; "Official and Private Documents and Correspondence of Lee Harvey Oswald," p. 1, sec. 1a, FBI, record no. 124-10086-10419, US National Archives.

24. Interviews with Soroko, German, Lavshuka, and Shushkevich, and in February 2010 with Anna-Teresa Sadovskaya, whose brother was an acquaintance of Oswald. Clearly Oswald enjoyed his new name. He began introducing himself as Alik, and he encouraged others to address him by that name (author's March 2010 interview with Ernst Titovets).

25. Interviews with Titovets, Lavshuk, and Makovskaya.

26. "Oswald Diary in Russia," 6. Memo from CIA deputy director for plans to Rankin, J. Lee, April 21, 1964, includes a map of the center of Minsk and a legend, which identifies the locations of the Hotel Minsk; the Minsk headquarters of the KGB and Interior Ministry, or MVD; the Minsk Radio Factory; and the residences of Oswald and people in his life, among other places.

27. "Oswald Diary in Russia," 6. Interviews with Titovets, Skop, and Eduard Sagindikov (February 2010). All construction details and other specifics pertaining to the design and layout of Oswald's apartment in Minsk come from Eduard Sagindikov's *Tekhnicheskiy Passport na Kvartiru Zhilishnovo Fonda Respubliki Belarus* (or, simply, his "apartment passport"). Sagindikov, who has lived in the apartment since 2001, allowed me to view the passport. He noted that the layout of the apartment today largely mirrors that of the early 1960s, when Oswald lived there. Sagindikov also said that when he removed a wall, a few years back, to create a passageway between the kitchen and the bedroom, he evaluated the structural integrity of all the walls in the apartment. His estimation was that there had not been any changes to the interior layout of the apartment since its construction; the faded wallpaper and chipped paint support this view. It's noteworthy that none of Oswald's writings, including his diary, makes any mention of any neighbors or life at 4 Kalinina Ulitsa.

28. Interview with Skop provided information for this entire section.

29. Interviews with Titovets and Oleg Nechiporenko (March 2010). Memo from CIA deputy director for plans to Rankin, J. Lee, April 21, 1964.

30. Interview with Nechiporenko.

31. Interview with Titovets.

32. Author's interviews with Oleg Kalugin; Nechiporenko; Shushkevich; Tennent Bagley (December 2011); Jack Tunheim (2010); Vladimir Adamushko, a historian of Soviet Russia at Belarus State University and an archivist in the central government in Minsk; and Igor Pavlovsky, a historian of Soviet politics at Moscow State University. Until 1994, Shushkevich was among the most powerful people in Belarus. Toward the end of the Soviet era, he was a member and then the first

deputy of the chair of the Supreme Soviet of the Belarusian Soviet Socialist Republic; in 1991, with Leonid Kravchuk of Ukraine and Boris Yeltsin of Russia, he signed the document, in a hunting lodge a few hours west of Minsk, that formally dissolved the Soviet Union. After the 1991 communist collapse, he served as head of the parliament (and, in effect, leader) of Belarus. Tunheim noted that Oswald, in fact, did attempt at one point to build an explosive in his apartment, although that plan seems to have gone nowhere. Titovets addresses this matter in his memoirs; see Chapter 21, "The Hand Grenades," in *Oswald: Russian Episode* (Minsk: Mon Litera, 2010). He downplays its importance, but it clearly worried the authorities.

33. Information used throughout this section comes from interviews with German.

34. "Oswald Diary in Russia (Extra Days)"; see the June 19 [illegible year] entry, p. 22.

CHAPTER 7

1. Norman Mailer remains the only outsider who claims to have seen the entire KGB file on Oswald, which is believed to include extensive details about Oswald's everyday activities and indicates that there was a peephole and listening device in Apartment 24. Ernst Titovets, in his memoirs (*Oswald: Russian Episode* [Minsk: Mon Litera, 2010]), reported on Oswald's fears that he was being listened to and, in the course of several interviews, from February to June 2010, discussed the KGB's round-the-clock surveillance of Oswald, made easier by the location of his apartment, the windows peering over the river, and the apartment's configuration. Eduard Sagindikov, who now lives in Apartment 24, said in a February 2010 interview that stories about the KGB's monitoring of Oswald were well known in the apartment building. A recent *New York Times* dispatch on Apartment 24 (November 2, 2012) noted that the KGB had installed a listening device in the ceiling and a peephole in a neighboring apartment.

2. "The Collective" in "Compositions on 'The Collective' and Minsk, Russia, with Foreword and Autobiographical Sketch of Oswald," pp. 41–42, FBI, record no. 124-10086-10419, US National Archives. Author's March 2010 interview with Sergei Skop, who helped flesh out my understanding of Oswald's sense of place in Minsk, his daily routine, and his psychological state during the first few months in the city.

3. In his diary entry dated "March 17–April 31," Oswald writes that he met "Pavil Golovacha" ("Oswald Diary in Russia," record no. 124-10086-10419, US National Archives). As of mid-March, Golovachev was working in the Experimental Department, according to his *trudnaya knizhka*, or "workbook of work." Then, on April 1, he was transferred to the Department of Devices. This means that Oswald and Golovachev almost certainly met on one of the eleven workdays in the latter half of March. I am grateful to Anna Zhuravskaya, Golovachev's sister, for showing me his *trudnaya knizhka*. It's curious that Oswald met Golovachev nearly six months after arriving in the Soviet Union and that he met his second good friend, the medical student Ernst Titovets, six months later, and that he met his third good friend, Yuri Merezhinsky, also a medical student, six months after that. It is unclear

whether Golovachev, Titovets, and Merezhinsky were strategically inserted into Oswald's life in regular, six-month intervals, one after the other. Still, the pattern is noteworthy given the extent to which Oswald's life was regulated and monitored.

4. "Oswald Diary in Russia," 6; "Official and Private Documents and Correspondence of Lee Harvey Oswald," pp. 5–6, sec. 12–14, FBI, record no. 124-10086-10419, US National Archives. See also Titovets, *Oswald: Russian Episode*, 322, in which the author discusses the Oswalds' last night in Minsk. Golovachev alludes to having been at the railway station in Minsk to bid the Oswalds farewell in one of his subsequent letters to Lee and Marina ("Official and Private Documents and Correspondence of Lee Harvey Oswald," 5, sec. 12).

5. Most of the information in this section comes from Anna Zhuravskaya (author's interviews, 2010); Alexei Zhuravsky, Zhuravskaya's son and Golovachev's nephew, in a March 2010 interview; and Maya Gan, Golovachev's sister, in a July 2010 interview. Also, Golovachev's *trudnaya knizhka* was very helpful. To a lesser extent, I have drawn on Oswald's comments and on Ella German, whom I interviewed in February and March 2011.

6. Interviews with Zhuravskaya, Zhuravsky, Gan, German, and Titovets.

7. See Golovachev's September 15, 1962, letter to Lee and Marina, in which he asks Marina for "a detailed press clipping of a technical nature concerning the outer space vehicle 'Mariner 2.'" In the letter he also gives Marina advice about getting a motor for her record player, and he asks for "maps on radio—technical and other technical subjects and the magazine *Life*" ("Official and Private Documents and Correspondence of Lee Harvey Oswald," pp. 5–6, sec. 14); interview with Zhuravskaya.

8. Interviews with Oleg Kalugin, in January 2010, Oleg Nechiporenko, in March 2010, and Stanislaw Shushkevich, in February and April 2010. Titovets, in an interview, discussed what he described as Golovachev's loquaciousness. Anna Zhuravskaya agreed with Titovets that her brother was voluble, but she added that his level of engagement depended a great deal on whom he was speaking to.

9. Titovets, *Oswald: Russian Episode*, 209. Titovets was not the only one to see Pavel this way. German, when I interviewed her, said the same thing that she liked about Oswald—that he seemed more mature, more serious—was the thing that was missing in Golovachev.

10. Interview with Titovets. See also Titovets, *Oswald: Russian Episode*, 204, 206.

11. "Oswald Diary in Russia," 7.

12. Interview with German. The U-2 incident and its aftermath have been written about extensively. Among the best accounts are Michael R. Beschloss, *Mayday: Eisenhower, Khrushchev and the U-2 Affair* (New York: Harper and Row, 1988); William Taubman, *Khrushchev: The Man and His Era* (New York: Norton, 2003), Chap. 16; and Powers's account, Francis Gary Powers, with Curt Gentry, *Operation Overflight: The U-2 Spy Pilot Tells His Story for the First Time* (New York: Holt, Rinehart and Winston, 1970). One sign of the seriousness with which Oswald viewed the U-2 incident would come on July 27, 1963. Then living in the United States, Oswald gave a talk on his Soviet experiences at the Jesuit House of Studies,

at Spring Hill College, in Mobile, Alabama. According to an FBI summary of Oswald's talk, "When the U-2 incident was announced over the factory radio system, the workers were very angry with the United States, but not with [Oswald], even though he was an American." It's noteworthy not only that Oswald mentioned the U-2 incident but that he remembered details about it. See "FBI Report on John J. Sweeney (Scholastic in Jesuit Training), Spring Hill College," December 1, 1963, Warren Commission Hearings, vol. 25, p. 14, US National Archives.

13. "Oswald Diary in Russia," 7–8.

14. Interview with Nechiporenko. Golovachev, who was interviewed by the PBS program *Frontline* in 1993, said of the KGB: "I was met by one of their people, and it was like this. He said, 'Your country asks you—your country demands. There is a foreigner here. It's in the country's interests for security,' and so on. That was early on, but I told him about it a year later. I had three or four meetings with the KGB people. They gave me little assignments to provoke [Oswald], saying, 'Try this out on him and see what he says'" (transcript of November 16, 1993, *Frontline* broadcast). It's unclear what, if anything, Golovachev actually told Oswald. It seems unlikely that Golovachev could have been so open with Oswald about his work with the KGB and expected Oswald to have sustained a correspondence with him after Oswald left the Soviet Union—but that is what happened. One suspects that Golovachev, in the interview, sought (misleadingly) to minimize or even trivialize his importance to the KGB.

15. "Oswald Diary in Russia," 8.

CHAPTER 8

1. See "The Defector Study," March 1979, House Select Committee on Assassinations, record no. 180-10147-10238, US National Archives.

2. This was the word of choice among Stalin apologists, who generally conceive of the Soviet leader as a *diktator* or *vozhd* (not a mere "ruler" or "authoritarian") who did what had to be done at a very difficult period—albeit with some "excesses."

3. Author's interview with Alexandra Lavshuka, March 2010.

4. "Oswald Diary in Russia," p. 7, record no. 124-10086-10419, US National Archives.

5. "Compositions on 'The Collective' and Minsk, Russia, with Foreword and Autobiographical Sketch of Oswald," p. 11, FBI, record no. 124-10086-10419, US National Archives. It should be noted that it is unclear when, exactly, Oswald completed various essays and fragments, so we cannot say with certainty that the criticisms of Soviet life that he catalogues in them were formulated during this period, in late 1960 and early 1961. However, it was during this time that Oswald became acutely aware of much of the absurdity and unhappiness of life in Minsk.

6. "The Collective," p. 39, in "Compositions on 'The Collective.'" Oswald does not include citations with his essay, so it's impossible to confirm his facts and figures. But what matters is Oswald's perception of Soviet reality, which had clearly acquired a sarcastic undertone that was very much at odds with his initial, ideological fervor.

7. This section draws heavily from interviews with Ernst Titovets, February to June 2010, and Ernst Titovets, *Oswald: Russian Episode* (Minsk: Mon Litera, 2010), 333–334.

8. In one of their early conversations, according to Titovets's memoirs, the two men discussed German idealism and epistemology. Titovets did most of the talking, but Oswald managed to make his case admirably—"no technical terms, just plain English." See Titovets, *Oswald: Russian Episode*, 123, and Chaps. 13 and 32. I got a glimpse of Titovets's closed nature the first time I met with him, at the Chelyuskintsev metro station in Minsk. It was early evening in February 2010, and when I arrived at the station, Titovets was there. I expected we'd head for a café— somewhere indoors. But Titovets said he felt like taking a stroll through nearby Chelyuskintsev Park. We walked and talked for an hour, but I couldn't take any notes because it was freezing, and I had to wear gloves. It was also snowing, making it difficult to use a recording device. What's more, even if I had taken off my gloves and scribbled a few notes, the snow would have turned my notepad into an inky mess. None of this prevented Titovets, who tends to speak quietly and with great precision, from learning a good bit about me.

9. Titovets, *Oswald: Russian Episode*, Chap. 9.

10. Ibid., Chaps. 10–12.

11. "Oswald Diary in Russia," 8.

12. Titovets, *Oswald: Russian Episode*, Chap. 14. Titovets has cleaned up Oswald's diary entry. The original reads: "a growing lonliness overtakes me in spite of my conquest of Enna Tachina a girl from Riga, studing at the music conservorie in Minsk. After an affair which lasts a few weeks we part" ("Oswald Diary in Russia," 8).

13. For all quotes in this paragraph and, more generally, a sense of Oswald's alternating feelings about the women he encountered in Minsk, see "Oswald Diary in Russia (Extra Days)"; see the "Nov. 1961" and "25 Dec 1961" entries, both on p. 22.

14. Oswald is probably referring to Enna Tachina, who appears as No. 88 in the CIA's list of "names of persons in the USSR known to or mentioned by Lee Harvey Oswald and Marina Nikolayevna Prussakova Oswald" ("Name List with Traces," January 20, 1964, CIA, record no. 104-10021-10067, US National Archives).

15. "Oswald Diary in Russia," 8, and "Oswald Diary in Russia (Extra Days)," esp. the "25 Dec 1961" entry, p. 22. It should be pointed out that Oswald here refers to Korobka as "Nell Rogrobakc."

16. "Oswald Diary in Russia," 8.

17. Author's interviews with Ella German, February and March 2011.

18. Ibid.

19. Ibid.

20. "Oswald Diary in Russia," 8, and "June 19" entry in "Oswald Diary in Russia (Extra Days)"; interviews with German.

21. "Oswald Diary in Russia," 8.

22. Interviews with German.

23. "Oswald Diary in Russia," 8–9.

24. In an interview Ella said—in Russian—that Oswald "made himself liked to me. That is all." It's worth noting that Russian relies much more heavily on passive constructions than does English. This is important because it signals a psychological and cultural difference between the Russian and the English speaker. It points to a different way of thinking that is probably untranslatable. On an everyday level, then, Oswald almost definitely conceived of their relationship differently from the way Ella did. This is not to say that Oswald could not have had a successful relationship with a Russian speaker—he was just a few months away from meeting his Russian-born wife. But it does hint at the many complications he would have encountered.

25. Interviews with German.

26. "Oswald Diary in Russia," 9. It's curious that, in his interview with the FBI, Yuri Nosenko told the Americans that the Soviet authorities never considered granting Oswald citizenship. In what might be interpreted as a bit of intergovernmental-agency sniping, Nosenko said that, in the wake of Oswald's suicide attempt in Moscow, the American was permitted to stay in the country only because of the intervention of the Ministry of Foreign Affairs or the Soviet Red Cross, which was separate from the KGB. (See the February 26–27, 1964, Nosenko interview, from "Collection of Documents Supporting the Warren Commission Report," CIA, record no. 104-10085-10010, US National Archives.)

27. This transition is reflected in Oswald's diary. Titovets, in an interview, also pointed out that this was a "complicated period" for Oswald.

28. Interview with Titovets.

29. "Oswald Diary in Russia," 9. Memo from J. W. Holland (District Director, San Antonio, Immigration and Naturalization Service) to Deputy Associate Commissioner, Travel Control Central Office (Immigration and Naturalization Service), January 31, 1962, record no. 104-10085-10010, US National Archives.

30. Interview with Titovets.

31. Composition 1 in "Five Untitled Compositions on Political Subjects," p. 10, FBI, record no. 124-10086-10419, US National Archives.

32. Interview with Titovets.

33. This is particularly true of his five untitled compositions, as well as his "Untitled Composition on Communist Party of the United States," "Speech," and "The Atheism System." "The Collective" comes closest to anything akin to an argument.

34. Interview with Titovets.

35. Composition 1 in "Five Untitled Compositions," 2.

36. Ibid., 2–3.

37. Titovets, Oswald: Russian Episode, Chap. 35. In Oswald's writings, the word "Athenian" never appears, nor does his description of the "Atheism System" ever make reference to any Greek thinkers. But his system, as it were, does sound more like what we would imagine an "Athenian System" to be rather than an "Atheism" one, in that its central concern is balance: taking the very best, as Oswald saw it, of both the capitalist and Marxist systems and fusing them into one, idealized,

Athenian-style polity. There has been speculation that Oswald meant "Athenian" but misspelled it. There is good reason to think this may be true, but there is no way to know for sure. It should also be noted that after the assassination a copy of Homer's *Iliad* was found among Oswald's possessions (see "Interviews with Robert Lee Oswald Relating to Personal Effects of Lee Harvey Oswald," March 16, 1964, HSCA, record no. 180-10116-10245, US National Archives).

38. "Speech," from "Six Compositions," p. 3, FBI, record no. 124-10086-10419, US National Archives.

39. All the information in this section, on Oswald's reflections on the state and his criticisms of communism and capitalism, come from "The Atheism System," "A System Opposed to the Communist," and "A System Opposed to the Capitalist," from "Six Compositions," 3–5.

40. The use of the term "surplus value" is typical of the superficiality and fragmented nature of Oswald's thinking. As a general matter, he is fond of incorporating terms in his speech and writing that suggest Marxist affinities without ever explaining how those terms fit into any argument. In the case of his Atheism System, for instance, he appears particularly concerned with the theme of exploitation. While he never explicitly discusses exploitation, the Marxian link between the labor theory of value and the exploitation of workers is implied. That said, one suspects that the "implication" is almost accidental. It is as if he has stumbled on this connection without really grasping it.

41. The complete subtitle reads: "A System Opposed to the Capitalist in that: No individual may own the means of production, distribution or creation of goods or any other process wherein workers are employed for wages, or otherwise employed, to create profit or surplus profit or value in use or exchange."

42. "The Collective," 56.

43. Ibid.

44. Yevgeny Yevtushenko perfectly captured this fear in his 1962 poem "The Heirs of Stalin."

CHAPTER 9

1. "Oswald Diary in Russia," p. 9, record no. 124-10086-10419, US National Archives.

2. Ibid., 9, 12. Author's interviews, February to May 2010, with Anna Zhuravskaya, Sergei Skop, Leonid Tsagoiko, Filip Lavshuk, and Galina Makovskaya.

3. Information for this chapter comes from several sources, including Ernst Titovets, *Oswald: Russian Episode* (Minsk: Mon Litera, 2010), Chap. 24; and interviews with Katerina Merezhinsky, Yuri Merezhinsky's niece, in January and February 2010; Anna Zhuravskaya; and Sergei Khrushchev, the son of the Soviet premier and a senior fellow at the Watson Institute for International Studies at Brown University, in February 2011. I am also indebted to the staff at the Palace of Culture, who allowed me to roam through the entire building so that I could see the auditorium, orchestra pit, ballrooms, and corridors that Titovets makes reference to in his book. And I appreciated hearing the stories shared by the librarians

at the Museum of the Great Patriotic War, next door to the Palace of Culture; their memories of October Square, when it was still called Stalin Square, added a great deal of depth to my understanding of this place in the early sixties. Least helpful was Oswald, who made only a brief mention of this night (March 17, 1961) that proved to be among the most important of his two and a half years in the Soviet Union ("Oswald Diary in Russia," 9).

4. Titovets, *Oswald: Russian Episode*, 223. Titovets's treatment of Merezhinsky, like that of Golovachev, is mostly accurate but a little unfair. His envy and outright disdain are palpable at moments. Titovets had had few, if any, of the advantages that Merezhinsky had had, but Titovets had acquired considerable knowledge, recognition, a comfortable apartment, a family. Merezhinsky, by contrast, died prematurely and with few accomplishments to his name.

5. Interviews with Anna Zhuravskaya and Katerina Merezhinsky.

6. "Oswald Diary in Russia," 9.

7. "Testimony of Mrs. Lee Harvey Oswald," Warren Commission Hearings, February 5, 1964, vol. 1, 91.

8. Oswald describes the palace in some detail in "The Collective," pp. 28–29, in "Compositions on 'The Collective' and Minsk, Russia, with Foreword and Autobiographical Sketch of Oswald," FBI, record no. 124-10086-10419, US National Archives.

9. Titovets, *Oswald: Russian Episode*, 226–227.

10. Ibid., 221, 223.

11. Ibid; author's interview, in April 2010, with Ernst Titovets.

12. Titovets, *Oswald: Russian Episode*, 231.

13. Information for this entire section, unless otherwise indicated, comes from Marina Oswald's testimony before the Warren Commission. (see "Testimony of Mrs. Lee Harvey Oswald," vol. 1, 84–92.)

14. Ibid., vol. 1, 85–86.

15. See Titovets's transcript of his interview with Merezhinsky, in *Oswald: Russian Episode*, 247. Priscilla Johnson McMillan, *Marina and Lee* (New York: Harper & Row, 1977).

16. "Testimony of Mrs. Lee Harvey Oswald," vol. 1, 92.

17. Titovets, *Oswald: Russian Episode*, 231–232.

18. Ibid., 260.

19. "Testimony of Mrs. Lee Harvey Oswald," vol. 1, 90–91.

20. Interviews, in February and March 2010, with Titovets, Stanislaw Shushkevich, Oleg Nechiporenko, and Oleg Kalugin.

21. Interview with Titovets.

22. "Oswald Diary in Russia," 9; "Translation: Soviet Medical Records on Lee Harvey Oswald," CIA, record no. 104-10534-10041, US National Archives.

23. "Testimony of Mrs. Lee Harvey Oswald," vol. 1, 91.

24. "Oswald Diary in Russia," 9. For more on the Soviet reaction, including that of the state-controlled media, to the Bay of Pigs on the day after the start of the invasion, see Seymour Topping's dispatch, "Moscow Blames U.S. for Attack," *New York Times*, April 18, 1961.

25. Ibid., 10.

26. Ibid.

CHAPTER 10

1. See Oswald's discussion of the Moskvich—he uses a misleading transliteration, "Moskavich"—in "The Collective," in "Compositions on 'The Collective' and Minsk, Russia, with Foreword and Autobiographical Sketch of Oswald," p. 27, FBI, record no. 124-10086-10419, US National Archives.

2. "Oswald Correspondence in Russia to His Mother and Brother, Robert Oswald," letter no. 8, FBI, record no. 124-10086-10419, US National Archives.

3. Lest anyone suspect Oswald was intentionally portraying Soviet life in a more cheerful light, the better to avoid the attention of the KGB officials who presumably read all his mail, consider that subsequent letters to his brother strike a much harsher, anti-Soviet tone.

4. In a December 14, 1961, letter to his brother, Robert, Oswald wrote that he had not received a letter, presumably from Robert, containing "certain questions." "Its quite possible they destroyed it," he wrote, referring to the Soviet authorities (see "Oswald Correspondence in Russia," letter no. 13). Titovets, *Oswald: Russian Episode* (Minsk: Mon Litera, 2010), Chaps. 16, 20.

5. Author's interview with Ella German, March 2011.

6. Ibid.

7. "Letter from Lee Harvey Oswald to Robert Oswald," May 31, 1961, Warren Commission Hearings, vol. 16, pp. 827–829, US National Archives.

8. *Report of the President's Commission on the Assassination of President Kennedy* (Warren Commission Report; hereafter WCR), Appendix 13, 706, US National Archives. "Oswald Diary in Russia," p. 10, record no. 124-10086-10419, US National Archives.

9. Lee Harvey Oswald, "Handwritten Letter to Embassy," December 1, 1961, CIA, record no. 104-10007-10419, US National Archives.

10. "Letter from Joseph B. Norbury to Oswald," December 14, 1961, Warren Commission Hearings, vol. 16, p. 681, US National Archives.

11. Author's interview with Jack Matlock, April 2010.

12. Author's interview with Ernst Titovets, February 2010. He said that he did not recall the exact dates of the recording sessions, but he did recall that he wanted them spaced apart by a year to allow for enough time to gauge any improvements in his accent. He had hoped that, by then, spending so much time with a native English speaker would be apparent.

13. I have relied, throughout this section, on Titovets's recordings and, to a lesser degree, on his account of the recording sessions.

14. "Oswald Correspondence in Russia," letter no. 10. "Oswald Diary in Russia," 11.

15. "Letter from Lee Harvey Oswald to the American Embassy in Moscow," January 5, 1962, Warren Commission Hearings, vol. 16, pp. 688–689, US National Archives.

16. Interview with Matlock.

17. WCR, Appendix 13, 709–710. By the time Oswald wrote his letter to Connally, on January 30, 1962, Connally was no longer secretary of the navy but governor of Texas. Still, the irony is unavoidable: Connally was sitting in the same car as John F. Kennedy when Oswald shot the president and, in fact, was seriously injured by one of the bullets that passed through Kennedy.

CHAPTER 11

1. "Oswald Diary in Russia," p. 10, record no. 124-10086-10419, US National Archives. Anna Zhuravskaya said that Pavel Golovachev did not know that the Oswalds were planning to leave Minsk. Nor was Ernst Titovets kept abreast ("Oswald Diary in Russia," 12). Indeed, Oswald had limited the number of people he told about his plan to leave the Soviet Union since at least March 1961, when, according to his diary, he told Alexander Ziger, who agreed that this was a good idea but urged him to keep quiet about it ("Oswald Diary in Russia," 9).

2. Author's interviews with Ella German, February and March 2010. German provided information used throughout this chapter.

3. Ernst Titovets, *Oswald: Russian Episode* (Minsk: Mon Litera, 2010), 165. German backed up Titovets's account of the incident.

4. "Letter from Lee Harvey Oswald to Marguerite Oswald," January 2, 1962, House Select Committee on Assassinations, record no. 180-10092-10411, US National Archives.

5. "Letter from Lee Harvey Oswald to Marguerite Oswald," February 1, 1962, House Select Committee on Assassinations, record no. 180-10092-10414, US National Archives.

6. "Testimony of Mrs. Lee Harvey Oswald," Warren Commission Hearings, February 3, 1964, vol. 1, 5. It's worth recalling the comments made by Dr. Renatus Hartogs, the psychiatrist who evaluated Lee at Youth House, in New York (see Chapter 1, note 3).

7. "Letter from Lee Harvey Oswald to Marguerite Oswald," February 15, 1962, House Select Committee on Assassinations, record no. 180-10092-10416, US National Archives.

8. "Oswald Correspondence in Russia to His Mother and Brother, Robert Oswald," letter no. 16, FBI, record no. 124-10086-10419, US National Archives.

9. The government agency that seemed to have the most reservations about Oswald was the Immigration and Naturalization Service. Its concern was never stated explicitly, to my knowledge, but only suggested in the ensuing holdup at the agency involving Marina's visa. Had there not been any concerns about Oswald and his loyalty to the United States, the delay would not have happened. This is reflected in the correspondence between INS and State Department officials. (See the letters from J. W. Holland and Michael Cieplinski cited in notes 10 and 17 below.)

10. Memo from J. W. Holland (district director, San Antonio, Immigration and Naturalization Service) to deputy associate commissioner, Travel Control Central Office (Immigration and Naturalization Service), January 30, 1962.

11. Ibid.

12. "Oswald Correspondence in Russia," letter no. 17.

13. Ibid.

14. *Report of the President's Commission on the Assassination of President Kennedy* (Warren Commission Report; hereafter WCR), Appendix 13, 711, US National Archives. See also "Oswald Diary in Russia," 12.

15. "Oswald Diary in Russia," 12. Once again Oswald is blending together, in his somewhat confused manner, English and Russian. "Po-Russki" in Russian means "in Russian."

16. Letter from J. W. Holland (district director, San Antonio, Immigration and Naturalization Service) to US Embassy, Moscow, February 28, 1962, record no. 104-10008-10029, US National Archives.

17. Letter from Michael Cieplinski (acting administrator, Bureau of Security and Consular Affairs, Department of State) to Raymond F. Farrell (commissioner of Immigration and Naturalization Service, Department of Justice), March 27, 1962, record no. 104-10003-10234, US National Archives.

18. "Oswald Diary in Russia," 12.

19. WCR, Appendix 13, 711.

20. Letter from Robert H. Robinson (deputy associate commissioner, Travel Control Central Office, Immigration and Naturalization Service, Department of Justice) to Michael Cieplinski (acting administrator, Bureau of Security and Consular Affairs, Department of State), May 9, 1962, record no. 104-10008-10058, US National Archives; WCR, Appendix 13, 712.

21. Titovets, *Oswald: Russian Episode*, 321–323. In his memoirs Titovets clarified what he regarded as the misperception created by Oswald's March 1962 diary entry in which he voiced fears of telling Titovets of his forthcoming departure because Titovets, Oswald said, was "too good a young Communist league member" ("Oswald Diary in Russia," 12). The diary entry, and the absence of any further mention of Titovets, suggests that the Oswalds left Minsk without saying good-bye to Titovets and, more importantly, that Titovets was not the friend, or *druyg*, he had made himself out to be. "The only plausible theory that I can think of to justify Lee's diary entry was that he might have wanted to protect me by creating a good image of his friend in the eyes of Soviet officials," Titovets wrote.

He was no fool to realize that for a member of Komsomol to have an American for a close friend might reflect negatively upon his friend's reputation. . . . If I knew nothing about the Oswalds going to the States, it would have cleared me of failing to report and persuade Marina, another Komsomol member, against leaving the Soviet motherland as the moral obligation of a Komsomol member should have dictated me to do. I can well visualize Lee chuckling under his nose while making that entry about myself. He must have thought it very clever to thus gallantly extend to me his protection, just in case—the only favor he could do me before leaving Russia."

Titovets noted that Oswald sent him a postcard the day he arrived in Moscow, May 24: "I'm very sorry I did not see you again before we left, but I came over to your place but you weren't there" (*Oswald: Russian Episode*, 325).

22. According to Titovets, the Oswalds stayed at Pavel's apartment on their last night in Minsk because Marina wanted to make sure that the apartment at 4 Kommunistichiskaya Ulitsa was taken over by a friend: "In their thinking, the authorities, on having been confronted with an accomplished fact, would give up and let the friend have the apartment. (As it turned out later it was a naïve move. The authorities simply evicted the squatters right off)" (*Oswald: Russian Episode*, 322). See also WCR, Appendix 13, 712.

23. Among other sources, this photograph can be found in Titovets, *Oswald: Russian Episode*.

24. "Letter from Lee Harvey Oswald to Marguerite Oswald," April 22, 1962, House Select Committee on Assassinations, record no. 180-10092-10419, US National Archives.

25. "Letter from Marguerite Oswald to Mrs. James/State," May 25, 1962, CIA, record no. 104-10008-10064, US National Archives; "Letter from Marguerite Oswald to Haselton/State," May 25, 1962, CIA, record no. 104-10008-10063, US National Archives.

26. "Testimony of Mrs. Lee Harvey Oswald," vol. 1, 98; WCR, Appendix 13, 712.

27. "Telegram from US Embassy in Moscow to Secretary of State," May 31, 1962, CIA, record no. 104-10196-10301, US National Archives.

28. WCR, Appendix 13, 712.

29. "Speed Letter from George H. Haselton to Marguerite Oswald," June 1, 1962, CIA, record no. 104-10008-10070, US National Archives.

30. "Letter from Robert I. Owen to Marguerite Oswald," June 7, 1962, CIA, record no. 104-10008-10071, US National Archives.

31. WCR, chap. 7, 395.

32. See "Five Untitled Compositions on Political Subjects," record no. 124-10086-10419, US National Archives.

33. Composition 3, p. 11, in ibid.

CHAPTER 12

1. Author's interviews, in March and April 2010, with Ernst Titovets and Stanislaw Shushkevich.

2. Allen Matusow's discussion of the election of 1960 and Kennedy's abbreviated presidency in *The Unraveling of America: A History of Liberalism in the 1960s* (New York: Perennial, 1985) captures this sentiment nicely (see esp. Chaps. 1–2). Another sign of the intensity of this feeling of national resurgence came with the 1962 midterm elections, when Democrats fared much better than expected (given that they controlled the White House) and key Republican critics of the administration were defeated. These included Senator Homer Capehart from Indiana and Representative Walter Judd from Minnesota; Judd had delivered the keynote speech at the GOP's convention in 1960. Another loser that year was the president's onetime opponent, Richard Nixon, who had sought the governorship of California (Rhodes Cook, "The Midterm Election of '62: A Real 'October Surprise,'" *Sabato's Crystal Ball*, September 30, 2010, http://www.centerforpolitics.org/crystalball/).

3. One wonders if Frost really believed that the 1960 election was "the greatest vote a people ever cast." Did Frost really believe that the election of 1960 (an election that had been marred by charges of vote tampering, at the hands of the victor, in Illinois and Texas) was the greatest vote *any* people had ever cast? Robert Faggen, a professor of literature and Frost expert at Claremont McKenna College, observed in an April 2013 interview that Frost had a penchant for "hyperbolic irony," and "Dedication" is no exception. Faggen added that there are many layers of meaning and subtext at work in the poem. In particular, the words "golden age," in the last couplet, point to a darker, underlying force. Golden ages traditionally precede decline, and in this sense the end of the poem should be viewed as an admonition. The Kennedy moment, Frost seems to be hinting at, will not last long.

4. By contrast, Dwight Eisenhower, hewing to a more traditional theme, began his inaugural in 1953 with a prayer asking God for the power "to discern clearly right from wrong." Like his predecessors, Eisenhower never said anything in his inaugural about doing "God's work."

5. "Interview of Mrs. Lee Harvey Oswald," Warren Commission Hearings, February 3, 1964, vol. 1, 10.

6. *Report of the President's Commission on the Assassination of President Kennedy* (Warren Commission Report), Appendix 13, US National Archives, provides a detailed account of Oswald's entire post-Soviet period. See 713–740. All information, including quotes, in this section comes from this source, unless otherwise noted.

7. "Questions and Answers Beginning 'Why Did You Go to the U.S.S.R.?,'" from "Six Compositions," pp. 5, 7, FBI, record no. 124-10086-10419, US National Archives.

8. "Testimony of Marguerite Oswald," Warren Commission Hearings, February 11, 1964, vol. 1, 207–208.

9. "Testimony of Mrs. Lee Harvey Oswald," Warren Commission Hearings, February 3, 1964, vol. 1, 6.

10. Ibid., vol. 1, 10.

11. Ibid.

12. "Testimony of George Bouhe," Warren Commission Hearings, March 23, 1964, vol. 8, 360.

13. Interview with Hazel Oswald, November 24, 1963, FBI, record no. 157-10003-10350, US National Archives.

14. "The Collective," in "Compositions on 'The Collective' and Minsk, Russia, with Foreword and Autobiographical Sketch of Oswald," pp. 3–4, FBI, record no. 124-10086-10419, US National Archives.

15. José I. Lasaga, a Miami psychologist, wrote a paper on the "psychological motivations in the assassination of President Kennedy" immediately after the president's death, and it was circulated at the White House in late December 1963. In the paper Lasaga wrote: "Up to about the middle of September, Oswald was a Marxist agitator who boasted at all times of his way of thinking, and who took advantage of everything within his reach to make propaganda to further his ideas. . . .

But, as of the month of October, everything changed. He stopped writing letters proposing plans of action to the Fair Play for Cuba Committee. He refrained from speaking in public. He ceased to boast of his Marxist convictions. He seemed an ordinary man dedicated only to work during daytime, to listen to radio or watch television at night, and to peacefully spend his weekend with his wife and children." Lasaga concluded that Oswald had already decided to assassinate the president in his service of the Marxist cause and that this had focused him and filled him with a preternatural calm. This was only partly true. Kennedy's November travel schedule was not public information in October, so Oswald could not have been preparing to kill him; he didn't know he would be in Dallas. But Lasaga was correct that a strange calm had settled in, and he was correct that this calm pointed to a new determination in Oswald, but that determination was not ideological. It was more fundamental: it was psychological. It had to do with Oswald's confrontation with himself, and it was going to explode soon (see "Possible Psychological Motivations in the Assassination," House Select Committee on Assassinations, FBI, record no. 180-10043-10187, US National Archives).

16. "Letter from Pavel Golovachev to the Oswalds," September 29, 1963, Warren Commission Hearings, vol. 21, 255–257, US National Archives.

17. Author's interview with Ruth Paine, January 2010.

18. Testimony of Mrs. Lee Harvey Oswald, vol. 1, 22; interview with Mrs. Charles F. Murret, November 30, 1963, FBI, record no. 157-10003-10357, US National Archives.

19. William K. Hartmann, "Repeatability of Proportion Measurements of Faces and Other Objects from Photographs," House Select Committee on Assassinations, July 1978, record no. 180-10116-10245, US National Archives; Ellis Kerley, University of Maryland, "The Oswald Photographs," House Select Committee on Assassinations, August 11, 1978, record no. 180-10116-10255, US National Archives.

EPILOGUE

1. Yuri Nosenko's interview with the FBI, February 26–27, 1964, "Collection of Documents Supporting the Warren Commission Report," CIA, record no. 104-10085-10010, US National Archives.

2. Author's interviews with Anna Zhuravskaya and Alexei Zhuravsky, March 2010.

3. Author's interview with Sergei Skop, February 2010.

4. Ernst Titovets describes his trip to Moscow, which overlapped with the Kennedy assassination and Oswald's death, in *Oswald: Russian Episode* (Minsk: Mon Litera, 2010), Chap. 34. Also helpful here were interviews with Titovets, April and May 2010.

5. Titovets said that it was a Saturday, but the assassination happened on a Friday.

6. Titovets, *Oswald: Russian Episode*, 351, 357.

7. Ibid., 363.

8. Ibid., 361.

9. Author's interview with Tennent Bagley, December 2011. He discussed the Nosenko case at some length in *Spy Wars: Moles, Mysteries, and Deadly Games* (New Haven, CT: Yale University Press, 2007). Bagley very helpfully shared with me chapters from his unpublished manuscript (tentatively titled *Secrets of the KGB*), which goes into greater detail about the Nosenko case, the CIA, and the nature of Soviet and American counterintelligence in the 1960s.

10. I am greatly indebted here to Stephen Donadio of Middlebury College. His comments on alienation in postwar American life and letters helped shape thoughts about Oswald in the role of antihero. There is an extensive literature on the American contemplation of America in the postwar era, starting with C. Wright Mills, *The Power Elite* (New York: Oxford University Press, 1957); David Riesman, *The Lonely Crowd: A Study of Changing American Character* (New Haven, CT: Yale University Press, 1963); William H. Whyte Jr., *The Organization Man* (Garden City, NY: Doubleday, 1957); and a slew of related works on American popular culture and consumerism, including Irving Howe, *Politics and the Novel* (New York: Columbia University Press, 1992), and Lawrence Lipton, *The Holy Barbarians* (Mansfield Center, CT: Martino, 2010). A very useful cross-section of criticism of the American scene in the early 1950s can be found in *America and the Intellectuals: A Symposium* (New York: Partisan Review, 1953), which stemmed from the symposium "Our Country and Our Culture" held in 1952 and organized by the magazine *Partisan Review.* The updated edition of Albert Parry's *Garrets and Pretenders: A History of Bohemianism in America* (New York: Dover, 1960) includes a colorful discussion of the Beat generation.

11. Author's interviews with Titovets, Ella German (March 2011), Skop, Leonid Tsagoiko (March 2010), Filip Lavshuk (March 2010), Alexandra Lavshuka (March 2010), and Stanislaw Shushkevich (April 2010), among others.

12. The first televised presidential debate, on September 26, 1960, neatly illustrates this rather simple dichotomy pitting action against inaction, Kennedy against Nixon (and, by extension, the Eisenhower administration and the perceived lethargy of the whole decade of the 1950s). In his opening remarks Kennedy repeatedly stressed the need for forward movement. "I should make it very clear that I do not think that we're doing enough, that I am not satisfied as an American with the progress that we're making," Kennedy declared. "This is a great country, but I think it could be a greater country, and this is a powerful country, but I think it could be a more powerful country." Nixon, responding to Kennedy, sought to fend off charges that the United States was "standing still." Strangely, the debate, which was centered on domestic affairs, did not delve deeply into the ideological differences between Republican and Democratic "action." It assumed the desirability of action—whatever that might entail—and it put Nixon on defense. (Kennedy's well-known vitality and crispness contrasted with Nixon's plodding, sometimes didactic style. Nixon's five o'clock shadow, which he attempted to cover up with Lazy Shave powder, naturally reinforced this dichotomy.)

13. Benjamin C. Bradlee, *Conversations with Kennedy* (New York: Norton, 1975), 10.

14. Joyce Hoffmann, *Theodore H. White and Journalism as Illusion* (Columbia: University of Missouri Press, 1995), explores the construction and maintenance of the Kennedy myth. The Field Poll data is from the California Poll and Field Research Company, Mervin D. Field (director), October 25, 1961. Two days later, the Field Poll released results from another survey that asked the question: "How likely do you think it is that the U.S. will be involved in an all-out atomic war within the next year or two—very likely, rather likely, or not likely?" Nearly one in four respondents believed that nuclear war was either very likely or rather likely to happen by 1963. The Gallup poll information is from Hazel Gaudet Erskine, "The Polls: Kennedy as President," *Public Opinion Quarterly* 28, no. 2 (Summer 1964): 334–342. There's an argument that can be made that Kennedy's popularity simply mirrored economic performance, which picked up markedly in 1961. But there are too many points, from the end of World War II to the present, at which political standing and economic performance diverge—Eisenhower in 1954, Johnson in 1965 to 1966, and, in fact, Kennedy in 1963—and there are far too many economic variables—job creation, interest rates, mortgage rates, inflation, and so forth—to establish a clear correlation.

15. David Halberstam, *The Best and the Brightest*, 20th anniversary ed. (New York: Ballantine, 1993). Discussions of the style and symbolism of the Kennedy White House are found throughout Theodore C. Sorensen's well-known biography of the president. See *Kennedy: The Classic Biography* (New York: Harper Perennial, 2009).

16. "Five Untitled Compositions on Political Subjects," pp. 8–9, FBI, record no. 124-10086-10419, US National Archives.

17. I am taking my cue here, in part, from Lionel Trilling's discussion, in the preface to *The Liberal Imagination*, of liberalism as "the sole intellectual tradition" in the early years of the postwar era. Trilling understood liberals to fall, broadly speaking, into two camps: moderates who hewed to traditional, democratic values and the more dogmatic, "illiberal" liberals who, he feared, had come to dominate the public discourse (and were inspired by Stalinist Russia). See Lionel Trilling, *The Liberal Imagination: Essays on Literature and Society* (New York: New York Review of Books, 2008), xx–xxi. Trilling's 1947 novel, *The Middle of the Journey* (New York: New York Review of Books, 2002), illustrates this divide between the center and the hard left more vividly. See also Michael Kimmage, "*The Middle of the Journey* and the Crisis of Liberalism," *New England Review* 30, no. 1 (2009). The essay also appears in Kimmage's *The Conservative Turn: Lionel Trilling, Whittaker Chambers, and the Lessons of Anti-Communism* (Cambridge, MA: Harvard University Press, 2009).

18. William Barrett, *The Truants: Adventures Among the Intellectuals* (Garden City, NY: Anchor Press/Doubleday, 1982), 155.

19. *Report of the President's Commission on the Assassination of President Kennedy* (Warren Commission Report), Appendix 13, 684, US National Archives. Oswald's coworkers at the Experimental Department, including Lavshuk, Skop, and Tsagoiko, made this point repeatedly. They wanted to know what America looked

like—the size and shape of the buildings, the landscape, people, farm animals, cars, bicycles, buses, bridges, roads, storefronts—but Oswald never talked about anything concrete. He preferred to discuss abstractions that, for the most part, they didn't know about and found boring. The few fragments of his writings in which Oswald devotes much ink to the United States comport with this same tendency. Consider, for example, his first "untitled composition" ("Five Untitled Compositions on Political Subjects," 3):

> Their are two great represenative of power in the world, simply expressed, the left and right, and their factions and concess. Any practical attempt at one alternative must have as its nuclus the triditionall idealogical best of both systems, and yet be utterly opposed to both systems. for not system can be entirely new, that is where most revolutions industrial or political, go astray. And yet the new system must be opposed unequipily too the old that also is where revolutions go astray.

His November 26, 1959, letter to his brother, Robert, sounds a similar tone. "It is because the government supports an economic system which exploits all its workers, a system based upon credit which gives rise to the never ending cycle of depression, inflation, unlimited speculation (which is the phase America is in now) and war," he wrote. "In this system art, culture, and the spirit of man are subjected to commercial enterpraising, religion and education are used as a tool to surpress what would otherwise be a population questioning their government's unfair economic system and planns for war" ("Oswald Correspondence in Russia to His Mother and Brother, Robert Oswald," letter no. 6, FBI, record no. 124-10086-10419, US National Archives).

INDEX